T0123417

The

H.O.P.E.

Tribe:

Honoring Open, Perceptive, and Empathic Children

Insights and Practical Strategies for Raising
Intuitive, Empathic, and Spiritual Children.

VALERIE LYNCH

BALBOA.
PRESS

A DIVISION OF HAY HOUSE

Balboa Press books may be ordered through booksellers or by contacting:

Balboa Press
A Division of Hay House
1663 Liberty Drive
Bloomington, IN 47403
www.balboapress.com
1 (877) 407-4847

Because of the dynamic nature of the Internet, any web addresses or links contained in this book may have changed since publication and may no longer be valid. The views expressed in this work are solely those of the author and do not necessarily reflect the views of the publisher, and the publisher hereby disclaims any responsibility for them.

The author of this book does not dispense medical advice or prescribe the use of any technique as a form of treatment for physical, emotional, or medical problems without the advice of a physician, either directly or indirectly. The intent of the author is only to offer information of a general nature to help you in your quest for emotional and spiritual well-being. In the event you use any of the information in this book for yourself, which is your constitutional right, the author and the publisher assume no responsibility for your actions.

Any people depicted in stock imagery provided by Getty Images are models, and such images are being used for illustrative purposes only. Certain stock imagery © Getty Images.

Print information available on the last page.

ISBN: 978-1-9822-0536-2 (sc)
ISBN: 978-1-9822-0535-5 (hc)
ISBN: 978-1-9822-0557-7 (e)

Library of Congress Control Number: 2018906442

Balboa Press rev. date: 06/08/2018

Table of Contents

Part Three: How Do We H.O.P.E.?

Dedication

This handbook is written for all children, all souls yet to be on this Earth, and the adults who have been entrusted with the care of them. It is for myself, my son, my daughter, my family, and my HOPE Tribe. Many thanks to my 'home base', Carol, the woman who believed in me so much that the spill over has given me renewed faith and belief in myself. Thanks to Sylvia, a gentle kind and loving soul that has visited (she resides on the other side) me frequently to give me strength, courage, support, and love on my journey. Thank you to my loving sister for all her emotional support during all the trying times in my life, helping me to seek balance, soulful expansion, and being a shoulder to cry on when the growing pains and 'the shifts' caused tears. I love you.

Mission Statement

From spirit to Earth, this book is inspired to help empower adults and children to see the positive outcome of connecting through the power of hope, believing, and trusting in our own experiences. More specifically, this book speaks to creating a HOPE tribe of believers, so that our children can live soul-actualized lives in a way that is productive and meaningful within our current social constructs. Robert Holden said, "If you are alive you need help". Too often we stay isolated, disconnected, and alone, especially in parenting. The HOPE Tribe is not just a book, it is a "living idea". It is meant to share strategies and insights and be a starting point for people to begin discussing empathic, sensitive, and perceptive children. It is a change agent, a dialogue starter, a shift maker, and a means for parents and others to begin implementing strategies to help their children cope and be the best they can be.

Purpose and Function

This book's purpose is to be an initial conversation starter, an introduction into a shift that needs to be made in our society's mindset regarding young people. This book will in no way provide all the information on this topic, however, my hope is that this book will not only give parents some ideas and strategies for fostering their child's intuitive, empathic and spiritual side, but will also inspire dialogues in families, communities, and schools about how we demonstrate 'believing' in our children. After reading this book, I hope people are 'moved' to create their own HOPE tribes and to begin conversations of their own about how to live out the tribe's values. As you read please keep in mind that this is merely a guide and handbook for practical insights and strategies. This is meant to be an easy read that gives ideas for relating, connecting, and building tribes. Further dialogue and research will be useful as well for many topics and ideas discussed in this handbook.

How to Read This Book

When reading this book, it is important to know what you are looking for, your launching point. Some will be looking for immediate strategies for the child in their life. Others will want to take more time and read the book from front to back in an orderly fashion. There is no correct way to utilize this book. It is a resource. The hope is to inspire a parallel process. This parallel process starts with meeting you where you are at, just as you meet a child where they are at emotionally, spiritually, and behaviorally. The goal is to provide support in whatever way you are needing it in this moment.

With this said, it is recommended to read the book in its entirety at some point. In reading the book in its entirety, one will gain a deeper understanding. It will be essential to comprehend the premise of this work and how it relates to the foundational concepts within the strategies. If you find yourself skipping ahead to explore a strategy or a chapter that is 'speaking to you', I suggest that you make a commitment to return to the pages you've skipped, as this book is about a process. When working with a child it is the process that often leads to the greatest connection and the best use of the strategy.

The book looks at the impact of supports on a child. These supports range from organizing a Tribe of believers, recognizing a style of interacting, the importance of relating between adult and child, and internal supports that a child can integrate for future use. Remain open to where you find yourself and what you are looking for. Soulful inquiry for each member of the H.O.P.E. tribe is seen as paramount. Personal growth and discovery is aimed to be the outcome.

Wayne Dyer states that "believing is seeing" so believe that you have found this book for a reason. Prepare to believe and see. Take notice of what comes up for you. When we explore deep within we live outwardly more aligned with that energy. This energy creates the way we relate to the world. From this positive energetic plan, we are able to call into existence those in our tribe who will serve our greater good and highest self. Enjoy the process.

Part One

What is the H.O.P.E. Tribe?

Chapter 1

The Journey

How did we get here?

"Hope is the conduit for miracles"-Gabrielle Bernstein

Let me first share what inspired this book. Gabrielle Bernstein said it best, "Hope is the conduit for miracles". This quote changed me as soon as I heard it and has stuck with me in a profound way. It has helped shape how I choose to live my life. I haven't always been a hopeful person. Believing my limiting and negative self-beliefs has been my habitual pattern until about a year ago. Sometimes it really is life's greatest pain that brings about the greatest positive change. My family has been through several struggles the past few years and it has rocked my world in a way that required soul level healing and a new way of living and perceiving life. This struggle has forced the issue of seeing how my negative self-talk keeps me from living from a true joyous place. In the past I approached life from a perspective of scarcity rather than abundance. I've had to do a lot of soul searching, a lot of tear shedding, and a lot of looking at how my beliefs shape and create my life. Dr. Wayne Dyer has said that 'believing is seeing'. So true. For if we truly believe we will see. So lately, I have been "seeing" this book on shelves at book stores, "seeing" it in the hands of mothers and fathers on airplanes as I travel, "seeing" it in the hands of teachers as they ponder what is needed in their classrooms, and 'seeing' it provides support to all who read it. Our thoughts are powerful tools in our life, and all too often we ignore them, alter them to meet societal views, and change them to a more negative story out of fear. These negative thoughts and stories prevent us from living a self-inspired, soul-actualized life. Living a soul-actualized life is one that is lived based on daily soulful expression, living your unique life purpose, being true to your life's path while living in deep alignment. A convicted soul-actualized person realizes their strengths, their limitations, their purpose, and how to interact in a world without selling out to false beliefs. My greatest inspiration for this book is a result of a collision between past and present. This collision consists of the past, a glance back in time at my childhood as well as the present, seeing my own children for who they truly are. I am ready to live my best life and my greatest hope is that my children will do the same. For children to really learn to live a soul-actualized life, they need a tribe. They need believers, supporters, and champions for their individual talents, skills, and abilities. Children need people who help them navigate their world and act as facilitators for their own dreams and aspirations. In a material world like the world today, a tribe can help children decipher between operating on a fulfilling soul-level and one that is driven by ego.

Feeling alone, foreign in this world, and separate somehow from my family, as a child I felt incredibly 'small'. Childhood was emotionally difficult for me. The emotional tension was like a rubber band stretched so thin it threatened to snap. My current reality was so far from an ideal place that I found myself lowering my expectations, falling victim to the destructive programs taught to me, and fearful of "making it out". We tend to forget that children are in fact people, too. We try to put an age on when a child becomes a person. For example, "when you are an adult you can talk to me about that." or "you don't need to worry about that until you are older". And perhaps my least favorite, "you are too young to understand". Parents make similar comments to their children when they themselves are cautious of addressing a certain situation, topic or issue. Examples might include, discussing curfew, a child's wants, what your child will eat for dinner, where babies come from, why there is mean people in the world, and why natural disasters occur. This projection decreases connection, filling a child's spirit with guilt for questioning and exploring their own inner wonder. We forget that children are little people, smaller versions of adults. Yes, they need guidance, but they don't need to be molded out of an attempt to control or out of fear. We can learn so much from our children, their souls completely open. Perhaps this is the fear of parents? If we open the dialogue, will we lose our own identity as the "person in charge". What might happen if we let go and lose control? The irony is that this may be the best lesson of all and children have the power to teach it. All too often our world tries to treat children as extensions of their parents or change them into who the world thinks they need to be. As my children would say, children become like "little minions". Children can be left feeling like they are here to do someone else's work and not their own. The meaning of 'work' here is a child's soul purpose, their life calling, their imprint on this world, their legacy, and what they have to offer. I do not ascribe to the parenting mentality of 'do as I say not as I do' nor do I believe that children should 'be seen not heard'.

Nothing is worse, at least in my humble opinion, than feeling completely alone even when surrounded by people. I felt alone as a child and rarely felt understood. As a young child I remember desperately trying to get my parents and siblings to see and acknowledge me. So desperate for connection, my seeking mind and spirit did what it needed to survive, it allowed me to see that I was not alone. What I termed, because that was the only understanding I had at the time, an "imaginary friend" was not imaginary at all. She was my spirit friend, someone who I grew very close to and someone who joined my very own "hope tribe". Despite my family's efforts to tell me 'my friend' didn't exist, I would not listen. I listened to music with her, set a place at dinner for her each night, and talked with her daily. I called her 'Cinco'. Yes, like the number 5 in Spanish. The synchronicity is that the number 5 in numerology is a number that represents the five senses, including sight, hearing, touch, smell, taste, as well as the five elements, we know them as earth, air, fire, water, and spirit. The number 5 also brings attention to how "change is inevitable" if we wish to learn and explore. Cinco had dark eyes, dark hair, and dark skin. She is beautiful. You see she is still here, with me, encouraging me to keep going, put my thoughts on paper so the world may hear my voice. A voice that so long ago was told was "too tiny" but now holds the power to fuel a revolution for children. Some would say that my imaginary friend was just a symbol or a therapeutic representation of a stressful or tumultuous time in my life. Those who know the deeper story know that I am a survivor of childhood abuse and trauma. I had to face these questions and accusations. Was she "real" or "imaginary"? According to common beliefs backed by articles, imaginary friends are just that… imaginary. But I knew Cinco was different. While she was there to share my deepest pain and to comfort me in times of overwhelming loneliness, like many say about their "imaginary friends", she also had a body, mind, heart and soul. I could see her in the corner of my pink walled room, a shy timid concerned young girl, giggling joyfully to cope with her own anxiety. She became my trusted sidekick, attending school with me, sharing stories and ideas, giving me a sense of security that something "imaginary" could never do. A warmth would come over me, a slight tearfulness evoked by true connection filling my eyes. A true connection that came from the spirit realm. A child who had come, fully in spirit and soulful expression, to do what no one else could. Cinco knew me, all the in's and outs, all the scary stuff, my deepest fears and dreams, she held them for me, waiting for the right time to unleash them and allow my own soul to serve. Our connection is deep and our purpose intertwined. No one can discredit her "realness" and while not all children who claim to have an imaginary friend will be experiencing a spirit or soul from the other side, some will. This does not mean that we need to bombard our child with questions that create a sense of concern about their experience, it simply means we must be open to the idea that their experience holds possibilities of contact with another realm.

Fast forward a year. I began to have more experiences where I would hear a song on the radio and have 'apparitions' (unknown to me at the time of what they actually were called) and 'people' would appear. I could see them in their lives as if it was happening in the moment, but I knew the people were no longer living in the physical realm. They had crossed over, passed away. Interestingly enough, I was never afraid and always felt at peace with these 'visitors'. In ways I felt safer with them than with people in my own physical realm. Their visit was one of peace and brought a message of hope. I remember during Desert Storm the song 'Show Me The Way' by Styx would be played on the radio often, even nightly at one point. I would hear it and soldiers would line up in my room. It was an odd feeling as a child, not sure what to make of it. It was as if they were right there with me. Even with an active imagination, I knew this was different than creating something in my mind. This experience, and others, would guide me later in life. Even today I get chills as I write this, fully aware of how these memories propel my desire to connect with others about life beyond what we perceive as "real" and by bringing awareness to these experiences.

It was a big concept for a young girl to understand, only 12 years by this time. "Show Me the Way" became my guiding force, a song that encompassed my experience and was shared with others often. It played an integral part in my process of healing my past trauma, the war that raged within me. Here are a few lines from the song that speak to my experience, lyrics that signal the need for a HOPE Tribe.

...And I feel this empty place inside so afraid that I've lost my faith
Show me the way, show me the way
Take me tonight to the river
And wash my illusions away
...That I wake up each morning and turn on the news to find we've so far to go
...And if I see your light, should I believe
Give me the strength and courage
To believe that I'll get there someday

The lyrics shine an illuminating light on the need for this HOPE tribe guide. A guide for finding hope within a tribe of believers, those not afraid to remain childlike, curious and open to the mysteries of life. As implied in the song, we do **not** want our children to lose faith. **We can't afford for them to.** Intuitive and empathic children have such meaningful roles to play in our society and in our communities. The world is full of illusions, ones that try to ignore our spiritual nature and make life something more material and ego focused. The HOPE tribe wants to dispel these illusions and move from an ego-focused mindset to a more open, holistic, love inspired, and soul engaged way of living. The children of tomorrow are the holders of this idea. The adults of today will either inspire or hinder this work. Children must be encouraged to live out their inspiration in a way that touches the masses and speaks to the interconnectedness of all. The HOPE tribe becomes about putting hope into action. To live H.O.P.E. is to Honor Open Perceptive and Empathic children in a way that values them for who they are, promotes their growth, gives meaning to their experiences, and allows them to live out their soul's meaningful work. For the past 17 years, "Show Me the Way" has been my mantra, my prayer, my guiding light. The words remind me of who I am, what I stand for, my hopes and fears, and my deep desire to help heal others. For now, my soul's purpose is to give back in a way that honors children's stories while offering helpful strategies to promote intuitive and empathic living.

As a child an Angel came to me. She visited often, and I enjoyed her presence. She sat with me. She had a maternal energy, comforting and nurturing me in difficult times. One day, ridden with heartache caused by intense loneliness, she sensed my deep despair. She came to me and gently said, "someday I will guide you home". Like a guardian angel, she assured me that she would help me find my place in this confusing world. Under her wings, I would find my "home". This powerful journey is not over by any means, however, I believe she has delivered her promise. I am home. It is through this delivered promise that I remain hopeful and trust that the process will continue to heal, not only my wounds but the wounds of the world around me.

My childhood, full of events once thought 'random' but now wholeheartedly known as orchestrated by a loving universe, led me to the idea of the HOPE tribe. These events, too many to name, may seem small to my audience yet in the mind of a growing girl attempting to make sense of a dark and often hopeless world, were profound. As a sixth grader I remained after school to talk with my teacher. This event that in the moment seemed miniscule, changed my life forever. This profound event, will forever stay etched in my memory, providing me so many gifts and remarkable learning about life. My teacher never openly shared that he was homosexual, but I 'knew'. This "knowing" would be confirmed years later when I returned to the elementary school for a brief visit. This 'knowing' is something I am good at. Even back then, as a child, and still holds true to this day, I can tell people about their siblings, past events, their emotional state and all sorts of personal information. I did not know how I knew, I just 'knew'. And on that day when I returned, I knew I needed to make my "knowing" known. My sixth-grade teacher was sitting at his desk. I approached him. Tears welled up in my eyes. Looking puzzled, he asked if I was okay. I assured him that I was but that I had something to share with him. The words leapt from deep within almost without pause. I told him that his twin brother was okay, happy, safe, and in Heaven. My teacher began to cry. He was engaging in a process of his own "knowing" about life. I was unaware that his brother had passed away. and he was grieving, wanting a sign of peace and hope. Sharing this message, facilitated by spirit, brought him that very peace and hope he was desperately seeking. It was a beautiful feeling, a real-life miracle. This miracle continues to spur me on. This experience has helped me learn to trust myself, take risks and recognize the healing power of connection. I never shared this story with my parents, and most of the time I have kept these things about myself hidden. I felt completely torn between living a life I thought I had to and living the life I thought I was meant to. I remember thinking that I wanted to be with people, connect to their stories, and help 'heal the world'. As a young child, the best way for me to honor this side of myself was simply just to share that "I wanted to be a nurse and help people heal". I felt like super woman. I could use a gift to change the world for better. Somewhere along the way I lost that feeling, believing what others told me, conforming to an idea of what I thought I should be. And here lies my purpose, the reason I write. I write for me, as well as the child within, my own children, and all children who have gifts beyond our understanding stifled by a society built on old ways of thinking. I write to live my dream, I write to express my soul purpose. I write to give children a voice.

Anita Moorjani, a Hay House contributor and world renown author of her near-death experience, said: "not living your personal dreams is also debilitating to our children, especially if they are empaths or sensitive beings. They will respond to your energy, not necessarily what you say. They will know if your actions are congruent with what you truly believe, your passions, and if you are living your soulful life". While children are the keys that unlock the doors to new worlds, the adults in their lives shape the keys, form the patterns to be congruent with various locks. Parents, teachers, and other adults shape each child's heart, mind and soul. Through this shaping process, adults allow for children to birth their true selves and unlock the mysteries of life or succumb to the predetermined ways of the past. As Dr. Wayne Dyer shared, "my children are your children" and "all children are OUR children". Raising empathic children calls forth the need for a tribe, a collective responsibility that allows each child to use their keys for their highest good. We all belong to each other, a tribe, human kind, to care for another is to care for self.

It is 2017. I have two wonderful children. My inquisitive 8-year-old boy and my clever 5-year-old girl are my greatest teachers. Their presence in my life has been extraordinary. Each day they show me what unconditional love feels like. Both of my children are 'sensitive', said with a positive connotation unlike the worlds typical portrayal. My daughter, a social butterfly, is excellent at 'reading' people's feelings and emotional states. My son has abilities beyond the commonly discussed or accepted 5 senses. He can sense people's emotions, is keen to changes in energy, takes on other's emotions in his body, sees auras, intuitively knows accurate information about people and places, and, according to him, has 'seen God'. As a baby I noticed 'differences', a uniqueness, about him. His behavior and demeanor might be comparable to a philosopher unraveling the mysteries of life. It wasn't until recently, about 4 years ago, that I started to put it all together. It is from this noticing, that I learned what it is to be an empathic child, and that I was a blessed mother of two. In chapter 3 we will explore common characteristics of empathic, intuitive, and highly sensitive children. As a mother I will not discount what my children feel, perceive, and or experience. I am working hard at this goal. It is difficult to navigate the world's differing perceptions, limiting beliefs, and stereotypical expectations. I grant myself peace because I am not perfect, and know I will make mistakes, however through this process I stay connected to this goal.

I write this book as a tool. This is a tool for parents, caregivers, grandparents, counselors, teachers, therapists, and others who believe in the precious mind and soul of a child. A guide for supporting children who originate from the Divine's love, a place where social constructs and ego has yet to take over; a place where connection to the greater good and to the spirit world has not been stuffed down, deemed impossible or socially unacceptable.

The H.O.P.E. Tribe: Honoring Open Perceptive and Empathic Children as a title for this work poured from me, divinely inspired from a place deep within. I wholeheartedly believe that my spirit guides, my Guardian Angel, other souls (like Sylvia), and God are the inspiration and co-authors. They have given me signs along the way to not only guide my writing but provide emotional support during difficult periods of the process. This book, The H.O.P.E. Tribe, is only possible through an authentic tribal effort. For my tribe, I am forever grateful.

Through this process, I discovered that one of my Spirit Guides is a Native American woman, appearing much like Pocahontas. She comes to me with long flowing black hair, a beautiful headdress, traditional clothing, and beads from the Earth around her neck. She stands tall, proud, and with great wisdom. I feel a breeze, one you might feel standing on top of a rock in the mountains after a climb or scramble, one of great accomplishment and pure connection to the journey. It's brisk, cool, and all encompassing. She speaks articulating a tribal mentality. She talks about the connection to the Earth, to the 'village', to the animals, the sun, the moon, and the plants. Her message is one of interconnectedness and sharing gifts for the greater good. In contemplating the title of this work, she appeared to me and guided me to the ideas of the Hopi Indians. I found it synchronistic that Hopi is just one letter off from Hope.

Metaphysically speaking the number 1 is symbolic. Not only will this be my first book, but in numerology, the Number 1 is like the first breath of the universe, Om and the I Am, symbolic of the Initiating Force. Like those first moments after child-birth, it is the first breath, the first cry, the 'first', the number 1 where you allow yourself to fall, be 'all in' love, with a little person that has been entrusted to you. The excitement continues as parents see all "the firsts" that follow. This book is like that first. Like, the first when we realize that a child is a gift and that their gifts are unique, special, and are given to them for a reason. The idea of the HOPE tribe has become my baby, my breath. Symbolism grew as I pondered the title, The HOPE tribe and the number 1. For example, in the Tarot, the number 1 relates to the Magician. Magicians embrace a deep knowing that they are difference makers and act as the change agents of our world. It doesn't take long to see the connection. They instinctively draw people, animals, and/or purposeful situations into their lives. They possess an interesting perspective on life, one that attracts attention to illusions and works to uncover the truth behind the universe and its mysteries. This one letter difference symbolism supported by metaphysical beliefs in numerology and Tarot, prove potent. It is from these discoveries that I have come to fully validate the name, the HOPE tribe, that will bring about an awareness of the spiritual realm and its influence.

As I began to write I became more conscious of how much our children and families need 'the tribe'. The tribe, created by Source, the very source that created each of us, binds us together in manifesting the Divine purpose. The HOPE tribe's mission is to keep that purpose at the heart of our soul's work, protected from negative words, thoughts, or behaviors. Should the "tribe's" children accumulate soul scars along the path, the HOPE tribe helps heal these wounds, reconnect a child to their soul gifts, embrace the heartfelt journey, and provide a safe base for reclaiming who they are. The HOPE tribe understands the communal effort needed to increase the power and influence of one.

Due to my very own "Pocahontas", support from numerology and tarot, my own need for hope, and a deep desire within, the emergence of this book became a reality. It is from these things and the combination of many events, stories, concepts and thoughts, including the Hopi Indian influence, has brought life to these pages. First and foremost, the subsequent words are not an attempt to explain and understand the lifelong legacy and spirit of the Hopi Indians. The breadth of such work would call for another book. However, the following discussion, is simply a way to express my thoughts about the power of returning to an ancient tribal idea that can lead us on a spiritual path facilitated by loving spirit guides.

The Hopi Indians, descendants of the Ancient Pueblo People, have a deep-rooted culture with strong tradition in their religion, spirituality, morals, ethics, and values. These complex rituals and ceremonies are beautifully performed 'for the tribe' and to benefit the entire world.

The name Hopi, derived from Hopituh Shi-nu-mu, translates to "The Peaceful People" or "Peaceful Little Ones". As we continue to dive into this topic of raising spiritual and intuitive children, I trust the meaning of the Hopituh Shi-nu-mu will resonate with the notions cultivated in the HOPE Tribe. Just as the Hopi name implies, the HOPE tribe involves those who believe in peace, champion the greater good, and demonstrate unity so that all in the "tribe" prosper. The tribe is rooted in a tradition of openness, acceptance, trust, and empowering children to use their soul gifts.

The HOPE tribe is a village, a community dedicated to raising children in ways that honor their perceptions, their truth, their experiences, and their stories. Our world needs these "tribes". The HOPE tribe seeks to uphold the proverb that "it takes a village to raise a child" by revealing that safe communities are only created through the mutual understanding of those within. The HOPE tribe is rooted in the Divine's love. The essence of love is honor, respect, openness, and appreciation for all people, especially children whose voices tend to be silenced or under recognized. The members of the HOPE tribe must operate from these core values to uphold the mission. With this comes a vow from all who 'join'. This responsibility entails remaining open, curious, and non-judgmental. This open-minded approach promotes the acceptance of truth. Suspended judgement reveals that no one "truth" can ever be identical to another. Curious dialogue allows for heartfelt learning from each other, the best tool available to manifest the values of the tribe. Members of the HOPE tribe understand the limitations of individualism and the promise in collectivism. To commit to the tribe is to support the tribal goal of increasing soul actualization of its youngest members. A tribe is only as strong as its weakest member. In modern societies many would quickly label children as the weakest members. This pedestrian way of thinking has no room in the philosophy of the HOPE tribe. Children must be viewed as the extraordinary people they are and permitted to spread their gifts among the world. The tribe calls for the allowing of sensitive and highly attuned children to be who they are, to challenge society in a peaceful and profound way, and to remain true to themselves.

Children today are raised, taught, and guided based on socially constructed falsehoods about distorted truths claiming to be absolutes. All too often I hear parents say, "you don't feel that way", "you're not sick", "you didn't see that", and so on. I am no stranger to this discrediting way of being raised. It is so easy to discount a child's perceptions, feelings, and experiences. It is about a mindset shift, a transformation, an evolved worldview. While this change is desperately needed and most would agree, this shift requires a reprogramming of sorts. Many openly state their misery with the current reality we find ourselves in, yet when asked to probe deeper, we become stuck, often paralyzed, falling back on old "tapes" circulating like broken records. Like mentioned before, the HOPE tribe is about action and moving toward a collective programming that honors all members of the living system. The most difficult part is that the collective whole is currently operating from an ego centric soul 'less' mindset. When we live soul "less" we live in depravity, a paradigm that labels people, doubts abundance, and makes our life's focus a human experience rather than a spiritual one. It leaves people, including children who are perhaps most susceptible, feeling empty, untapped, and under-utilized, as if their soul has lost connection to the deep life force.

In life I want my children to 'trust their intuition and self' more than anything else. The universe always delivers what we need just at the right time, it is just whether we are willing to pay attention to it. Children need help navigating these nuances of spirit, learning to trust their guides, succumbing to the power that resides within, and honoring their desires. Parents of highly sensitive, intuitive, and empathic children need to pay attention to what is going on for their child. Simply noticing is not enough. Parents are mentors, assisting their children in the integration of experiences across all domains. This mentorship promotes self-confidence and an ability for a child to trust themselves first, then others. Like myself, some children will find this mentorship outside the walls of their home. Some parents will be unable to make this shift, yet their children possess a knowing that is beyond the physical. The HOPE tribe answers this call. Those in the tribe will attract those who need them most.

The HOPE tribe awaits. The tribe, full of the people around us, angels, ascended masters, and spirit guides, requests your membership.

These forces, energies, and spirits, as an integral part of the life force (God/Universe/Prana/Source Light/the Divine/whatever you choose to call it), orchestrate experiences on Earth that surpass anything we could imagine. The HOPE tribe gives up on total control, offers gratitude for the gifts and abilities our children are blessed with and acknowledges that Spirit works hard for us to reveal our true potential.

This is not about whether or not you believe in Angels, God, an intelligent universe, unicorns, dragons, or fairies, but rather your belief in our children, our key to a wondrous, peaceful future. Our world is changing. Our world is a very different place, almost unrecognizable from when I was a child. Our children are forced to maneuver among situations and stimuli that we never had to deal with. On top of that, researchers, metaphysical healers, and other professionals are noticing an increase in our children's extrasensory abilities. Many feel lost, searching for ways to guide our children in the right direction. With no Global Positioning System designed to offer optimal routes toward soulful alignment available, the HOPE tribe will provide a 'home base', a gathering place and starting point for believers. The HOPE tribe, a network of supporters, is available to advocate, comfort, fortify and reassure you and your child.

We must answer the call NOW. Our world needs to embark on a new journey, one filled with wisdom of the past, beauty of the present, and hope for the future. Our children need us to believe in them. They are the link, the loop that keeps us connected. It is evident a new way of thinking is being summoned for our ever-changing world. With more children being diagnosed with various disorders and mental health conditions (Autism, Sensory Integration Disorder, OCD, ADHD, and more) suggests that our traditional ways of connecting to our environment are insufficient and hurtful. With little understanding of the why, we can only say for sure that we know something must change. If we continue in the same manner our children will suffer, causing all connections to erode. Without connection there is no life. The HOPE tribe can act as the life force needed to be a "conduit for miracles". Miracles born from a collective tribe of people, joined for empowering children to live fearless of being different, proud to be who they are, and strong in their truths.

We live in a world of standards, meeting them and staying within them. If you look at schools and their curriculum it is easy to see how we measure success, skills, abilities, talents, and what we are supposed to do with our lives. Children are sent messages all day long through academic standards, media, and family guidance on what they should do, who they should be. If we let children direct their lives a little more, (this does not imply decreasing expectations or not setting limits for our children), we may be amazed at the talents that emerge that we never knew existed. Peace and happiness would flow from a soul felt place where children knew they belonged, not just trying to fit in, and creative expression would guide the child and those whom they touch in profound spiritual and eye-opening ways.

I am guilty of saying to my child, "why don't you like...", or "don't be so sensitive". These words make me cringe. Despite my efforts I have found myself trying to change my children for mere social acceptance. One thing I hope parents, and those who guide children daily, myself included, hear is that we are not perfect. We may find ourselves fighting against our own social constructions, how we were raised, and the implications of the social circles we find ourselves in, but the first place to start is by honoring. Honoring ourselves, looking at our own thoughts and beliefs. Honoring our children, noticing their strengths and talents. Honoring the connection, between us and our children and the world. And honoring life as a soulful journey. Offering services to schools, communities, and groups of HOPE tribe members in the future may be an idea to continue the journey of this book and its mindset. This would provide more information, skills, and strategies for fostering intuitive living among our children and their families.

Chapter 2

The Members

Who is a part of the H.O.P.E. tribe?

"If you are alive you need help" Robert Holden

The HOPE tribe is a collection of people and spirits. The spiritual realm plays an integral role in the HOPE tribe. This realm consists of spirits, angels, ascended masters, and so many more. The tribe is spiritual, one without boundaries of time and space. This realm challenges worldly ideas of what and who our children are supposed to be. However, this does not mean that the tribe loses its connection to the world. The tribe must operate in this world. More importantly the tribe must learn how to remain connected without being swayed back to traditional limiting ways of being. My son will often say, "I am not a robot". This is a profound statement. I believe children feel this way most of the time. Children often go through the motions, are seen not heard, are given little control over their own environments, and are forced to reside in boxes. While robots resemble humans and are able to perform tasks required of people, they cannot connect with others, engage in authentic relationships, and do not possess the capacity to feel. Robots don't have a spirit or a soul. I won't remember an "interaction" with a computer, but I will recall a conversation with another human being, a person with a story, personality, hopes and dreams. Our stories, interpretations, wishes and fears, drive genuine connection. It's this connection that aligns us to the greater good, the universe. it's the connection to the universe that allows for the use of our soul gifts, giving meaning to our lives. Our connection to the universe solidifies the connection among our children and ourselves and allows them to live a confident soulful life. Living confidently, sure of our purpose, brings children great joy, a joy that is contagious. We could all be robots, but our tribe values connection, talents, and gifts that are given freely and shared for the greater good.

The tribe encourages children to embrace their intuition and creative energies. Belief in every child's abilities is the launching point for trust. Trust allows our children to express themselves in a way that promotes integration of body, mind and spirit. The HOPE Tribe is built on a belief system, a way of interacting and connecting with children that allows for extrasensory perceptions and experiences, fostering intuitive living. Aiding children in trusting their intuition promotes creativity, self-respect, self-acceptance, expansion, and mind-body-soul integration. The tribe is not exclusionary., There are no "others". It it is easy to group people by labels, assigning meaning to them, allowing our egos to select who we associate with and who we care for. Truth of the matter is, we are all connected. It's scary for some to see it this way, but to care for another is to care for self, and vice versa. We need to reconnect our modern tribe to the indigenous one. A revival would create a wisdom, an interdependence among its members. The tribe see's the benefit of all who participate, what everyone can bring, and invites the Divine to guide and facilitate expansion in a way that is loving and meaningful for the world. The HOPE tribe honors open-minded, perceptive, and empathic children and provides guidance to parents and others who directly support them.

The H in HOPE is the heart of the tribe. It stands for Honor and is the cornerstone for the tribe, bringing all members together. It binds members and promotes a safe place to explore who children really are, complete with their divinely inspired gifts and abilities. As a parent I want to 'honor' my child, in our world this can be difficult. Ralph Waldo Emerson wrote "life's greatest accomplishment is to be yourself in a world that is constantly trying to change people". Imagine a world where everyone lived up to their full potential, where we didn't shy away from acting simply because of fear of what others might think.

What morals, values, ethics, and ways of going about our daily lives would change for the better? Honor comes from living authentically and wholeheartedly. Discounting what a child believes, hears, sees, experiences, feels, is dishonoring their soul, their self, their sense of who they are. To Honor someone is to stand beside them while they stand up for their convictions, believing in them when others don't or can't, and holding their experience with respect, even if it isn't our own. If we shut our children down, if we tell them their experience is wrong, they begin to change who they are. When children choose to change, they shift, become jaded and muddle their self-concept with others. They begin to be someone other than who God/the Divine/The Universe created them to be. Before Honoring begins, we must first uncover what we wish to honor. What follows is a way to define those aspects we wish to honor in our intuitive and spiritual children.

Chapter 3

The Language

What is the common understanding?

"Language by its very nature is a communal thing."--T.E. Hulme

While I do not typically believe in labels because they tend to isolate rather than connect, at times labels provide for a foundational understanding important to ensure that children get the support they need. In addition, labels can help parents develop a sense of awareness regarding their own exceptionalities and their child's unique gifts. What follows are loose definitions and characteristics of certain common terms. This common language will help create a shared understanding among the tribe and support learning needed to access the strategies shared later. The following is not meant to "label" people, but rather offer up common terms and brief definitions to support deeper inquiry. I encourage all tribe members to do further research that could benefit children, self and families.

Spiritual

To be spiritual is to be a child who is more interested in relating to others on a soul or spirit level. According to Lisa Miller's website, these children have a 'positive active relationship to spirituality" (2017). This relationship is characterized by an active belief in a Higher Power.

Higher Power can be named God, Divine, Universe, or nature. This connection to higher source has protective qualities for children and is viewed as helpful in decreasing maladaptive behaviors such substance use and abuse, reducing emotional tension that lead to anxiety or depression, and increasing their meaning and purpose.

Due to this deep desire to connect on a more soulful level, typically spiritual children lack interest in material things. With this said, children are children, and they will have their wants. Spiritual children still ask for toys, still desire material things, however, there is a different quality about them when it comes to this. Their lack of attachment to an item is how this quality is expressed. (https://en.wikipedia.org/wiki/Spirituality) Spiritual children typically have more ease in letting material things go, don't tend to hoard or have hoarding tendencies, and appear to have less emotional reactivity to the loss of an item. A spiritual child's wants for material items are not deep rooted nor based in lack or scarcity concept. 'Things' don't fill them in a way that attachments to things might for another child.

Intuitive

Intuitive children use what feels to be true as their guide. In The Highly Intuitive Child Catherine Crawford shares that intuitive children 'feel the vibe instantly in their body' and can pick up on energy in a room. (Crawford, Catherine. 2009) They utilize instinctive reason over conscious reason to acquire knowledge. This knowledge may come without proof or evidence. Often times intuitive children may not even be aware of how they obtained the knowledge. One may hear intuitive children use the phrase, "I don't know" more often than not. They truly may not 'know', for they may be relying on instinct, perceptions, or a feeling rather than rational thought or reasoning to access "knowing". The term intuition is linked and translated as "consider" or "to contemplate". (https://en.wikipedia.org/wiki/Intuition) These 'contemplators' 'consider' what they feel as a resource to understanding the environment prior to engaging the prefrontal cortex.

Empath

A child who is empathic has a high level of compassion and empathy. Simply put, it's the ability to feel with or what other people may be experiencing. This can literally be a "walking in their shoes" experience, where it is difficult for the empathic child to know what is their experience vs another's. This ability increases a 'oneness' mentality. Dr. Judith Orloff reminds us that children who are empaths 'see more', 'hear more', 'smell more', intuit more', and 'feel more'. (The Empath's Survival Guide, 2017) Often times empathic children feel connected to people but can't explain why. Sometimes empathic and intuitive children don't know themselves well enough to even know what they like, dislike, or desire in a situation. Conversations about likes, dislikes, and their strengths on a consistent basis will help with increasing their self-awareness around this and eventually will aid in a deeper understanding of their emotional states. As an empath myself, I can instantaneously pick and absorb physical and emotional energy in a room. I find myself drawn to certain individuals and guided by Spirit to engage with them. This engagement can range from a simple hello, to providing a message, as I am also a Psychic Medium. For children this may be noted as who they may gravitate towards in a room, whom they wish not to sit close to, or other comments they make about individuals they come in contact with. For my children, their bodies give off a physical indication of energy they respond to in another person. They will sway, lean away from a person, or move closer to an individual depending on different energies they are sensing.

Sensitive and Highly Sensitive

A child who is considered sensitive or highly sensitive are said to have an overactive response system. They can react to situations prior to thinking first. They tend to act upon a feeling or sensation they have. These children also may complain about aspects of their senses that others don't take notice of. These complaints may stem from textures in foods, textures in clothing, smells, noises, and different types of lighting. A good reference for Highly Sensitive People or HSPs is Dr. Elaine Aron.

A discussion has been started and addressed by Judith Orloff, the author of The Empath's Survival Guide, about the difference between empaths and HSPs. Empathic children will take the experience to a deeper level, meaning they can sense subtle energy and absorb it into their own body. This can occur with people, animals, and environments. The internalization of these emotions or even physical pain can cause an inability to know what is their discomfort or someone else's. Judith Orloff has created a diagram of The Empathic Spectrum. Judith Orloff has published useful information regarding empaths and techniques for coping. Seeing children on a spectrum is helpful when appreciating every person's uniqueness and personal expression of gifts, talents, and abilities. I would recommend further reading in this area for parents who believe they are empaths, and/or for those who are discerning whether their child is or is not. (https://www.psychologytoday.com/blog/the-empaths-survival-guide/201706/the-differences-between-highly-sensitive-people-and-empaths) Another online resource that can provide some assistance or guidance is https://exemplore.com/auras/Indigo-Crystal-and-Rainbow-Children

Star Child

Star Children are a group of children that are born to 'rebuild the Earth through compassion and kindness'. According to several websites and David Wolfe, these children are known to embody the energy of grace, purity, truth, and wisdom. Their perception of Earth is that ALL life on it is sacred. (www.DavideWolfe.com). This group of children is split into different subsets according to their generation and attributes. This typically relates to specific decades a child is born, what personality traits that express, and past life experiences. The following are the individual subsets defined more in depth.

Indigo Child

Another popular term is Indigo child. An Indigo child is a child believed to be in the next stage of human evolution. An Indigo child is believed to have paranormal abilities like telepathy, empathic abilities, and are often viewed as more creative than their typical peers. Indigo children are known as the older generation of new age children, typically born in the 1970s. (https://en.wikipedia.org/wiki/Indigo_children) Indigo children often find themselves in a position in life that is focused on increasing the integrity of systems. Being big picture thinkers, these children are motivated to "recreate fundamental ideas" and altar systems for good. Such examples of systems can include education and government. Indigo children are said to embody 'spirits of a warrior' and are drawn to ending old ways of thinking. (David Wolfe)

Crystal Children

Bringing harmony is a Crystal child's purpose. Crystal children can be like Indigo children, however are often less assertive about their beliefs. These children tend to be more blissful in nature, and even tempered. Holding a balance between intensity of their passion and using emotional disposition to inspire harmony. They are said to be born mainly to Indigo children who are now intuitive and empathic adults. Crystal children can be highly sensitive and empathic. They operate on a higher frequency. This often times can manifest itself as a decreased need for verbal communication. Perhaps a child began speaking later in life (not until the age of 3 or 4) or don't see the need for verbal communication in the same way others do. An example is if a child gravitates towards another form of communication. Like my son who enjoys sign language, American Sign Language and the one he has created himself. Also noted by Doreen Virtue is that Crystal children often know best when it comes to what will serve them for their greatest good, which can make parenting even more difficult. Remaining open to what a child states is in his/her best interest will serve both in the relationship. These children tend to think outside the box, and beyond their years providing strategies that touch the deepest parts of them and allow soulful expression.

Rainbow Children

David Wolfe, describes Rainbow children as the "highest example of true potential". (https://www.davidwolfe.com) The goal of Rainbow children is to serve others. It is believed that Rainbow Children are the rarest of Star Children, having never lived on this planet. Rainbow children are "new souls". Due to the fact that Rainbow children are thought to be completely spiritually evolved, they are often misunderstood. They are about service and giving. The greater good at the forefront of their hearts and minds. Rainbow children have an ease about them when it comes to emotional expression. They already act in accordance with their spiritual peak. It is thought that Rainbow children possess a life purpose to heal and re-balance humanity. Rainbow children are the youngest and newest generation of spiritual children. Many Rainbow children are born to a Crystal child. This provides H.O.P.E. that at least one parent will be more apt at understanding their Rainbow Child. (https://www.angeltherapy.com/blog/indigo-crystal-and-rainbow-children) https://exemplore.com/auras/Indigo-Crystal-and-Rainbow-Children)

The names given to these children, were given based on aura coloring, energy patterns, and generational birth order. Doreen Virtue discusses this on her website www.AngelTherapy. Please see the table below to better identify the characteristics associated with each. It is thought that each group, or generation, have a stronger ability in certain areas that correspond with their aura color and their specific energy pattern. Many times empathic, intuitive, and sensitive children have parents who are as well. This is not always true. Ultimately, it is important that we seek to understand ourselves while attempting to understand our child more. If you believe you or your child is one of these types of special children, especially Crystal or Rainbow, please read further about their unique talents, abilities, and perceptions of the world. There is a list of resources in the back of this book to offer more insight into what it means to be a child or parent with these capabilities. Again, it is critical that we realize the truth in the proverb "it takes a village to raise, [parent, foster, and inspire] a child".

Type of Star Child	Typical Characteristics
Indigo Children	• Energy field shows darker purples and blues
	• Strong willed and stubborn
	• Have problems with authority
	• Intuitive, often psychic
	• Creative and unafraid of trying something new
	• Easily frustrated, may struggle being patient
	• Thrive with clear boundaries and structure in child rearing years
	• Might be insecure
	• Goal = break down traditional thinking ('shake things up')
	• May be diagnosed with ADD, ADHD
Crystal Children	• Energy field is clearer and more transparent
	• Typically born to Indigo Parents
	• Can be emotional and some might name them as "touchy-feely"
	• Decisions based on intuitions or feelings
	• Allergies and sensitivities are common
	• Seek and enjoy solitude
	• Maintain lasting friendships
	• Make good counselors or mediators
	• Usually have a musical nature about them
	• Connect easily with children, animals, and those in need
	• Choose comfort over "fashion"
	• May feel overwhelmed by crowded and high-energy places
	• May identify themselves as homosexual or be on a spectrum for how to enjoy sexual experiences
	• May love water
	• Are often healers and have a calming nature about them
	• Goal=build new world foundation
	• Might be termed "on the spectrum" because they can be seen as self-absorbed/contained

Rainbow Children	
	• Energy field has varied shimmering colors
	• Others may say that they are "in their own world"
	• Are known to be very loving and generous
	• Are brave and overcome hardship
	• Care for others
	• Can be telepathic
	• High energy in all domains, physically and psychically
	• May have larger eyes
	• Delayed milestones such as late to speak (may be 3 or 4 years of age)
	• Views the world in a fluid fashion, including gender
	• More secure and do not tend to care what others think of them
	• Goal=continue building new world, create new ways of existing, Earth is number 1 in all they do

https://exemplore.com/auras Indigo-Crystal-and-Rainbow-Children

Spiritually Awakened Children

Understanding spiritually awakened children is better grasped when we simply discuss common traits. The following are common of spiritually awakened children. This is built on my own observation, as well as my research. In reading articles in Conscious Lifestyle magazine and listening to several of Dr. Wayne Dyer's videos regarding spiritually awakened individuals, I realized that I have been privileged to know many. Please visit the website https://www.consciouslifestylemag.com/spiritual-awakening-signs-and-symptoms/ for more information and further opportunities to explore.

This is not an exhaustive list, and I encourage you to add your own if you deem fit. Everyone's input and experiences are important and valuable and help create a shared understanding of what is meant to be a part of the H.O.P.E. tribe.

A spiritual child or an awakened child may have an intensified or 'different' perception of life. This perception may cause things to seem brighter, to mean more, and the person tends to find joy or contentment in the "everyday things" more than before. These children enjoy watching nature in action, are struck by the beauty of the landscape, or are in awe of the sight of a bubble. Generally said, spiritually awakened children have a deeper appreciation for their surroundings.

A spiritually awakened child may have a different perception of time, or a shift in time orientation. The present moment becomes very important. A spiritual child might talk about time as though it is much slower, or may not see the benefits of living by a clock. My son once asked, "why is there time?" From this question a very thought provoking, lengthy, philosophical discussion ensued about time, how it started, the social construct of it, and so on.

A child who has a heightened sense of awareness in regards to spirit, spiritual matters, or speaking of certain life forces, may be a spiritually awakened child. An intuitive child may begin to talk about nature in a very spiritual way. Even death, typically morbid and fear evoking, is viewed simply as a life cycle event that is necessary within nature. They may develop or exude an 'all is well' attitude. This connection is to all things (people, things, nature, places, natural cycles) and may become the norm. They may begin to see things as a web of connection, possibly even making comments like "hey that person's name is Jim and I met a Jim yesterday at…". While this seems insignificant to some, it is an outward indication of how a child's brain is working. This connecting dots between experiences is powerful.

In addition, a highly empathic or intuitive child may see the link between all things, express ideas and thoughts that speak to harmony and connectedness of life. A spiritual child may talk about a 'new and old self', or talk as if they are not the same person as before. Some highly perceptive children want to change their names or 'be completely a new person'. My daughter recently has begun to ask if she can change her name. Sometimes this is just an age appropriate expression of individuality and personality, and other times it can be a sign of a more awakened sense of soul self. Spiritually awakened children experience an increase in sense of connection.

An intuitive and empathic child that has undergone or is undergoing a spiritual awakening may display high levels of empathy and compassion. They feel what another is feeling. They cry watching shows about animals being treated unfairly. Overall they become more aware of what another living thing is experiencing and can even experience it within themselves as well. This is what we call an empath.

A highly intuitive or empathic child may lack group identity. At school they may "get along with everyone" (as a teacher has said about my son), not ascribe to any 'groups' and when asked may say that they "just do whatever they feel like doing that day in the moment". Spiritually awakened children have a universal, more global, outlook and tend to be more concerned with collective issues, how people's thoughts and action impact others, and are likely to embrace environmentally friendly choices.

They tend to have a moral compass that the live by and focus on. "Is it okay if I do that?", "is that the right thing to do?" Perhaps this lack of group identity speaks to the spiritually awakened child's tendency to live life by curiosity rather than engaging in judgement of others. They tend to be more altruistic and giving. Spiritually awakened children seek authentic engagement with others or engage for a "cause". Typically, spiritually awakened individuals have more authentic connected relationships, and tend to have less insecurities around being with others.

These children tend to be creative, have vivid imaginations, and are said to be able to just "be" and find enjoyment in inactivity. They are less prone to boredom or habitual worry. Spiritually awakened children may express more gratitude than same age peers. There might be less 'thought chatter' occurring, meaning a child's mind might actually quiet down. They may appear more spacey or look off into the distance or be referred to as a 'day dreamer'. This is often the space created for their creativity.

Spiritually awakened people and children may have a strong sense of detachment to things. They no longer seek to accumulate material things, and some children may even give some of their toys or books away without prompting. These children are able to identify and communicate what they do and don't enjoy.

These simple descriptions and attempts to define complex concepts, are necessary to build a shared framework. In order to offer support to all H.O.P.E. tribe members, common terminology is critical. This shared language improves collaboration and communication, allowing for authentic dialogue. Common terminology and a deeper understanding of key vocabulary creates a framework for knowledge translation and the ability to fully implement strategies discussed in future chapters. Words capture our thoughts and allow them to be translated into action. In hopes of building a solid framework, at times it is helpful to create labels. While labels can isolate, the wish is that the labeling in this chapter has provided a communal understanding that can act as a catalyst for deeper questioning.

Chapter 4

The Soul Kaleidoscope

How can a metaphor for soulful living guide us?

> When I have them working together, it's like a
> beautiful kaleidoscope. –Ornette Coleman

The idea of Soul-Actualization comes from more examination of the term self-actualization. A prominent psychologist, Abraham Maslow, began a dialogue about the nature of being human. Out of this dialogue, a new way of seeing human nature, a mindset that moved from seeing human nature in a negative light, to a "more positive view where man is motivated to realize their full potential" was born. (https://en.wikipedia.org/wiki/Self-actualization). According to Maslow, self-actualized people have the following characteristics and abilities.

Self-actualized people…

- Judge situations correctly and honestly. They are sensitive to dishonesty.
- Are aware of and mindful of human flaws, and are accepting and tolerant of others in a kind way.
- Rely on their own experiences, intuition, and judgement to form their views and opinions.
- Belong and not just aspire to fit in. True to themselves, rather than focusing on how others want them to be.

- Fulfill a personal mission, with passion and not egocentric in nature, operating from a view of the greater good.
- Are viewed as resourceful and independent.
- Tend to show and express gratitude and appreciation for all of life and nature.
- Form deep bonds and connections with others. Not superficial. May have a few close friendships over many superficial acquaintances.
- Value mindfulness, solitude, and are comfortable being alone.
- Are able to laugh at oneself, see areas of growth, and 'not take life too seriously'.
- Experience times of feeling at one with the universe, intense feeling of peace, or being full of light.
- Socially compassionate.

https://en.wikipedia.org/wiki/Self-actualization

Using Maslow's work as a foundation, soul-actualization is living from a place of self-actualization. Soul-actualization impacts ourselves, others and our world by being open to change beyond the physical world. Soul-actualization embodies all aspects of the term spiritual enlightenment. It creates space for conversations about manifesting a H.O.P.E. Tribe directly connected to the spirit realm as well as creating a tribe in the physical, human world. The spiritual realm is always operating **with** and **for** you. The spiritual realm includes but is not limited to, God/Source, Guardian Angels, Archangels, Ascended Masters, Spirit Guides, Members of your soul family, and spirits of those who have crossed over from your family line.

To summarize, Maslow's Hierarchy of Needs states that if more foundational aspects of self are fulfilled, a person can operate from a space where actualization is possible. Soul-actualization then, is when you reach self-actualized living but are open to your spiritual enlightenment allowing your soul blueprint to extend out leaving a legacy. This legacy is when your soul's work continues from 'the other side'. An example of this is Dr. Wayne Dyer and Louise Hay, whose Earthly legacies continue to transform the lives of people, through books, videos, word of mouth, and more. Their souls continue to visit the Earth, to create change, influence good, and continue their soul's message and purpose despite physical death.

Prior to and during the process of writing this book, both of their loving spirits came to me. Louise Hay first revealed her spirit to me as Lulu. They continue to teach me from the spirit realm. Being in my spiritual H.O.P.E. Tribe, they held me accountable to soul self when ego-self began to mutter negative self-talk. I was reminded of affirmations that would provide the strength to move forward and was shown how fear is just False Evidence Appearing Real, a well-known acronym shared by Dr. Dyer. I wholeheartedly believe that Dr. Dyer and Louise Hay are in my tribe and am so thankful for their loving presence.

There is no delineation between our spiritual and earthly tribes. They are one! The Tribe extends beyond space and time of this physical realm and existence. My experiences and contact with the other side has shown me the great support the Universe offers. Our soul strength, soul purpose, and soul-actualization is infused with Source, with love and light. The Source bestows blessings. The blessing is that we can never be separated from it, we can only fail to recognize it. The Source, love and light, is always available. We must be vulnerable enough to embrace and trust it. It flows through us and when we embrace where our full potential originates it allows us to operate from a soul-actualized space.

Spirit graciously gave me a symbol. This symbol reminds me to live from a soulful place. Spirit knew that I needed a visual representation, a symbol that would help me visually understand. Providing a tangible symbol can aid in better articulation of and comprehension of a more abstract idea. This diagram visually demonstrates how the Earthly realm and the spiritual realm come together to impact soulful living. The diagram is titled Soul Kaleidoscope. The Soul Kaleidoscope accounts for all aspects of a child and integrates mind, body, and spirit.

<u>Soul Kaleidoscope</u>
A Kaleidoscope of Color
Diagram to help understand aspects of
H.O.P.E. children and soulful living

"A **kaleidoscope** is an optical instrument with two or more reflecting surfaces tilted to each other in an angle, so that one or more (parts of) objects on one end of the mirrors are seen as a regular <u>symmetrical</u> pattern when viewed from the other end, due to repeated <u>reflection</u>. The reflectors (or <u>mirrors</u>) are usually enclosed in a tube, often containing on one end a cell with loose, colored pieces of glass or other transparent (and/or opaque) materials to be reflected into the viewed pattern. Rotation of the cell causes motion of the materials, resulting in an ever-changing viewed pattern." (https://en.wikipedia.org/wiki/Kaleidoscope)

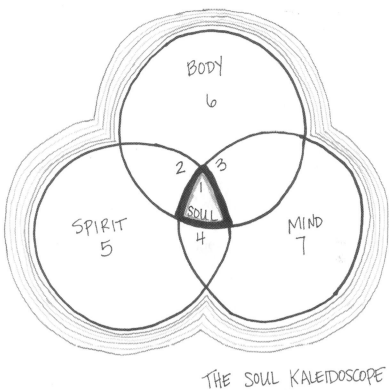

THE SOUL KALEIDOSCOPE

An explanation will reveal how colors, numbers, and all aspects of a person come together to create a beautiful picture that is unique and bright. The image of a young child looking through a cardboard kaleidoscope and turning it was the symbol that was downloaded to me from spirit. During this download, a short movie reel in which a child's face lit up in amazement and awe played repetitively. With each turn of the kaleidoscope the child's eyes widened, awaiting what would be created next with a small twist of the wrist. The idea that not a single person has the same experience with a kaleidoscope is profound and meaningful. A kaleidoscope is a strong metaphor for the experience of life. All experiences are different pictures presented through the kaleidoscope and viewed by the eyes who look through. What is seen, felt, and what images come to mind are different for each person. It is like a unique fingerprint, unique blueprint, and ultimately reveals our unique soul print. This kaleidoscope image aligns perfectly with my interpretation of a childlike holistic view of the world.

Looking at the diagram from a numbers perspective, the number 1 is of utmost importance. Number 1, the triangle at the very center, represents the soul. It is Number 1. The soul is a special place and needs to be the primal force behind Earthly living if we are to live self and soul-actualized lives. Number 1 represents the number of creation, represents the love and light that we are, the connection to Source, to the Creator.

While studying this diagram you will notice the three larger circles. These circles represent the ideas people more readily discuss when we describe a 'holistic' approach to self. They are mind, body, and spirit. The goal is to see 'holistic' become 'wholistic' where the 'w' is the "what we are". The 'what we are' is our essence, our soul, Divine love, pure good. The number three, according to worldnumerology.com, represents the creative child. Living with the soul in the leader position, the number 1 (triangle representing the Soul) then informs the three large spheres representing mind, body, and spirit. The process of allowing the soul to inform the other domains, creates interconnectedness and flow. Flow is the soul's expression of the interworking's of the pieces, inspired by the Soul. This expression shows itself as a child's unique set of gifts, talents, and abilities.

When a child is conducting their life from the mind, body, spirit domains without Soul as the motivator, the result may appear creative and full of talent, however there is a lack of connection to soul. Lack of connection to the number one, creates distance between self and Source. A gap is created, leaving Soul purpose drifting and untapped. Another possibility is for a child's ego self to overshadow soul self. This may limit the child from reaching their full potential, losing their connection to Source, changing an inner drive to match Earthly or human expectations, and changing who they are to meet societal pressures or to simply want to fit in. When soul leads and directs, passion and authentic living stays at the forefront. Love and a child's soul blueprint becomes the igniting force. The child is intrinsically empowered and their sense of belonging to Source, self, and creation is not muddled or confused with human conditions and human perceptions of success, happiness, and joy.

For purposes of this diagram and discussion, spirit and soul are viewed as different. Unfortunately, the typical way of describing a person (as mind, body, spirit) leaves out a few key pieces of the spiritual realm. Often, orchestrated events by spirit and Angels, and a perspective of Soul as an extension of God (God in all of us), are neglected. Spirit is more of Divine intervention, guardian angels, and spiritual influence **on** the soul. For example, spirit guides, ascended masters, angels, and spirits who have crossed over from your family line can contact a person, can help orchestrate events, and provide signs and symbols. The soul encompasses spiritual abilities, sensitivities, and Divine breathed talents that keep us connected to spirit no matter our connection to the Spirit Realm. Soul being connected to Source light and love is not dependent upon how we chose to relate to the Spiritual realm. Being infused with pure good is our birthright and is never stripped from us. Believing in and utilizing our God breathed unique talents with the assistance of the spirit realm is an action, a decision, or a way to express soul self.

The mind is our cognitive ability, our IQ, organic neurochemistry, our thoughts, our ability to process information, and a human's mental faculties and abilities. Body is the physical Earthly body. This can include our actions and behaviors, physical attributes, and our genetic make-up. Our body is the vessel by which we physically express our soul. Our mind is our mental expression. With assistance from the spirit realm, the other two domains align in unison. Form here we have the ability to embrace soulful living.

The other spaces labeled by numbers two through seven, can represent a child's energy centers, or chakras. These energy centers, when aligned, reflect the soul (the source light and pure love energy) and does so in a way that is pure, with little refraction and little interruption. Each chakra has an associated color. It is my belief, that each person has an energetic field around them, an aura, or "Rainbow air" as my son would call it. This colored energy can speak to a person's physical, mental, and spiritual state. When our energy centers are balanced our 'light is radiant', 'colorful', and we are operating from the pure prism of love or white light. As James Van Praagh would say, we are all souls having a human experience so some 'refraction' and interruptions will occur. Simply put, refraction is a phenomenon of light being deflected when passing through one medium to another. As it relates to a child's soul and living, refraction can be external or internal influences that are perceived as negative or 'deflect' away from the soul's essence. Negative thought patterns and generational maladaptive or dysfunctional relationship patterns, as a few examples, can cause interruptions to soulful living. Source, love and light is overshadowed by human ways of behaving, relating, and integrating, refracting the original state of who we are and changing it to more of who we think we should be. However, if these are minor or a child can realign themselves in adaptive and healthy ways, larger interruptions or 'refraction periods' will not disrupt their soul trajectory on a large scale. Thus, the soul is able to remain the guiding force. This is when positive affirmations, the concept of Law of Attraction, staying connected to our Source, and spending time in meditation to connect to our core, helps our children cope, become mindful stewards of their bodies and minds, and continue living out their soul blueprint.

The soul is the 'glue', what keeps us connected to Divine Light, and is the source of our greatest joy. The H.O.P.E. Tribe's mission is to rediscover the soul. Its purpose multilayered, like that of a child. One, to keep the current socially constructed views that inhibit our children from living a soul-actualized life at bay. Two, teach our children how to combat these ideas that attempt to make life robotic, stuck, and soul deflated rather than soul inspired. Three, the tribe hopes to be a physical manifestation of 'oneness' and promote authentic connectedness among its members.

The soul is difficult to define, a concept that is not tangible. No one can touch it. Despite it being intangible, it is possible to still be 'seen'. Soulful living manifests itself in other ways. Look around at the kaleidoscope of life. There is evidence that soulful living is not only possible but is in action. What does a person who is living their soul purpose look and behave like? How does it feel when you are in the presence of this person?

Closely related to the term 'spirit', soul is more abstract. Our society focuses on producible, tangible, and scientifically proven evidence. Such evidence is deemed only 'factual' if founded by 'valid' and 'reliable' instruments and measures. When did the collective whole, the human race, lose sight of the validity and reliability of personal report and subjective experience to determine happy and soulful living?

Our soul is like a fingerprint, there is no other like it. As a group, humans have created robotic systems and logical paradigms to explain aspects of life. These explanations have left out variables that account for Soul. While, science is important and helpful to us as people, the soul can't always be defined in scientific terms, often leaving it left unaccounted for. Empathic children don't fit within psychological explanations often provided. To see empathic children as being 'blessed' or in tune with our originating Source could actually spur more scientific research, if we overcame our fear of unknowing. Such research is needed in areas of spiritual matters, enlightened ways of thinking, mindfulness and the impact of these aspects on daily living, health, and a child's success trajectory.

For those of you reading this book this is most likely exciting news. Yet for others it creates intense fear; fear of the unknown, uncertainty about what is 'certain', and difficulty acting in accordance with a belief that others might not ascribe to. Living to fit in has taken precedence over belonging to Source, Self, and then other. In addition, living to fit in has squashed our personal inquiry into matters that are deemed "invalid" or "unreliable" using common scientific thinking and methods for "knowing".

To reiterate, our soul is our essence. The soul is 'who we are'. It is even deeper than our talents skills and abilities. We are Divine breathed and Divine inspired light, energy, and an extension of our Source, our Maker. Our 'soulprint' is a space within a physical shell that has no limits. It is our 'differences'. Our soul, our unique soulprint, allows for our extraordinary self to be a **difference maker.** Everyone one of us has this power. This is the aspect of children we don't want to hinder or cut off. This is where their purpose, true joy and inspired soulful living originates.

Using a two-dimensional diagram is problematic in that it cannot do the "soul" justice. Ideally the "soul" would be represented by a three-dimensional prism. The prism I image would be the center piece, white as a diamond, filled with radiant light and Divine love shining down **on, in and through it**.

This prism is like our crown chakra. When the crown chakra is opened, it receives. The crown chakra is depicted by the color purple, like an amethyst stone. According to The Complete Guide to Chakra Healing by Philip Permutt, the associated concepts with the crown chakra are spirituality, connection to the universe, imagination, awareness and optimism. (2008, pg 112-113) In short when our chakras, or our body's energy centers are balanced and aligned, then a kaleidoscope of color will shine **through** us. The colorful essence of soul reflecting pure white light of the Divine will shine out and through, across the other parts of the self. The word 'through' is important. Through implies that the space within is being filled and used by Source. Source is able to work through us to provide the world with our gifts and abilities.

Important to note is the use of a triangle to represent the soul. A triangle has multiple layers of meaning historically and mathematically. Originally the triangle was chosen to represent a multi-dimensional world (with some dimensions yet to be realized) encompassing the spirit realm, which extends beyond space and time. Triangles are one of the most basic geometric shapes. They have the strongest foundation. The strongest triangle is an equilateral, where the base sits horizontal and the other two meet up to join each other at a point, a single source. That single source represents the Divine, the Universe, God, or whatever you feel led to call it. It seems all to serendipitous that the center of our diagram is a triangle where three sides that represent the three circles that extend outward: mind, body, and spirit, are linked and overlap to depict the soul.

A triangle is also Delta, a letter of the Greek alphabet. Delta is the fourth letter. The uppercase Delta has two meanings in mathematical terms; 1) difference and 2) discriminant. Difference is defined as the amount one numbers differs from another. In regards to soul-inspired choice compared with programed-self choice, we want the difference in change to be small. We want there to be as little change to a child's soul as possible because we want them to live out there full and divinely inspired gifts and purpose. Finding the discriminant helps identify the number of real solutions there are in a quadratic equation. In the case of 'souls' the discriminant is endless. Souls are unique and no two are the same. Our unique soul is the 'special'ness in all people.

A triangle is also used in psychotherapy or other forms of relationship healing modalities to represent a three-person dynamic or system. This system, dysfunctional and unbalanced in nature, creates an 'odd man out' if not kept in balance. Unbalanced triangles in relationships can be used to decrease anxiety, increase 'perceived' emotional connection or attachment with another person in that same system. Perceived emotional disconnection is due to the triangle's unhealthy and incongruent way of relating. This triangulation between people, where authentic and pure connection is not the guiding force, also denotes how aspects of a child's self becomes incongruent and disorganized when the soul isn't the lead. If the soul takes a backseat, a triangle between the three spheres of mind, body, and spirit can't be created. Often a person focusing on one facet more than the others causes an imbalance.

When a child is operating from a fragmented place, the kaleidoscopes color will not shine. It will be unable to fully illuminate. The darker spots, missing pieces, and the dulled colors can indicate parts of the child's integration system that is over or underworked. Continuation of this can cause the soul to shut down. Some have the ability to read auras, rainbow air, with such detail they can identify areas of physical, mental, and spiritual disruption. This perceptive ability can allow a person to pinpoint areas for integration and tap into soulful desires that have been cut off from their current existence. When the soul leads, the mind, body, and spirit are working for the soul's desires. A person is not merely attempting to survive but looks to thrive.

The goal of the soul is to move from surviving to thriving. If we don't believe and trust our children's experiences, we are pushing the child to move outward in the kaleidoscope. Moving from soul as the guide, the other circles begin to work separately rather than together. Separated from source the spheres operate independently and create a triangulation. This unhealthy triangulation uses the mind, body, and spirit in a way that only focuses on symptomology rather than the deep seeded root cause for unwelcome feelings such as anxiety, disconnection, and a need to fit in. When shut down out of fear, uncertainty, or ignorance, a negative ripple effect across the kaleidoscope occurs. Stifled, unmotivated, and children with low self-worth are produced.

Most parents have the best of intentions. They want to protect, to keep their child from hurt, disappointment, or being teased. They want to guide them and help them be successful in today's world. So if the soul is living its true Source breathed existence, then the prism reflects the white light out across the entire kaleidoscope. All colors of the rainbow would be present. The soul embraces every color and how they impact our life. These colors would shift and change, just like when the kaleidoscope is twisted.

What causes these colors to change? External factors and internal thoughts can shift these colors. For example, when someone is reading someone's aura they are looking at their energy. As stated on Gaia.com, "James Van Praagh reminds us we are souls having a human experience and it is this frequency of spirit which vibrates creating the energetic field around us. The field around our physical body is our "aura". (2014) The shift and change need not be perceived as negative. Change is constant and inevitable. If when the kaleidoscope is turned, it is also tilted in one specific direction, the colors will fall to the side it is tilted toward. This changes the colors, their hue, and even leaving "unfilled" spaces where no color is present. This symbolizes when our soul isn't at the center. We lean, figuratively speaking, to one side. This can mean we are too focused on one core area rather than integrating them all into one. We may be focused more on the mind, (like negative thoughts or ego self), our body (focused on self-image in the eyes of others) or spirit, (making spirituality a religion or a religious experience and excluding others from the tribe based on culture and belief). When we experience the lean, the off balance, our aura can show us different aspects of where our 'rainbow' is less bright, has some 'darkness' or might be showing us the areas we are needing to draw our attention to.

The kaleidoscope reveals how change is exciting if we don't resist. Shifting and changing is a natural state of life. The shifts can be wonderful if balance is kept and source is the origination of our motivation. Letting go of our Ego self would allow our kaleidoscope to shift and change with ease. When we don't resist and we attempt to remain in balance by allowing our soul to lead, colors remain bright. Even when we see things change shape and form different patterns, we can still shine bright.

It is important to note that Ego self is still a useful part of self. Ego self can protect when we need to be protected. Ego self can help define more appropriate healthy boundaries. Ego self can be the action piece of soul passions. Ego has its place, but it's place is not as leader. Its place is as the supporting actor in the movie of life. The soul plays the lead role. Those who want to have the most authentic life possible allow the soul to be the center and their Ego to create the physical manifestation of that soul purpose.

In the diagram, the seven total spaces created by the three circles (mind, body, spirit) overlapping, represent the chakras. Chakras are the seven energy centers of the body. Each energy center has a color associated with it. They link mind, body, and spirit. When our chakras are in alignment then we are living from a pure balanced place. When discussing chakras with children, using the part on their body that it correlates with can help them better understand their energy centers and what physical, mental, and emotional cues can be linked to each one. Asking mindful questions about where different feelings resonate for them in their body will be important as well. Many activities in this book offer the opportunity to discuss the link between these bodily centers and other facets of self.

Below is an overview of the energy centers and physical location. Each chakra is listed with name, color its most associated with, possible manifestations (not exhaustive by any means) if in or out of balance, and affirmations that children can utilize when focusing on each energy center.

1. The Root Chakra-Color: Red; base of your spine; out of balance or overactive=anxiety, fear (even when there is not threat); in balance=peace, calm, connection to self and others

    1. Affirmation for kids: "My body and mind can be calm in this situation", "I am calm", "I am close to myself and others", "I have nothing to fear", "I will not listen to fear". "fear is ugly, courage is beautiful", "when I am calm, I act calm", "peace is when my body isn't 'jumpy'.

Have your child create their own affirmations. "courage is jumping off the high dive for the first time and finding out that I loved it!"

2. <u>The Sacral Chakra</u> Color: Orange; right below belly button; out of balance or overactive=addiction, addictive bxs, overeating, imbalance of pleasurable activities; in balance=harmony and balance in pleasurable activities

    1. Affirmation for kids: "balance is a great place to be", "moderation", "enough is right where I am", "too much of a good thing isn't possible, too much of a bad thing makes me feel yucky", "I am like a scale, and both sides are equal", "I only do that which gives me great joy AND is healthy for my body". Have your child create their own sacral chakra affirmation: "balance is bliss"

3. <u>The Solar Plexus Chakra</u>: Color: Yellow; from center of belly button to top of breastbone where ribs connect; out of balance or overactive=difficulty with emotional regulation (anger, frustration, or quick to react), less empathy and compassion; in balance=power, able to make choices and decisions, love, compassion and empathy

    1. Affirmations for kids: "I am able to make good choices for myself", "a choice is just that, a choice, not right or wrong, it is what I do with my choice that makes it right or wrong", "anger only serves me if I use it well and for good", "pause before acting", "I can learn something from every place I find myself", "every person can be a teacher to me", "I am open to feeling and then acting from a calm mind space". Have your child create their own affirmation: In response to "when does hitting happen?" "Hitting happens when I don't ask myself why I am mad first". "what is a possible affirmation to say to yourself each day or in a situation where you start

to feel yourself getting angry or frustrated?" "I can be understood and heard without hitting".

4. The Heart Chakra: color: green; right over heart center of body; out of balance or overactive=poor boundaries, putting others first; in balance=see and practice love for self and others, health and healing chakra

    1. Affirmations for kids: "when I love myself I am a giver", "I make healthy choices for my body", "exercise all of myself: my body, my mind, my spiritual muscles!", "giving to self is important, too", "saying 'no' is sometimes a gift to me and the other person", "saying no is okay to do", "I choose things to do with my time that interest me", "I choose kind and thoughtful people to hang out with". Have your child create their own affirmations. "I want to be around people who like me for me!"

5. The Throat Chakra: Color: blue; right in between collarbone; in balance=speak clearly, and from your personal truth; authentic communication; out of balance or overactive=feelings of not being heard, speak loudly, interrupt others

    1. Affirmations for kids: "I say what I mean, and mean what I say", "I act like the person I say I am inside", "I don't change who I am just because others want me to", "I can speak clearly and people will understand me", "I am good at sharing my stories with people", "People understand me better when I understand myself", "To tell the truth is my greatest gift". Have your child create their own affirmations: "I am a truth teller"

6. The 3ʳᵈ Eye Chakra: Color: Indigo; between eyebrows; in balance=feel balance between physical and spiritual world, receive information through extrasensory perceptions (as well with 5 senses), intuitive, perceptive; out of balance or

overactive=not grounded, living too much in a different realm, obsess about spiritual matters or engaging in metaphysical healing in an obsessive manner

1. Affirmations for kids: "I am here for a reason", "I have a lot of work to do on this Earth", "Taking care of my responsibilities will help me be who I want to be", "When I complete my schoolwork I am helping the world because I am learning what I need to so I can be my best self", "hard work brings great rewards", "I am connected to everything", "taking care of myself, others, and the Earth are important", "I am ME, hear me ROAR!" Have your child create their own affirmations. "I am the best me there is, so I am going to use it!"

7. The Crown Chakra: color: Violet-white; top of head, crown; this chakra is associated with being a spiritual warrior; recognizing and obtaining strength and purpose through the God Source. Ultimate goal!

     1. Affirmations for kids: "I am love", "I am a creation of God", "God loves me so much he put me here", "I have a big purpose in life", "I have a soul job to do", "I share light and love in the world", "I want to make the world a better place". Have your child create their own affirmations. "Love and I are best friends"

Working your way out from the middle of the diagram, the triangle or piece that representing the soul, to the larger spheres, and then to just beyond, the furthest most place of the diagram are the colors of the rainbow, 7 rings wrapping around the entire diagram three overlapping spheres. The 7 rings then are the 7 chakras, each associated with its color. We start with a layer representing the base chakra, characterized by the color red, and end with the crown chakra, often associated with the colors violet or white. This rainbow reminds us that when our soul radiates source light there is a positive ripple effect. This ripple effect

44

goes beyond ourselves, beyond our physical world and extends out to the spiritual realm.

The diagram, when viewed in its entirety, depicts the inner workings of a child on all levels. The Soul Kaleidoscope embraces all aspects of human existence and highlights the importance of a child's soul. With each turn of the wrist each child is revealed a new story to tell. Full of colors and images, their personal kaleidoscope is a unique 'soulprint', containing their God given talents. When the kaleidoscope is held gently in human hands, the kaleidoscope does what it is intended to do. If the hands take over out of fear or control, the kaleidoscope is less likely to create with internal spontaneous serendipitous meaning. When our "hands" shake, grip the kaleidoscope with a suffocating clasp, or attempt to "control" the shifts, we lose the authenticity of the moment. We lose the ability for the soul to lead us. We lose our connection to the Source, Divine, love and light.

Chapter 5

The Manifestations

How do I know if my child is a highly sensitive, intuitive, or empathic?

"People need 'aha' moments, they need awareness, they need things that actually shift and change them."-Jack Canfield

The fact that you are reading this book right now, is a true sign that there are signs in your life that you or your child has the qualities of being highly sensitive or empathic. As you have been reading, you have probably been sensing some relief, realizing that you and your child are not alone. You are gaining more insight on "why you might 'fit' with some better than others, why you might have been viewed as the black sheep of the family, and why you might have always wondered why you felt different. It might be as if all the pieces are finally coming together.

Raising children is the most difficult and important job our society has. It is my hope that this book has already began the awakening process for those who are parents or who are called to serve in roles that mimic parenthood. When we begin to look at our children from a new lens, we are able to find comfort in our efforts. Furthermore, the great news is that the H.O.P.E. Tribe supports a process, from management to mastery. When we recognize that our children need us to "let go" of the control that often comes with "managing" them, ensuring that they get the perfect grade, they have the perfect behavior, etc., our children can begin to engage in a learning process. This process promotes self-inquiry and allows our children to move from "being controlled or managed" to "mastering" their purpose.

As a parent of a highly sensitive or empathic child, you might find yourself wondering if you are "doing it right". The fact that you are learning more about your child clearly shows that you are "doing it right". This inquisitive search is a sign that you are on the path to helping yourself and your child "master" the "assignments" given in life. You may still be questioning, which natural empaths do, if the title of highly sensitive or empathic or intuitive fits for your child. The following are more ways in which these capabilities and traits may manifest themselves. It is important to note that this is simply a way to dig deeper. We are all unique beings. It is impossible to cover every sign, characteristic, trait, or example. Therefore, these guiding questions have been provided to aid you in your journey, as a starting point.

In addition to this point, I would like to speak a bit more about maladaptive behaviors. If soul purpose is stifled or there is 'refraction' (as discussed in The Soul Kaleidoscope chapter) children can manifest maladaptive behaviors. These behaviors don't serve them well. While they had a purpose, it is in the best interest of the child to learn more about their actions and ways to adapt their behaviors to align with their soul purpose. The strategies in Chapter 10 will offer ways of helping children do just that. Whether outwardly viewed as negative or positive, there are some common characteristics that speak to how a child with extrasensory perceptions shows up in the world. When we place judgement and label a behavior as "good" or "bad", we have the potential to contract a child's heart, stifling their purpose altogether. I prefer to simply name the behavior, discover its purpose, determine how it serves the child, and evaluate if it needs changing or not. While I do not have the time in this book to do this concept justice, it is something to ponder when helping our children move towards mastery.

Here are some starting points to decipher if your child may be highly sensitive, intuitive, or empathic. Following are some common characteristics and traits these children tend to display. They are loosely organized into four categories. These categories are mind, body, spirit, and soul. Before digging deeper some general questions, you might want to ask are:

- What might I notice, or what might catch my attention if my child is intuitive, highly sensitive, or an empath?
- What might their behavior look like?
- What activities are they drawn to?
- What do their thought processes look and sound like?

Mind

Does your child strongly dislike surprises even ones you would consider 'fun'?

Highly sensitive, intuitive, or empathic children typically don't like big surprises. They prefer to know what is coming. Birthdays and other special occasions can 'feel' different and even bring about a level of anxiety that is hard for some to understand.

Does your child appear to read your mind?

Parents will report moments of possible telepathy. These parents say "it was like they just knew what I was thinking". The child may even say that they did. Telepathic communication and interpersonal energetic communication, which may be nonverbal, are strong between these children and their sensitive parents. They tend to just 'know' what the other is needing, thinking, and wanting. It is important to navigate this carefully, as this doesn't always translate to the outer world. Children with these types of abilities or relational dynamics can be left thinking "they know everything" and "they know what others are thinking and feeling". The danger in this comes if it creates difficulties socially. It is important socially for them to learn how to navigate age appropriate relationships and how to check in with their self and others about interactions and situations. Sometimes these children are viewed as egocentric, or even narcissistic in nature. They don't hesitate to tell you what they think, what you are thinking, and they can act in accordance with what they believe a person should do, coming across as "controlling or demanding".

Does your child seem to be 'wise beyond their years'?

You may notice people making this comment about your child. Being referred to as "an old soul" is commonplace. Their conversations may be full of broader ideas, more developed critical thinking skills, above average vocabulary, and even demonstrate a very clever sense of humor. Abstract and more global thinking may also be present. They typically are labeled as "bright" or "gifted" children. This label generally comes with a higher or above average IQ but does not have to in this sense. Being avid readers, they read above grade level. Their focus tends to gravitate towards humanitarian type ideas and goals that seem beyond their age or ability to influence.

Does your child respond positively to logical and natural consequences?

Remembering that intuitive and empathic children sense, feel, and perceive another's experience, informs the type of intervention that would work most effectively. Using non-harsh forms of discipline tend to create better and longer lasting outcomes. Gentle reminders, logical and natural consequences are received with more ease by intuitive and empathic children. Subtleties in facial expressions, body language, and other environmental stimuli can add anxiety or emotional reactivity to a situation. 'Taking things personally' is often how these children are described by adults and even other children.

A seemingly common situation can bring about great anxiety and emotional response for an empathic child. One child, an elementary age student, gave his mother his backpack to carry. Nothing out of the ordinary is occurring. His male teacher approaches and says gently "that is your backpack and it is your responsibility to carry it". The teacher kneeling down, and speaking in a gentle tone, was caught off guard when the child burst into tears. Both the teacher and the child's parent were left speechless for a moment. What just happened? The sensitive child 'felt' the words, the meaning of them touching a deeper part of him. The child quickly emotionally assessed the messages behind the words, illusions erased and all that was left was raw disappointment in the child's body. This disappointment was his own, his teacher's, and his mother's and therefore it was magnified and intensified. The child had assigned emotional meaning to the interaction based on the disappointed energy that was flowing through him. It wasn't until the teacher, the child, and his mother had a discussion that the conversation could be teased out. That moment became a teachable moment, one where a discussion ensued and 'real life' practice was allowed for facilitating how the child could check in with self and other to ensure that what he was feeling matched that of the situation and the others involved. The teacher's typically smiling face was not present during that moment, informing the child of the meaning behind the statement. The mother was in fact feeling disappointed and frustrated, as she had been attempting to motivate her son to increase responsibility for his things. The boy also heard a critical voice inside his head, his own negative self-talk, that triggered his own level of disappointment, intensifying the disappointment he was absorbing from the adults. A deep sense of overwhelm resulted.

Empathic children have filters that are more porous. A good metaphor is a coffee filter as compared to a spaghetti strainer. Coffee filters, laden with tiny microscopic holes, hold onto the smallest things. This does not change the pot of coffee. In fact, it is required for a good pot of coffee. Spaghetti strainers have big holes, allowing for big and small things to fall through. Empathic children's filters have large spaces and holes This allows many things to fall through, making it unclear what is their own and what is someone else's. Their filter doesn't sift out all the subtleties of interactions that don't belong to self. Even when the task requires the coffee filter, the child still uses their spaghetti strainer. Therefore, the pot of coffee is changed, too much is allowed in. The child is left trying to filter or sift through the contents after the fact rather than before. They absorb everything in the moment. They feel first and then think. This way of absorbing can make them appear more emotionally reactive, immature, or sensitive. It is their neurological system, it's in the wiring. The positive part of this "filter" dilemma is that they have an amazing ability to pick up on so many subtleties of their environment, when others never even recognize they exist.

Does your child tell unusual stories?

Sometimes children have unusual stories in general. The difference here is that, while it may seem to fit a situation, the details don't quite add up. You may not be aware as to how the child received the information. Typically, once the information is checked out it is factual with great accuracy. There is a school that is situated on a ranch near my home. A man founded this ranch some time ago and has since passed away. It is a local historical sight and most locals know of the ranch. A child who is thought to have the ability to perceive spirits who have crossed over began talking openly about 'seeing' the ghost of the man at school. This child talks about him in ways that hint to conversations with this deceased person. The child becomes adamant that the man is searching for his tools and the child feels a burning desire to help him find them. Another example of an unusual story involves a young girl, age 7. She came home from school and told her parents that she 'randomly guessed' another child's middle name. The information was verified. The intuitive child shares that "she just knew it" and has had several of these experiences. One highly sensitive young boy would spend hours in his room talking to 'Einstein'. When asked what he and Einstein were discussing his response would be about life events of Einstein, relativity, mathematical equations, and E=MC squared. The boy's mother was amazed to verify the accuracy of his statements and was astonished at how her young son was able to discuss these 'big' ideas.

Does your child seem to always have questions?

H.O.P.E. Tribe children are curious creatures by nature! Most children go through a phase of asking 'why' around the age of 3. As with other traits, empathic and intuitive children take things to a deeper level. The 'why' questions have a more profound quality. The answers to the 'why' are followed by another 'why'. These children have a deep desire to understand the workings of life and can appear to have a relentless approach to their questioning. They just can't seem to find rest in the typical answers to such 'why' questions. Not only do they tend to ask more of these questions, the questions tend to be thought provoking for even the adult being asked. The questions can be difficult to answer, as they can be deep psychological or spiritual in nature. Adults have to gauge how much information to share with the child, deciphering what is age appropriate. Sometimes these questions require the adult to explore their own personal beliefs. Questions can revolve around religions, and the origins of life. While all kids go through phases, these children seem to never really leave the question asking phase. Their questions are not in line with what their typical peers are curious about, and seem to be, again, "beyond their years".

Does your child prefer to be alone, or appear to be socially anxious?

Parents worry that their empathic child is 'anti-social'. First and foremost, it is important to note here that highly sensitive and empathic children do not respond well to these types of labels. In fact, most sensitive children 'look deeper' than labels themselves. To be labeled in such a way would be even more demoralizing than it would to another child. In order for these children to balance their system, integrate information, and soothe themselves, they typically prefer alone time. They may retreat to a certain spot, read a book, literally hide, or ask to go home from a park unexpectedly. Alone time is the way many H.O.P.E. tribe children give themselves space from all they have been absorbing. They seek time to integrate, shed, and recognize how to move forward. We all want our children to have a strong sense of social aptitude. Allowing our highly sensitive children this preference of alone time aids them in better social navigation. Appropriate social navigation is a direct result of healthy integration of self. This integration process may look and 'feel' different for empathic and intuitive children. Often times, this process requires alone time or simply a significant reduction in external stimuli.

Does your child appear to be obsessive or compulsive?

Trying to decipher and integrate all that is coming at them, can look like obsessive compulsive symptoms. They may want things to be predictable and even ritualistic at times. The idea that doing the same routine will help decrease negative or unwanted sensations may prompt these children to be more rigid or engage in daily routines that are serving as 'perceived' anxiety reduction. These children can receive spiritual downloads, which can include seeing apparitions, having premonitions, and hearing things that others cannot. Their systems are on sensory overload all the while trying to find their place with peers, family, and society. This shows up sometimes in interesting ways. A child may walk in the house and before even putting their things down take notice that a candle has been moved, a book is off the shelf, or that the smell means the dishes were done. They seem to notice everything. Big changes to their environment and circumstances can be very difficult to cope with. Handwashing or excessive desire to take a bath can be prevalent. A fascination with water, its healing properties, and the sensation it provides to the body can also serve as a technique for 'shedding' unwanted sensations or energy that has been absorbed. Compulsive behaviors can speak to how the body is integrating information. Deeper inquiry into the mind, body, and soul will allow for a greater understanding of the function and purpose.

Does your child act in a more 'cautious' manner than same age peers?

A two or three-year-old who mindfully contemplates stepping off a curb is an example of how this may look. Same age peers may just dart off a sidewalk into the street and not consciously be aware of the inherent dangers. Or a child may ask if they can cross a street when most children would just act. Highly sensitive, empathic, or intuitive children may seem to underreact. Their responses seem to be outside the 'normal'. These children may say things like, "I can jump like that at a trampoline park, but I am not so sure it is a good idea off the couch". Their friends may look at them with puzzled and quizzical looks. These looks almost seem to communicate "come on kid this is fun". Enjoying the activity becomes a process of deciphering elements of the activity. Participating in a safe manner and contemplating the effects of their actions increases the enjoyment if they decide to do it. A child may seem to "take a long time to warm up" in new environments due to this aspect. For example, if a highly sensitive, intuitive, or empathic child goes to a new trampoline park, they may walk around surveying the entire place prior to deciding to "play". They are taking in the nuances of the environment. They feel compelled to do this and if this act is stopped, they may become emotionally dysregulated.

Does your child have strong emotional or physical reactions to strangers?

Stranger Danger is a very pertinent issue, especially in today's world. Any stranger to these children are typically always seen as a 'danger'. This means they might clam up, retreat or hide, avert their gaze and not make eye contact. Some say they want to leave a situation, not talk or answer questions, and don't demonstrate their usual behaviors or attitudes in a public setting. Helping a child honor his thoughts, feelings, and perceptions when in the presence of others will allow a child to make more sound decisions about the people they trust and have in their life. (As a side note this concept can also be noticed in other settings. Since empathic children might not act in accordance with their true ability or there is a hesitancy to perform tasks in front of those they don't know well, it is important to be mindful when a child is being 'tested', 'assessed', or 'observed' for academic, behavioral, social or emotional reasons.)

Does your child have a strong dislike (or lack of attention to/awareness of) labels and stereotypes?

Many might believe that highly sensitive and empathic children, merely because of what the label implies, would recognize and draw attention to gender differences, cultural differences, and other aspects that differentiate. However, H.O.P.E children 'recognize' these things in a different way. It is a blessing that empathic and intuitive children can see people for who they truly are. They typically don't put emphasis on outward appearances and/or societal stereotypes. Gender differences may come down to only anatomy. H.O.P.E children will typically see the benefits of embracing both masculine and feminine qualities. Questions arise about why fashion is according to gender, or why race impacts relationship. A six-year-old was overheard telling peers that 'boys can marry boys'. He was defending homosexual men's rights despite having no personal relationship with anyone who identifies with this lifestyle. Intuitive and empathic children also may engage in or be drawn to activities that appear to be "of the opposite sex". Examples include, a young boy who wants to take a sewing class, a young girl who wants to only dress in 'boy' clothes, or a young girl who challenges the norm that a girl can't play in an 'all boy' sport.

Body

Does your child startle easily?

Loud noises cause alarm for these children. Some common examples include someone coming around a corner with heavy stomping, a coffee grinder, vacuum cleaner, motorcycles or certain types of cars, etc. Some may react by putting hands over their ears, hiding, or jumping behind furniture. It is clearly an overwhelm to their system. When there is little or no time to prepare the reaction is even more intense. Bystanders may even say, "what is wrong with them?" or "what's the big deal?" Simply put, these children have super sensitive systems.

Does your child engage what looks like excessive daydreaming?

H.O.P.E children can appear as though they are watching something that others can't see. They may be noticed staring off into space and daydreaming. This can even be recognized in infants. My son used to constantly have these 'staring episodes', even at 6 months old. I often wondered what he saw, checking behind me or around the room for clues. He also has these eyes that almost everyone who met him commented on. "He has beautiful eyes", "I would love to have eyes like that", "Oh my look at his eyes". I always thought he had beautiful eyes. People often commented when I was out with him that he just looked at them so deeply and with great intent, like he could see deep into their soul. These comments now mean so much more to me than they did back then. I wish "I had seen his eyes" sooner, maybe I would have changed some of the things I did or said, maybe I would have allowed him to be more of who he is and less of who I thought he should be. I now realize that I write because it is never too late to start discovering ourselves and our children. With each moment is a new opportunity, a chance to recognize what makes each child unique and different. Allowing these differences to be expressed is to embrace the idea of soulful living.

Does your child have adverse reactions to textures, specifically clothing?

"These clothes don't feel good." "Cut this tag off". "I don't like this underwear. There are too many lines in them." "Get it off get it off". "Yuck I don't like this shirt." "My legs hurt in these pants." "I got water on my sleeves while washing my hands, I have to change". These, and more, are common among sensitive children. My children are sensitive to clothing and have their own sensory sensitivities. Some have questioned if my son has Sensory Integration disorder. Dialogues with his pediatrician, a therapist, a speech and language pathologist, his teachers, and other parents have allowed me to explore this further. When all the puzzle pieces are put together here is my current belief about my son and his sensory sensitivities: I believe my child is highly sensitive and his 5+ senses are heightened due to a different style of integrating, relating, and filtering. Given his empathic and intuitive nature he receives downloads from other realms. He receives vibrational frequencies. These are in addition to already having a system that is hard wired to absorb energy.

Does your child complain about or have a heightened sense of smell?

Shopping for perfume with a sensitive child around can be problematic for the parent and the child. The multitude of fragrances and scents can wreak havoc on a highly sensitive child's system. Children with this sensitivity can endure somatic complaints (headaches, stomach aches, burning eyes, itching, dizziness, and more). The sensations they feel can then begin to influence their behavior. The behavior manifestations can become difficult. This then becomes difficult for parents. Parents may struggle to engage in a "soulful" intervention.

The child's body is reacting to the odors. These odors can produce thoughts, may come with images, bring on bodily sensations, or call in spirit. Odor is powerful. If we think about our own odor experiences it is easier to see how we can attribute thoughts, memories and behaviors with specific smells. (i.e. smell of a certain cookie reminding us of family time at the holidays, a smell of a food that causes our gag reflex) We can see how a child may struggle with interpreting these odors from a sensory perspective, especially if the system is overloaded. Even more difficult, is that these odors may carry multiple meanings. Sometimes a spirit makes itself known through these olfactory sensitive experiences. Sensitive children will generally notice smells well before others do. While driving on the highway, my child said, "I smell smoke". Ten miles later, on the side of the highway sat a car. The vehicle had caught on fire. While the fire had been put out, the smell of smoke lingered in the air.

Does your child have sleep problems?

Sleeping difficulties for a child can be hard on a family. Highly sensitive, intuitive, or empathic children can have difficulty settling down at night, may be fearful of the dark, talk about 'night ninjas', 'angels and ghosts', 'shadows', and other things that "visit" them in the night. They may want a light to stay on, have someone lay with them until they are asleep, experience nightmares or night terrors, and wake up several times during the night despite their age. They also may report vivid dreams and have difficulty sorting out if they were awake or asleep. These children often fight bedtime routines or can excessively cry as night approaches.

Intuitive and empathic children also report a tired feeling. This may be due to sleep disturbances. However, this also may be in response to energy absorption. When a child is constantly shielding themselves from taking on energy it is a tiring process. Their body is working somatically, mentally, and emotionally. Learning effective strategies for shielding is important. A child who is exhausted due to lack of adequate sleep is more susceptible to picking up on negative energy around them and this energy may be absorbed into their body.

Does your child have a compassionate heart beyond their age?

Empathic and intuitive children have compassionate and beautiful hearts. These children can sense distress of others, sometimes even on a global scale. I have witnessed children that have a sudden bout of dizziness, fear, and sadness. An interesting example of this was when a child had all three symptoms and simultaneously it was discovered that an earthquake happened in Mexico. The child lived in southern California. While the child was not physically present for the event, he clearly felt it.

It is vital for parents to monitor what their child is watching on television and computers. H.O.P.E children can become obsessed about other people's distress and it can feel debilitating to these children. The work and research on mirror neurons reveals that what we see, hear, and sense can trigger a brain response that 'mirrors' that of actually experiencing the situation. They might actually feel the hunger of the starving children, the pain of the injured person, or the cold winter weather for the homeless person. Often these children will want to help others. They become passionate about blanket and can food drives, giving toys to foster children, even asking if your family can adopt children. Highly sensitive children can have a physical or emotional reaction to hearing or seeing a news story, therefore traumatic news stories should be limited and/or discussed with your child in a soulful way.

Does your child seem to feel pain differently?

Above or below average pain tolerance can be an indication of possible heightened sensitivity in a child. Children who witness or experience trauma can have a higher pain tolerance. Much has been said about trauma and children with higher sensitivity levels (including psychic and intuitive children). It is worth noting that because they have endured or even cut off emotionally from physical or emotional pain, their bodies may not recognize it quite like others. For example, a child, who suffered from abuse and trauma, threw a pair of scissors towards the ground. The scissors bounced up and stuck in his shin. He didn't feel anything. He even walked around with the scissors in his leg until someone pointed out to him what had happened. This child also was known for taking tumbles and falls that the parents were sure to end in tears, yet never did. To this day, he says he has an extremely high pain tolerance. He now understands that he must be mindful when he is hurting. Taking his pain seriously due to a history of knowing he experiences it differently. If his body hurts, he knows he needs to pay attention. This person was assessed for any medical condition that might explain this tolerance, however, no known medical explanation was found.

While each child is unique, typically empathic children will be hyper-sensitive to pain. What some would consider small injuries, (stubbed toe, hang nail, scratch from playground blacktop, hit by a nerf ball), are extremely painful, whether actually sensed that way or just expressed in that manner. H.O.P.E children can sometimes take a longer time to recover, self-soothe, and resume the activity, if they even do choose resume.

With both sides of the spectrum being shown here, the real key is to ask yourself if your child's pain tolerance seems to be 'out of the norm' of what other peers his/her age experience. It is also very important that a child be medically assessed if their pain tolerance creates distress, problems, or any concerns for you or them.

Does your child enjoy activities that are less aggressive in nature and more individually based?

Many parents have fantasies about their child. Expectations of what the child will be like, or what they will do as a profession, seem to infiltrate parent's thoughts, beginning even when their child is an infant. Parents can hit an emotional wall that forces them to look at the idea of their child being an extension of them. As parents we can get stuck here or we can look deeper at our children and see them for who they truly are. For example, a father who always wanted a football player may have to put those desires in check. H.O.P.E tribe children tend to prefer more individually based sports or interests. For example these individual based activities include, karate, tennis, robotics, chess club, debate team, and many more. For my child, karate combined his love for language and culture with an individual sport that allowed him to build self-confidence, self-esteem, while getting the health benefits of physical activity. The mindfulness act of karate was the draw for him. He would strike a "yoga pose", as he called it, whenever the moment called for it. Times I saw him do this most included, hiking in the mountains, playing at the beach, in the car in traffic, in the grocery store, and probably more when I was not around. Mindfulness tends to 'find these children', not the other way around. They may not be actively seeking it. Their energy is pulled towards activities that are more mindfully motivated, which includes arts and creative projects.

Does your child have a speech delay or did your child experience difficulties with speech?

Highly sensitive, empathic, or intuitive children can start out life with a delay in speech or atypical communication patterns. Again, it is important that any developmental milestone delay be addressed, discussed, and assessed. Talking with healthcare professionals, mental health therapists, and others about the development of your child is always important. Some of these children wait until later to use verbal communication, however, the parents will most likely report that the child was able to communicate with them easily through learned sign language, a system of signs or behavioral cues that intuitively communicated needs/thoughts/desires. Some people report that they had a telepathic sort of communication and understanding with their child and had no difficulties communicating despite lack of verbal communication, and other speech delays. I can speak first-hand about the communication connection I have with my son. Prior to him talking, I could intuitively know by the look in his eye, the sound of his cry, and the way in which he moved what he needed. The popularity of baby sign language and more knowledge about different vocalizations in baby's cries, have increased the ability of parents to communicate with their children in a more reciprocal way at an earlier age. I believe this promotes not only increased self-awareness for both parent and child, but also increases intuitive relating and building deep connections.

Spirit

Does your child express that they see colors around people or animals?

The child may talk excessively about colors (not age appropriate) or assign color to feelings, thoughts, actions or objects without having been taught to do so. This is a sign of an organic draw to color. A child might ask, "Why is that person "Red"? This question might arise after interacting or being in the presence a person who was upset. Some children state that they see 'round spheres', which my son has instinctually referred to as orbs. Reading auras is also an ability that some H.O.P.E children possess. My son became highly interested in what he termed 'rainbow air', how it looked around living things, and how it morphs and changes. Initially when I inquired about 'rainbow air', my son said, very matter of fact, "it's everywhere", and "we all have colored air around us." "The colors have meaning mom, and when you see dark spots that is not good", he told me. Intuitively my son is perceiving energy around people. He understands more deeply that this energy has significance and is related a person's human experience.

Does your child share stories about seeing people or animals others can't see?

Has your child: 1) told stories about seeing people or animals who others can't see? 2) reported seeing Angels or God? 3)talked about imaginary friends? 4) knew information about family members who have crossed over/passed away that they wouldn't have been told or had access to? 5) talked about themselves as if they have already lived a full life, possibly as if they had past life experiences?

One day I was shocked when my son said, "Mom, I saw God". I remained curious asked him what he saw. He replied, "it isn't like the pictures we see in the Bible or in paintings. It was just a bright golden glow with a black outline. It was warm and I don't know if it was a boy or a girl. I wasn't scared. I just knew it was God". I know several parents who say, "I think my son is psychic, sees spirits" or 'sees things that others could not see'. My son has also shared information about past creatures, some prehistoric and some mythologically based that, to my knowledge, he has had no access to information about. He has recently been interested in dragons and assigns his friends and his family members dragons he believes represent them. It wasn't until I researched more about mythological creatures, that I realized magi zoology is an actual area of study. Being a Dragonologist is possible in our world. He seemed to know this already but couldn't tell me how he knew it. He has always wanted to be an "animal explorer" or zoologist, and now his new love for dragons has provided another possible path. Even though I do not know much about the topic, I don't shut this down. I don't ask him to shy away from his interest.

Does your child have savant type abilities?

Savant type abilities may be present for H.O.P.E children. These can include self-taught musical talents and using music in a way that is beyond their age. Music can be a love or passion for these kids. It not only helps them express themselves, it allows for emotional release of possible energy and 'baggage' they have absorbed from others. I knew one child who was six years old and he processed his days through writing songs at night. They were amazing works of art and it won't be surprising if he is a well-known song writer in the future. Being an intuitive and psychic medium myself, I know that music can also send a person to a soul space and attract spirit. When listening to a song, I can see, "know", or even hear a spirit and receive information. If this is true for your child, it will be important to set up protecting and grounding rituals, which will be discussed later, in Chapter 10. Along with these activities, having conversations with them about their experiences, setting up boundaries around listening to music, and providing outlets for coping is essential.

Soul

Does your child create change wherever they go?

It appears that more and more children are interested in spiritual matters. More spiritual and empathic topics, such as environmental concerns, animal cruelty, and other Humanitarian efforts, are being collectively discussed. These discussions are taking place in homes, schools, and in our communities. In some regard, children are leading the way in these humanitarian efforts and have done so for several years. Recently a preschooler at the school I was teaching at, became extremely passionate about recycling. A four-year-old boy had a passion for recycling and helping the Earth. He channeled this into making posters and collecting items from classrooms weekly. These items were delivered to the appropriate places. According to his mother, this idea was completely his own. Her support was simply supplying materials and handling the logistics. A mother who never thought twice about using and discarding Ziplock bags, was now championing her son's cause. This four-year-old's concern for planet Earth is inspiring.

Another child was passionate about animals and their care. She became vegan. This change forced her family to look at their eating habits, their beliefs about animal treatment, and how consuming animal products effected the earth. It prompted other discussions with other families. A ripple effect occurred. My family became more interested in animal care and we began feeding the animals at a farm rescue near our home. This was all a response to this five-year-old's care for animals and a conviction that she now lived out.

These kids feel things at their core, their soul. They seem to be so set in their ways that nothing can alter their perspective. They have a vision, a soul purpose and they are driven to share it, and to live it. As Brene Brown states in her book Rising Strong, "It often takes only a single brave person to change the trajectory of a family, or any system for that matter" (pg 59). H.O.P.E children live bravely. They are inundated with information, whether sensory or spiritually downloaded, and are forced to face a world not easily explained or even "known" to typical people. Bravely living is done when a child can say what they believe and a parent honors them for their beliefs. This honoring helps them rise strong beyond the limits of society, above the pressures that tell them otherwise.

Does your child have a global curiosity?

Whether it be different countries, languages, religions, or traditions, these children often ask purposeful questions about globalization. On their first day of kindergarten, both of my children were instantly drawn to children whose parents were from India. The school they attend is diverse. However, the 'pull' and draw to first generation children from India was interesting. Due to being the first generation in America, these children still actively participate in their culture and traditions from India. My daughter was completely fascinated by her new friend's bindi. My son wanted to learn everything about India and the Hindu religion. Being open, I became more curious myself. It became a wonderful way to explore another culture as a family, as well as converse with and get to know other families. A unique connection formed and a greater depth of understanding followed.

As I sat with a psychic medium, I was not surprised when she shared that my son was a monk in a former life. A favorite hobby of my son was spending hours on Google translate looking up different words in different languages. His favorite was writing words in Japanese and Chinese. Keeping in mind that he was only four when he started enjoying this activity is what makes it so unusual. My son mentioned that he understands multiple languages. He linked his interest to linguistics to 'hearing voices in these different languages'. He stated that 'people, although others could not see these people, talked to him in different languages regularly. He wanted to understand them, so he took an interest in their language, researching and learning to write it. As a way to honor my son's linguistic ability and passion, I wanted to share Hope written in Chinese.

The symbol of this word is powerful. We see it in tattoo form, hanging on walls, used on cards and stationary. This beautiful symbol gives rise to the need of a H.O.P.E Tribe. One that embodies the meaning of the word to its fullest and brings people together.

Does your child have an intense love of animals?

At the age of three, my son's favorite animal was the Red River Hog. These animals aren't usually highly sought after or the most loved. Typically, the only people fond of these unpopular animals are the zoo volunteers and employees, not the three-year-old visitors. Mapping out our family's trip to the zoo looked something like this: Red River Hog first, our must see. Then to the naked mole rats (yes, you read that correctly!), flamingos, then condors, all the aviaries, reptiles, and then (if there is time) on to the more popular animals like the lions, giraffes, monkeys, bears, and elephants.

My son's love for the 'less thought' of animals was endearing. He cared about them. He said they were "cute" when most people barely took notice of them. He had a soft spot in his heart for the animals that were 'different', society deemed as not 'cool', and who did things a little different. I love this about my son. His demonstration of love for the less loved animals at the zoo has taught me so much about acceptance and finding beauty in everything. Now I can say, and really mean it, that a naked mole rat really is one of the cutest things I have ever laid my eyes on. My son even asked Santa Claus for a Red River Hog stuffed animal. He was thrilled to see that little hairy swine sitting by the Christmas tree on Christmas morning that year. We still have it. To honor my son, and the unpopular Red River Hog, we will always keep it. A good reminder of beauty, uniqueness, and going against the societal grain for love. A way to truly live what we believe to be right.

Overcoming the Naysayers

Some people argue the above-mentioned characteristics are not valid. They claim them to be too vague, or a characteristic that can apply to every child. Adults who stick hard and fast to traditional western medicine may view these traits, perhaps this entire book, as a way for parents to not seek medical or psychological treatment, avoiding a diagnosis, and claiming a child is 'spiritual' to deny a parenting style or ignore behaviors. While this list can be seen in every child, the distinguishing factor is the impact it has on the child. Children who are truly intuitive, perceptive, and empathic will 'feel' these traits on a deeper and more purpose driven level. Many children love animals and talk about 'taking care of Mother Earth'. However, in these children a care for animals won't result in drastic behavior changes such as becoming vegan or vegetarian. A concern for the planet doesn't result in building a school wide program that works to recycle and participating in lengthy conversations with peers about the benefits of such work. Children who engage in an idea or belief on all levels, spiritually, emotionally, and physically are the ones who will embody what it means to be highly sensitive, intuitive, and empathic. Simply stated, the ways these characteristics manifest is much more profound and persistent compared to same age peers.

It is important to know that many intuitive and spiritual children will have parents who are as well. Some, however, will not. Yet embracing our children's strengths and abilities is about them and not us. A child will know they are being honored when their experience is not embellished nor discredited. With all of this said, embracing our children's interests, no matter how unique they are, is simply embracing soul. It teaches children to listen to self, to honor self, take pride in their talents, and helps them see their unique contribution to the world. I can't state it enough, honoring our children is what the H.O.P.E tribe is all about. In honor we find hope. To honor something is to believe in it. o believe in something gives hope to the holder of that belief.

The strategies in Chapter 10 highlight ways to embrace, discover and harness, without controlling, these unique characteristics. Helpful tools for children to perceive situations from the unique way they experience life are provided. Children in the H.O.P.E. Tribe will resonate with animal imagery, find meaning in the use of color and nature, and utilize symbolism as ways to more fully comprehend their abilities. It is my wish, that the activities in Chapter 10 bring healing to those children who are in need of finding their place in the world.

Part Two

Why is the H.O.P.E. Tribe needed?

Chapter 6

The Implications

How does H.O.P.E. show up in our lives?

"Where there is love there is life; where there is life there is hope."
Allan Stratton

In order to truly embrace H.O.P.E. we must be able to identify how the need shows up in our world. When we look at situations, we may write them off using traditional un-evolved ways of thinking. These conventional responses keep us and our children stuck in a world that is afraid to "see" what cannot be tested, is not tangible, may not make complete sense, and does not allow for every dot to be connected. Our world is good at turning its back on newness. It is resistant to change. We are programmed to believe specific ways. When we join the H.O.P.E. tribe we challenge this thinking. We look for ways that a new way of being and interacting in the world has been there all along. We see that when something shows up in our world, we can look through a different, often more empowering lens, that encourages connection rather than isolation. The need for H.O.P.E is seen everywhere when we open our eyes. The implications of being part of the H.O.P.E. tribe is that we begin to think differently, experience parenting and relationships differently, and become more present in our worlds by necessity.

The Importance of Finding Your Tribe

A child who is an empath is believed to be able to perceive or experience the emotions of others. A child with extra-sensory perceptive abilities has a sixth sense, an ability to receive information beyond the known traditional senses. This ability means they are capable of sensing emotions of those around them in a way that is unexplainable by science or psychology. Many parents of these children find themselves feeling overwhelmed, lacking an explanation from science or psychology. In an attempt to explain this phenomenon further, I will share a brief story.

Recently, my son had a friend over for a playdate. His friend shared a story about an acquaintance eating a live goldfish. My son burst into tears and desperately cried out "why, why would they do that?" "Mom that poor fish, why?" he questioned. "I can feel that fish mom, that is horrible, terrible, sad," he lamented. Everyone was surprised by the intense emotions my son expressed. This situation could have been filled with anxiety and even embarrassment, however, I chose to honor his feelings and look deeper. In that moment I felt proud that my son felt comfortable sharing such deep emotion in front of me, his friend, and his friend's mother. His sensitivity to the topic warmed my heart, revealing his compassion for all living things. His friend's empathic response signaled the arrival of my own HOPE tribe. They both sat quietly, letting my son cry his tears. Then his friend's mother said, "I just love his heart. It is a beautiful thing". My son smiled and allowed himself to work through the moment. Play resumed shortly after. There was no teasing, no challenging his emotions, and perhaps most significant, no attempt to squash the moment or shut it down. In that moment, it was crystal clear, I sat among members of the HOPE tribe. My son and I were safe.

I tried to imagine how others might mock him, tease him, gossip about the 'episode', or quickly find any reason to leave and disconnect. In an instant, the tribe grew. The tribe in that moment became not only about my son, but about me as well. I wanted to belong somewhere where my child would be held in great esteem for who he is, what he experiences, and what he has to offer...a beautiful heart. It was a powerful moment, one that offered reassurance for the HOPE tribe and ushered in an even deeper desire to fulfill my calling to write and share this with others.

New Ways of Being

Most would be astonished to learn that being empathic happens at a cellular level. This kind of "being" shows up on scans and medical imaging as a reactive neurological system. Empaths operate in a completely different way, from distinct filters, unwilling to block messages otherwise seen unnecessary. As with my son, empaths can be labeled as "overly sensitive" and even diagnosed with a sensory integration disorder. Sensitive and empathic children can have reactions to bright lights, certain sounds (especially loud noises), smells, and certain places, typically crowded ones. If we pause, and look beyond the surface, we will see what empathic and sensitive children endure. Integrating, processing, and assimilating sensory overloaded experiences can be challenging for sensitive children. My son was terrified to go in public restrooms because of the self-flushing toilets and not being prepared for the loud noise it would cause. Post-it notes to cover the sensor became a must have for me as his mother. Understanding his level of discomfort and even pain with loud noises was what prompted the use of innovative strategies to ensure joyful living.

He covered his ears at sirens, loud music, or in crowds of people. It was hard to watch and at times I found myself wishing he didn't have to endure it, wishing his sensitivities away. However, instead of wishing parts of him away, I decided to approach his day WITH him. WITH made it less about me and more about him. After much self-work and deep inquiry about my own emotional reactions to his 'challenges', I allowed myself to be a partner in discovering what would create more alignment for him.

Our interactions effect our connection. When interactions are informed by feelings of overwhelm, anger, frustration, confusion, and fear, connection is bypassed. The relationship is hijacked by 'trying to fix something' rather than remaining curious, finding reciprocity in the learning cycle, and searching for healthy strategies that benefit all.

I found so much appreciation and respect for who he is along the way. A time of reflection and introspection resulted.

Taking a look at oneself requires self-discipline, and self-compassion. As parents our journey is our child's journey as well. If we engage in what we ask of them, not only do we grow, but we understand their process and experience on a much deeper and empathic level. I had to begin asking and questioning my everyday beliefs and practices. Where was I sensitive? How did I feel when others shut me down? Who are the members of my HOPE tribe? Do I behave and act in accordance with what I truly believe? Am I living my soul blueprint, the fingerprint that separates me from everyone else and allows me to be uniquely different? What do I do that might change my child on a soul and cellular level? Am I okay with who he is, what he has been given? How do I come to terms with my own beliefs and what he believes, where do these beliefs converge and diverge? These are not easy questions to digest and yet this is where the true learning occurs. This work is the foundation and allows for the celebration of unique gifts.

The HOPE tribe becomes a sacred ceremonial ground for self-discovery while helping our children discover who they are. We must engage in this ritual together. Even if we don't deem ourselves as highly sensitive, intuitive, empathic, or spiritual, it is still our responsibility as entrusted caregivers to look deeply inside to decipher what is ours, what is someone else's, and how the way we live impacts our child's inner being. Some of the activities in this book will encourage that both adults and children engage together...connecting through a neurological reciprocity that changes both and allows a child to better understand how to navigate self in relation to others and to the world. The creation of a healthy, vibrant, gift-focused, tolerant, and accepting environment is critical to mastering the ritual needed to connect both parent (adult) and child.

New Ways of Thinking

Cells change based on their environment, internal and external. Therefore, the building blocks of life are altered in a profound way as the interplay between nature and nurture occur. The fabric of our being then is modified by interpersonal relationships, our surroundings, and one's ability to integrate information. Empaths and highly sensitive people have been shown medically to have atypical brain activity. This proves the organic and inherent nature of these traits; the hard wiring of abilities, and the neurological differences of extrasensory perception. The very essence of us is derived from these small cells; these molecular idiosyncrasies that speak to our unique nature. They are God breathed and inspired gifts that were given when we received our life force energy, our soul. That is powerful!

When we look at our child's extra-sensory perceptions from this perspective we are less likely to shut it down, get frustrated by it, and/ or try to change it. Rescuing our children from pain or discomfort is common place for parents. Helping our children deal with bullying, teasing, and others who put them down for their gifts is about coping. Truly asking them to change is shutting down their feelings or experiences. Not providing safe outlets to express themselves and putting them in uncomfortable situations, is a mere attempt to 'get them used to the normal way of being'.

We often engage in this "shutting down" without conscious awareness. For example, florescent lighting has been shown to negatively impact certain people, some of who are highly sensitive and empathic. These effected people can experience physical symptoms, such as headaches, due to this type of lighting. From uncomfortable physical sensations, emotional reactions often result. If a child begins complaining, or starts to lose more rational thinking, it might be due to lighting. While this is not true for all situations it warrants more curiosity. Shutting a child down who might be "reacting" to overstimulation to lighting, would be to force him/her into a room that is physically or emotionally debilitating for them. Discussions, seeking solutions, and understanding how external stimuli effect internal states of being is useful for optimal integration. This doesn't mean that our children don't go to school because of the lights they use. It means that understanding how our child's body reacts to a certain stimulus is organic and that finding solutions will address more of the true nature of the situation, as opposed to creating an emotional battle about it.

Often, I hear parents make insensitive comments about children's, their own and others, emotional reactions to different external stimuli.

They may label the child 'too sensitive' or the behavior 'as controlling or manipulative', rather than 'digging deeper'. These comments label behavior in a negative manner, create cognitive dissonance, and prevent emotional expression. Pay attention to your child's reactions and responses to see what the function of the behavior is, what does the behavior communicate. Behavior can tell us much about what a child believes and experiences. If your child knows that they are cared for, physically and emotionally, they will feel respected, leading to genuine connection and authentic discussions for solutions. So being mindful of external and internal stimuli can have a profound impact on a child's experience. Allow your child their experience, don't deny or embellish, give it the attention it warrants, and help find solutions. This process will be empowering for both you and your child.

Sensitive and empathic children can possess 'super senses', hearing the slightest hum, smelling the slightest odor, and feeling uncomfortable with certain textures. I can't help but recall a time when my son was completely unraveled emotionally and physically by the smell in a restaurant. His gag reflex activated, his eyes full of tears, his body unable to self-soothe, crying and desperately begging to leave. To be honest, I was annoyed and frustrated. The urge to shut him down, tell him to 'stop it', discount his experience and force him to react differently was there. I paused. I breathed. I pondered. What was the HOPE in the situation? How would the tribe view this? Ultimately, the HOPE was that we could all engage and connect over dinner. The goal was to enjoy our time together. The HOPE was to honor his experience, be open to his hard wiring, have empathy for him, and find a solution that would work for all. Long story short, we discovered that the smell of lemon cancelled that of the other odor and he was able to return to the experience and balance his system so he could participate fully in the activity of a family dinner.

Children will discount their experience if we discount it. This will increase their tendency to dissociate from parts of themselves. Soul purpose and their unique blueprint then is pushed further away. When children move further and further away from true self they become disconnected from true joy and love. They become programmed by other, not informed by their soul. This is dangerous. Moving away from joy and love is to move away from Source, the Divine light. The gap, the space created between soul self and 'programmed' self, becomes rabid for a feeling of connection, purpose, and hope. Unable to bridge the gap because soul self is so far removed, children can engage in maladaptive behaviors and negative thinking. These patterns are disruptive to their lives and send them on a 'soul less' trajectory. Such patterns can include decreased self-esteem and self-competency, addictive behaviors, and decreased social relatedness skills (inability to connect, empathize, and relate).

Speaking of "soul" purpose, arouses a story of a young boy, age 7, who shared his traumatic experience with me. His head got caught in a swimming pool filter. His mother confirmed the story and told me how she had to rescue her son from the situation. The most interesting part of the story was the way in which he shared his experience. He talked about it as if "he had experienced it from outside himself" and stated, "but I didn't die because I still have work here to do". He mentioned how he still becomes anxious when he thinks about it, but that he has ways of calming his body down. He spoke beyond his years about the situation, his wisdom light-years beyond his time here on earth.

He proceeded to tell me more about his life, sharing experiences that suggested he had gifts related to extrasensory capabilities. Some of these experiences included seeing people who have passed away, hearing voices of spirit, and being connected to a greater meaning for his life and his purpose. He is connected to his soul's purpose. He is ready for the journey. His mother shared that he was interested in space travel at the age of two. In digging deeper she learned that her son had several experiences beyond her understanding. Beginning at age two, he experienced soul's from the other side, one of which was Einstein. Unwilling to shut her son down, her thought became:

"I just told myself that it is a 50/50 chance he is in fact talking with souls in the spirit realm, and if he isn't well, he's got a great imagination".

She never has discounted his experience. She gives him ample time, space and outlets to express himself, and allows for him to have his own experience in this world. She is a tremendous example of allowing a child to live their soul purpose. Her commitment to allowing him to be him, even from a place of not quite knowing what she believes, is powerful and embodies the core principles of H.O.P.E.

New Ways of Feeling

Many empathic children can sense other people's emotions, energy, and physical symptoms in their bodies. For example, my son and I went into a supermarket. While in the check-out line I began to feel "drawn" to the woman in front of us. Being an intuitive, empathic person myself, I have these sensations often. The difference this time was that with no complaint before-hand, my son immediately started saying that his head hurt. When I asked more about it, using questions like "where in your head?", he stated on the right side and pointed to an area just above his right temple. We took 3 deep breaths together, and with the breaths he allowed it to leave his body. He stated that it was gone, the pain had disappeared. The woman was now gone as well. I began to question:

Could his headache have been a similar experience to my curiosity and being "drawn" to the woman in front of us? Could he be experiencing a physical manifestation while I was experiencing a more heart manifestation? Could the reason I was "drawn" to this woman have anything to do with a pain? Could my son be experiencing someone else's pain? These thoughts quickly entered my mind.

Then I began to wonder and question even further. If it was solely his pain, it would persist. If the pain left, this meant it was fleeting. Could it be someone else's? He said it was gone and no complaints followed. Now, I know that some skeptics would say "well, he just wished it away" and to that I would respond, "well good". We may never know how the headache came to be and that is okay. You see it is about teaching a child how to cope with distress, physical or emotional pain, discomfort, or a situation that is difficult without telling them what they are experiencing is wrong, inaccurate, or impossible.

Placebo effect is a real thing! Anita Moorjani and David Hamilton spoke to this idea. On a Hay House Radio Show they discussed how medically the placebo effect was shown effective. They shared ideas about healing sanctuaries, places where I describe as healing from the inside out and from the top (the Divine) down. They spoke of hospitals becoming more places for connection, holistic thought put into practice, and healing through connection to self, other and God. I believe that the H.O.P.E tribe needs to be a 'healing sanctuary', both emotionally and physically for children and those who support them. The H.O.P.E tribe would be a representation of ideas and beliefs so that smaller healing sanctuaries and tribes can be formed in a more tangible, physical way. If our homes became 'healing sanctuaries' our children would be able to create that atmosphere outside the home as well, with friends they choose, a mindset they work from, and situations they gravitate towards and even create for themselves.

Would it be crazy if my son was experiencing someone else's pain? No, I believe that children and people (since I have experienced somatic empathic responses myself) can carry, hold, or take on other people's symptoms, be it emotional or physical. This makes finding tools to cope, ways to rid themselves of sensations, or just understanding this phenomena of great importance to me. We will discuss strategies and how certain questioning can help children distinguish between what is theirs and what is another person's in a future section of this book. What I do want to relay now, is that typically if an empathic child is fine and has no somatic complaints and there is a sudden complaint, it is beneficial to ask more questions to decipher if it is their ailment or someone else's. Empathic children tend to 'feel' things first and then think. This 'feel then think' dynamic is opposite as others typically think then feel. Helping children understand this dynamic is imperative in aiding them in sorting out what they think and feel, who it belongs to, and a helpful strategy for coping. There are specific strategies to support children in understanding the "feel-think" mode of receiving information. Chapter 10 provides such strategies.

New Ways of Receiving

Another way H.O.P.E. might show up in our lives is through understanding "downloading". Beyond heightened sensitivities to our 5 senses, intuitive and highly empathic children can also sense things, receive messages, insights or receive downloads through sight, hearing, and intuitive 'knowing'. Downloads are when someone receives information beyond rational explanation by extrasensory perceptive abilities. Some might think it is merely an active imagination, and while these children do typically have great imaginations, this information is usually in response to something or is an antecedent to an experience. It can possess a random quality to it. Often making sense of it requires going to a deeper level and typically it feels as if "something is missing or doesn't seem to add up".

An example of such a phenomenon follows: A child, age of 3, pretends to call her great grandmother on the phone. The child uses the name of her great grandmother. The child's mother had never mentioned this person to her, had no pictures in the home, and proceeds to ask if any other family member has talked with her daughter about this distant relative who had passed away years before her daughter was born. To the mother's surprise, no one recalls having talked about this relative to her daughter. Clearly pieces have been "downloaded", however "something is missing and does not add up". Where did the child learn the name of this deceased relative? Could the child be in contact with her great grandmother who is visiting from the other side? While there may be very little information to support this occurrence there is equally not enough information to discount this experience.

"Downloading" has also shown up in my life through many experiences. I will share one from my son's developing psychic ability. My son woke up and before school he wanted to play his snap circuits, an electrical circuit game. In my mind I thought: "Well, this is different. He doesn't usually want to do something like this before school". I didn't mention anything to him regarding my puzzled reaction. I let my thought be observed and let go. After picking him up from school he said, "Mom, we did snap circuits in STEM club today, and I did them this morning before school at home. I didn't even tell myself to look into the future this morning and I still did".

The main channels for someone to receive 'information' is through extrasensory perceptions. Many times people will hear the words clairaudient, clairvoyant, claircognizant, and clairsentient. However, many do not know what is meant by these terms. In order to help assimilate this information and make sense of these terms we will use experiences of a fictional child, Claire, age 8. The experiences expressed as Claire's story are combined bits and pieces of living children's experiences and stories. Using a fictional child will allow us to construct a mental model and better explain how the "claires" (clairaudient, clairvoyant, claircognizant, and clairsentient) show up. Highly intuitive children possess all, a combination of some or one of the 'clairs'.

Clairaudience is clear hearing. This is hearing a message as actual words or by song. Example 1: Claire wakes up some mornings with a 'song stuck in her head' and at times this song is one she has no to little access to. The song may have preceded her generation, or one that is typically more accessible to older children via traditional channels of communication.

Example 2: Claire will hear something. It may not be the same as a typical person's voice but it is a definite 'hearing'. Claire will "hear" a phrase, number, letter, name, or a piece of information.

Clairvoyance is clear seeing. Claire sees fleeting or repetitive images in her mind's eye. Example: Claire begins to repetitively see in her mind the letter T, and then sees a flash of a picture of three girls with pigtails. Claire finds later in the day she meets a person named Tom, or while she is sitting with a friend she learns that her friend's grandfather Timothy passed away several years ago. My own clairvoyant experiences include seeing a black and white movie reel, which often symbolizes a past event or experience for the person I am with. Claircognizant is clear knowing. This is when we can't explain something, we just know it. Our intuition, our gut, something within us just knows. Example: Claire was out an about with her mother at a local store, and she just 'knew that another child whom was shopping in the store was ill'. This other child was a complete stranger, probably roughly the same age as Claire based on appearance. Her mother looked and there seemed to be no obvious signs of illness. Claire was sure of it and said "I just know he is mom. I think he has cancer". As Claire and her mother continued about their errand, her mother overheard the father of the boy tell another person that he had Neuroblastoma, a form of cancer affecting young children. This type of cancer attacks the sympathetic nervous system.

Clairsentient is clear feeling. This is a blending of sorts at the emotional (just knowing) level and the kinesthetic (physical, somatic) level. Clairsentient abilities include feeling differences in energy fields, ability to scan someone either with hands or mentally to find areas of physical complaint, physically taking on the pain of another person, or having a desire to place your hands (or continually wanting to ask about a particular place on a person's body) on someone at a certain place on their body. Example 1: Claire is sitting in class when her head begins to hurt and progressively gets worse. A classmate, who endured migraines on a regular basis was sent to the nurse's office. Claire was unaware of the medical needs of this student Example 2: Recently, while writing in a coffee shop, out of the blue my chest began to hurt. The pain started as a tingle, then got more and more intense. My chest began tightening and I started to have more labored breathing. I took 3 deep breaths and asked myself where the pain was coming from. Was this pain mine or not? I began to pay attention to myself and my surroundings. There were two women sitting at a table next to me. At that very moment they began talking about a memorial service that was scheduled for later that day for a fallen police officer who was shot in the chest. Immediately after I heard the words, the pain was released and then his spirit greeted me. The greeting did not last long, just long enough to validate that the feeling was in fact representing his death.

While there is not a recognized 'clair' for scent/taste it is still a way to receive intuitive information. A highly sensitive or empathic may begin to ask questions like, "what's that smell?" Example: Claire goes into a beauty shop and smells a 'rosy scent'. She is adamant that the lady helping us has a mother who wears a perfume like the one she is smelling.

When we belong to the H.O.P.E. tribe we honor all channels of receiving and expressing. The opportunities to H.O.P.E. are numerous if we allow ourselves to accept new ways of thinking, feeling and being in this world. These show up in our lives and they require a response that values their uniqueness. Without thinking about the implications of the H.O.P.E. tribe in our lives we miss a huge piece of who we are at our most spiritual and soulful level. We must be willing to wake up and be different in our world, not only for ourselves but for our children.

Chapter 7

The Ways of Protecting

Why do our children need to be protected?

> "There can be no keener revelation of a society's
> soul than the way it treats its children."
> Nelson Mandela

The H.O.P.E. Tribe is not just a title of a book it is a living idea. The principles and practices must be put into practice in your everyday life. Finding a village of like-minded, or at least open minded, individuals to help you on this parenting journey will be imperative to you and your child. For the skills one doesn't have another most likely will. An example of this concept is when our children feel more comfortable talking to someone else about deeper things. This is okay and is highly encouraged within the H.O.P.E. tribe mentality. The act of allowing them to share who they are with another is teaching them how to cope and integrate self. My son wanted to talk to his best friend's mother rather than me about something that was bothering him. I encouraged it. I would prefer he talk to her than no one. She is in my tribe and I knew that I could trust her with whatever he came to her with. I knew that she wouldn't shut him down, and if it needed more attention she would let me know. A tribal community allows for authentic sharing what you know, genuinely giving what you have, and receiving what others can offer. If you have picked up this book, or have ever had the thought that your child might have extrasensory capabilities then you are probably on target with your assumption. Intuitively, especially us mother's, we know more about our children than we think we do. Listening to ourselves as parents is also very important in helping our children cope with these abilities that at times can be overwhelming. Find a tribe of people close to you that you can talk to about these things.

After reading the definitions and brief descriptions in the previous section, you may find yourself asking more questions. It is important to note that your child does not need to have ALL of the aforementioned characteristics to be considered highly sensitive, empathic, intuitive, or spiritual. In addition, and of equal importance, it is recommended that children be assessed medically if they report somatic complaints. For example, vision problems, ringing in ears, extra sensitive to clothing or developing rashes (possibly from food allergies) may signal a medical concern or an energetic somatic response. It is also important that your child have support emotionally if needed. Perhaps psychotherapy, social emotional groups, whether in or outside of school, life skills group, OT, speech therapy, and others can be necessary as additional resources and supports for your child. Medical and other professionals can help us gain insight into the workings of our children's bodies. Often medical doctors, due to traditional training, underestimate the role of extrasensory capabilities and their impact on the physical body. Bridging the gap and working together will avoid the us vs. them mentality. We all have our special talents and abilities. Medical practitioners have their place in our lives for a reason. With this said, finding one that you and your child connect with is important.

Perusing the previous chapter might also leave you feeling affirmed and thinking "this totally describes my child". You may ask, "If this is my child, what does this mean for him/her?" It is a sad reality but bullying, teasing, and a culture of fitting in is everywhere. Empathic, highly sensitive, and intuitive children can be labeled as, "those who beat to a different drummer" or perhaps more unfriendly terms such as "weird", "strange", "peculiar", "odd" and can often feel misunderstood. Personally, I love the idea of being different, however, our children may not have the inner confidence to embrace their differences. They have to have support to honor the "beat they choose to walk through life with". They have to have time and space to explore "their style of drumming".

These children are susceptible to being called names based on emotional reactions, and the way in which they interact in the world. Since many empathic or intuitive children can fit in anywhere (and unfortunately, sometimes they feel like nowhere), they may lack a close group of friends which could help ward off or mitigate the effects of teasing and bullying. As a member of the tribe and as their parent, our role can be helping them create their own HOPE tribe at school or in the community. There is power in a community of support and this can be very beneficial way to collectively protect our children. Please see Chapter 10 to learn more about exercises, activities and strategies to help support your child in building a strong tribe that offers support and protecting qualities. *If you suspect your child is being bullied please seek resources and support.

Signs that a child is being bullied or excessively teased
Unexplained injuries
Lost or destroyed clothing, books, electronics, or jewelry
Somatic complaints (headaches, stomach aches, feeling sick or faking illness)
Change in eating habits
Difficulty sleeping or nightmares
Loss of interest in pleasurable activities, decline in performance at school not wanting to attend school
Changes in peer groups and social circle, avoids social situations
Feelings of helplessness
Any self-destructive behaviors (running away, talking about suicide, harming self, consistent abusive self-talk, alcohol or drug use)

**Stopbullying.gov

Another aspect that is needed for consideration of highly sensitive, intuitive and empathic children is the concept of "belonging". There is a difference between fitting in and belonging. To fit in is what the H.O.P.E tribe warns against. Fitting in often requires children to alter their soul self in order to be liked. They must ascribe to a limiting mindset which can suppress and stuff down one's soul purpose. To belong is a totally different experience. Belonging is knowing you are accepted, can offer your gifts without ridicule, and can receive openly. When we find a group to truly belong among, we are able to be our authentic selves and our differences are celebrated not criticized.

According to Brene Brown's Top 4 Life Lessons found on Oprah.com "fitting in is the greatest barrier to belonging. Fitting in, I've discovered during the past decade of research, is assessing situations and groups of people, then twisting yourself into a human pretzel in order to get them to let you hang out with them. Belonging is something else entirely – it's showing up and letting yourself be seen and known as you really are."(2017)

As parents we need to direct, facilitate, and lead conversations with our children about fitting in as compared to belonging. This can be a delicate and emotionally charged subject. Many of us might have faced our own battles with being teased, bullied, or struggling to find true belonging. If as a parent this brings up any emotional baggage or feelings for you, please try to express it, share it, discover, and uncover it. For when you do, you will be more open to helping your child find strategies for coping with his own belonging battles. Belonging battles are the ones worth fighting for. Finding where you can be YOU is a battle that should be fought. Oppositely, the battle to fit in is not worth fighting. When you are asked to fit in you are asked to change yourself. The outcome of the battle has already been decided and you have lost. Our world has begun to live from a 'fear mindset', especially when it comes to the idea belonging. We fear not having something or not having enough to 'fit in' with "those" people. We are afraid to notice differences and actually name them in a respectful way that calls positive attention and light to uniqueness. We have forgotten that it is OK and even beautiful to be different! Collectively we live in fear. We don't allow our children, or even ourselves, to be open, to embrace, and to learn more about differences. As a human race we tend to shut these conversations down. We are fearful of even talking about our differences. When a child asks more about another child's culture, ethnicity, or any other difference from their own belief system, we would be wise to respond by providing answers, seek to understand and open up deeper dialogue. This would serve our children more. This response helps them understand themselves, their values, their beliefs, and their connection to self and others.

This is the meaning and the why for The H.O.P.E tribe. My hope is that children find places of belongingness rather than simply trying to fit in. This place won't require them to sacrifice their soul, their self, in order to be a part of a community. My daughter shared a story of a girl in her kindergarten class. The girl asked for a 'gold bead' that my daughter was holding. The girl told my daughter that if she didn't give her the gold bead she wouldn't be her friend. While many see a simple gold bead, here in this story, the gold bead represents self, love, passion, soul gifts, beliefs, and so much more. I was sad to hear that my daughter gave her the gold bead even though she desperately wanted to keep it. When asked why she gave it to her, she simply and in a matter of fact way replied, "because I wanted her to be my friend". My heart broke. But then I said to myself, "take hope and turn this into a conversation, a connection place, a time we share what it means to fit in vs. belonging". So right then and there my daughter and I discussed this very issue, in kindergarten terms of course. We strategized ways she can respond in the future without giving her 'gold bead' away and still trying to keep a friendship she wanted, too. She could say something like, "I really want you to be my friend. I like playing with you. I also really like my gold bead. I want to keep it and I hope you will still be my friend".

I will be the first to admit that my children have seen me be a person who changes who they are for the feeling of fitting in. AND I have also been diligently working on this. I want to show them the true difference between fitting in and belonging. When you belong you must first belong to yourself. Then you can belong 'with' the outside world. When self-love and acceptance of our unique abilities and gifts allows us to find those who celebrate with us, one can live from a joyful and authentic place. 'With' rather than 'to' is highlighted for significance. For "belonging to the outside world" represents possession and relates to fitting in. Belonging is being 'with' others in a way that is authentic, unique, and pure. On Oprah.com, Brene Brown shared Top 4 Life Lessons. The following is a quote from Brene Brown regarding lesson one Fitting In Is Not Belong.

"Many of us suffer from this split between who we are and who we present to the world in order to be accepted. But we're not letting ourselves be known, and this kind of incongruent living is soul-sucking" (2017).

I want my children to belong in a way that is soul inspiring, where they receive positive energy to express their truest and purest self. The H.O.P.E tribe is where this belongingness can begin.

It is important that our children are given tools for dealing with teasing, bullying, or soul-sucking people they come in contact with. Listening to our children's stories about their school day, recognizing shifts in moods or behaviors, and being engaged in their school community can help prevent bullying or teasing. My children have participated in an anti-bullying class. The class was several hours in length, they discussed differences between bullying and teasing, how to address different situations through role play, and learned self-defense strategies. Both of my children seemed to have more confidence in themselves in dealing with difficult situations. I encourage parents who worry about their child's ability to deal effectively with challenging situations like these to explore more learning opportunities.

The thoughts of how I was bullied as a child are brought back to me. I was teased and taunted. I felt a deep loneliness within. My soul was wounded. My heart was intensely hurt. My wish to fit in was so much stronger than my will to belong. With a tribe, with H.O.P.E., I would have felt supported. I would have been less fearful to project my true self into the world. I would have gained self-confidence. I would have used the tribe as a sounding board, a place to gain ideas for combatting the cruelty that I endured. I would have been empowered, for a tribe is a collective community that backs its members and ensures their safety.

When we neglect ourselves and are required to give up pieces of ourselves to fit in, we lose ourselves. We are in danger of dying, not literally but our souls lay dormant and unable to express their true passions. As a tribe we need to restore HOPE. This H.O.P.E is that children can get back to their soulful self, soulful expressions, and creative energy. Our world is conditioned to see certain aspects of children while unconsciously destroying others. This fear drives children to be disconnected and become isolated compartments of themselves, isolated pieces seeking to become whole again. As we grow we tend to compartmentalize more and more, losing sight of true belonging and living our lives seeking approval and the need to fit in.

The enemy is a school of thought that children have to rid themselves of true soul experiences, and that children don't have the power to have perceptions beyond rational thought. Intuitive and empathic children are asked to cut off a part of them, a piece of them is asked to die a young death. Highly intuitive, perceptive, and empathic children are born into this world and sent into a battle of sides, a battle that doesn't allow for duality and differences. A battle that keeps children small and doesn't allow their voices to be heard. They need a H.O.P.E. tribe which operates from a place of love, understanding, and empathy so that they combat a worldview that says that this physical experience is all there is to life.

Our highly sensitive and empathic children fight internal and external battles all day long. These battles are characterized by experiences that others do not understand, demean, and discount because they cannot explain them. Others, while they may have the potential to experience these types of "spiritually awakened" moments, are fearful and unable to tap into these resources due to their frame of mind. This fear leads to anger which can lead to hate. This deep seeded fear and misunderstanding may eventually lead to actions which may impose suffering for others. This isn't to say that what empathic children endure is bad, it is not. It is beautiful, but can be confusing and difficult to integrate when you are amongst others who experience life in different and more traditional way.

If we all looked deep inside, did some soul searching, we would see a great desire to belong to the Divine. The good news is that we all do already belong to the Divine. We just have to want to recognize this connection. We don't have to 'fit in', we just have to live out our true and Divine inspired gifts. While we are always connected to source, to live truly connected and soulfully we have to live synergistically. Our actions must match our beliefs. Our feelings, thoughts, behavior create our experience. In order to be truly connected to self, other, and the universe we have to be internally aligned. Our bodies and minds need to match our soul. Our soul needs to feel free to be expressed through our body and mind without judgement from self or others.

The H.O.P.E. tribe is all about synergistic living. This type of living is expressed when we all work together in harmony. When we see the need for balance and wisdom for the greater good we are attempting to live in harmony. It is in this harmonic state that children get guided in a peaceful meaningful manner towards their soul purpose and where we are called to live out Divinely inspired gifts despite what the world might think.

Hope is a feeling of trust, a feeling of expectation and desire for a certain thing to happen, a wish, optimism. The H.O.P.E. tribe is just that, a place to start bringing all these things back for the sake of the generations to come. We need to bring our H.O.P.E. children back from a place of distrust to one of trust and soulful desire. It is time for conversations, real and difficult ones, to start. The H.O.P.E. tribe challenges its members to start talking about these issues for the sake of our children, the sake of our world, and to begin creating H.O.P.E. tribes all over the world.

Another way for us as parents to help protect our highly sensitive children is to talk with them about healthy and appropriate boundaries (physically, emotionally, and spiritually). Physically speaking our children need to know that physical contact, no matter with who, is always a choice. Their body is their body, and they get to decide who and how someone is touching it. I have heard parents, grandparents, and others speak to children in the following ways: "Well, where is my hug?" "You can open your presents after I get my hug." Let's remember that some children (and even adults!) may not be comfortable with hugging or touching for various reasons. They may simply not want physical touch in that specific moment. This choosing not to accept physical contact in that moment may be for reasons beyond our current understanding. Respecting our children's bodies and space, honoring their needs and wants regarding physical contact is important. It builds safety, trust, connection and ultimately honors them as a unique being.

Empathic children at times have difficulty deciphering between themselves and others. Having conversations regularly about boundaries, including emotionally, physically, and spiritually, will help them better learn where they begin and end, figuratively and literally. Talk about the word, "no". While it sounds so simple, it isn't always simple to say. We as parents know this! In our current society the word "no" has a negative connotation, often seen as a 'bad word'. Our children need to be able to take back the power of no. No simply states a personal boundary. In today's world boundaries and remaining true to self for the greater good is essential. Practice saying no through role play or psychodrama activities with your child. This practice will help children acclimate their bodies and become prepared for the visceral response that occurs when using or hearing the word "no". This practice helps ensure that children will use it when they want to stay true to themselves, perhaps they are not wanting to do something or something doesn't feel right. This will serve them well when they are combating teasing or peer pressure. And of course, there will inevitably be the need for the conversation about how saying no to eating your vegetables or cleaning your room isn't the same thing! During these "power of no practice sessions", talk with your child about meaning it, say it and mean it, and what that looks like. How does someone know you mean what you say? Providing social skills training, and role playing for your child (either provided by you or someone else) regarding what to do or say in situations can add to our child feeling safe and protected.

When we discuss the importance of boundaries, Ego can play a critical part. Anita Moorjani, a New York Times bestselling author and prominent Hay House speaker, provided an excellent point of view on the concept of Ego. Her thought was that people who are drawn to spiritual issues already live from a decreased sense of Ego. Therefore, their Ego isn't necessarily a "problem". This means they tend to think about life from a more abstract spiritual point of view. These individuals attempt to provide teachings, ideas, and projects that better the collective whole. She made a point that healthy Ego can help maintain healthy, appropriate boundaries. Healthy appropriate boundaries are necessary to have a purposeful human experience. Ego, when driven from a soulful place, allows us to be effective change agents.

With children it is important that when we are teaching soulful living, we are encouraging the integration of healthy Ego. Ego, while often viewed negatively, is on a spectrum, one end being complete egotistical narcissistic behavior and the other end being inability to identify self as having a human experience. To strip away a child's Ego would disserve them, us, and the greater good. The goal is to have a child embrace their Ego from a soulful place, where soul is informing the Ego. Therefore, we see the ego as necessary, and soul and ego working in harmony can make positive change. Ego separated from soul is when things go awry. When self isn't driven by soul connection, and when our path is diverted off of our soul blueprint and path, we are truly disconnected. These are big words and concepts for children. We can help them see the connection between their ego and self-worth by talking about soulful ideas, ways of expressing themselves, and supporting the follow through with projects or ideas. Ego helps protect in a way that is still in alignment with Source and provides motivation to carry out ideas. When healthy Ego is aligned with Source, a child is protected. This protection is a manifestation of appropriate boundaries.

The art of boundary setting resides in deeper understanding of self and other. It is imperative that parents don't try to fill in the gaps for their kids and at the same time don't make things fit that don't. In no way do I want a parent to try to make their child be something they are not. Trying to push your child into being empathic, highly sensitive or intuitive would be a disservice to your child's soul. The same holds true for parents who do not honor a child's intuitive nature. When we shut down our children, we are creating a deeper pain, a soul pain. Open, honest, and creative expression encourages decreased compartmentalization and increases the ability of the child to be who they truly are. This is our greatest gift of protection. When a child believes in themselves, exudes self-confidence, they can identify situations and people that will best serve them and their life's purpose.

They will operate from a place of certainty and trusting self rather than fear and confusion. This is essential, for if we are divided, broken, we will most definitely live an inauthentic life. We will be unable to trust our own experiences. We must help our children integrate who they are into the world. **Either we can let the world change them or we can let them change the world.**

True belonging, not separate from Source and connected to all, is when we act in socially responsible ways. Social responsibility promotes that which is best for the greater good. Ego conditions are left behind. Social responsibility requires connection to a community, a tribe. This tribe, one built on H.O.P.E., is essential for raising a socially responsible child connected to their soul gifts. We need a H.O.P.E. tribe that believes in and protects its children.

Chapter 8

The Navigating

How do we navigate social beliefs, constructs, and systems?

"Every child is unique, and it is through a child's creativity or innovative behavior that they can express their uniqueness."-Kay Kuzma's *Understanding Children*

Parents of highly sensitive, empathic and intuitive children, especially those parents who do not share similar abilities, need a tribe to support their children. Navigating our current world can feel lonely when we perceive things differently or from a different perspective than the general collective. Our children are dropped off at school, unless we are parents who choose to homeschool, and we trust that they are receiving the type of education we believe in. The type of education the H.O.P.E. Tribe supports is one in which social emotional learning and learning how our bodies process information, is valued and facilitated. This is a wave of the future and could not be happening at a better time. But for now, until our social world catches up with our spiritual world, our children have to operate in the current system.

Education in America is geared towards academic standards, and focuses little on teaching social relatedness, emotional regulation and the way our bodies process both external and internal information. Many children, and their parents, find it difficult to navigate the educational system and how to appropriately discuss their child's intuitiveness, empathic skills, and sensitivities in a way that is both effective for their child and doesn't create tension between parent and the system. Volunteering at your child's school can be a good way to assess, see firsthand, and determine if any changes would be beneficial for your child. Not all parents have the luxury of volunteering, and so communication with your child's teacher will be important. Better yet, if your child's teacher or school administration can be a member of your H.O.P.E. Tribe that would be the most beneficial.

When discussing aspects of your child's learning, it is important to approach the situation from a 'we are in this together' manner. The H.O.P.E. Tribe mentality is that we all have something to share and we bring unique gifts and personal strengths. Being open to hearing what school personnel have to say about your child's learning style, what they observe, and their limitations to certain adaptations will be useful when approached through teamwork. With this said, it is okay if you feel uncomfortable sharing certain aspects about your child with the school. The school does not need to know any details about your child's experiences if you or your child are not comfortable. The key is to be an advocate for your child, a parent who shares their expertise and teams with the school to help your child be successful. You do not have to label your child intuitive, spiritual, empathic, or sensitive in order to have conversations with teachers and the community agencies they are involved with. Simply discussing identified areas of need and possible solutions, as well as ways to help your child manage during their school day is sufficient enough.

In Chapter 10, I discuss the strategy of the 3 Cs. This speaks to Communication, Connection, and Creating Space. The 3 Cs can be utilized here when dealing with outside or external supports. Communicate openly and often with your child's school. Sometimes scheduling uninterrupted time to discuss your child's progress in school is helpful, and sometimes just popping in to let the teacher know your child is having a tough time is best. Consistent communication, if open, authentic, and mindful, will create the space for connection, no matter if it is planned in advance or simply spontaneous. The connection between home and school will allow for open solution-focused conversations.

This aids your child in succeeding in their academic environment and keeps lines of communication open for discussions about your child's strengths, abilities, and sensitivities. The 3 Cs are powerful. WE must engage in Communication, Connection, and Creating Space not only with our children, with our tribe, but also with other systems that may not view life from a similar mindset or point of view.

For example, others who do not openly share the common language among those of us who are open to the connection we have with the spiritual realm, may find the "language" uncomfortable. Often times, spiritual becomes synonymous with religion, which is definitely not the case. When using a new "language" to support and advocate for our children, we sometimes have to provide education. This might mean providing brief explanations of the terms we use. We may find it helpful to use concrete examples to show examples of what we mean. Remember with any "language" it is important to not put your beliefs onto another person. We want to support our child, however, we must be careful, as the parent, not to place our thoughts, needs and desires onto them. We must allow them to be co-creators of their worlds. Some of the following might be helpful words to use when discussing with people who may not ascribe to labels like "spiritual, intuitive, or empathic".

My child, or I…..

o   See(s) the big picture when it comes to…
o   have a heart for…
o   operate from a place of…
o   are/am open to…
o   believe that…
o   See(s) the benefits of following intuition or 'gut feelings' when it comes to…
o   Try to understand behavior and emotions at a deeper level…
o   Encourage self-expression by…
o   Promote individuality and celebrate differences by…
o   Be sure to create your own!

Through my own experiences of speaking with teachers about this process, new ideas were formed. Often our child is excluded from meetings at school, and conferences become about adult's perceptions of children. Often children are not present to share who they are and what they are doing. Allowing children to participate gives them a place to voice who they are, their needs, their strengths, and possible strategies. It also helps build positive self-esteem, helps them create boundaries, and helps them advocate for their own needs.

This is what authentic transparency is about. When we are transparent with our children, we create space for deeper more meaningful conversations. We build trust and relationships are strengthened. This also helps children 'belong to' their communities. They find a way of making sense of the systems they find themselves within and ultimately they belong to their own story. By providing a space for them to engage, participate, and be heard, we are intentionally connecting them to self, to other, to community, to collective, to Source. Parents can advocate for their child's involvement in the process, as well as advocate for increased social emotional learning curriculum in schools. In addition, parents can advocate for schools to operate from a trauma informed lens, increasing interoceptive activities, and allowing for creative and intuitive activities in school.

More and more teachers are saying things like, "I've never seen a kid like this before", "there is something totally different about them", "they are special", "they are beyond their years", "I don't know how to keep them from being bored and create a challenging, inspiring environment for them". They also have noted that children, "can't make a choice", "some kids seem overly giving or concerned about others". Some say, "we notice a lack of assertiveness", "we've seen that certain children lack self-identity and have emotional reactions at school that are atypical". I am assuming that I am not the only person who has heard this about their child.

Knowing myself, knowing my own empathic children, and knowing other children who are spiritual, intuitive, and empathic, I believe we are seeing more of these characteristics because we are seeing an evolving child. We must then adapt and provide an environment that meets the needs of our changing world, our changing children. I believe all children have something to teach us! H.O.P.E. Tribe members can organize a parent group at the school to discuss these ideas and ways to implement some of the strategies they use in their homes.

Our Parent Teacher Organizations focus on raising money for technology and nicer looking school amenities, however we may want to look at allocating funds to other ways of helping children be successful. Our children are evolving into more spiritual creatures who witness and engage in a deeper understanding of the world. They show a depth of intuition of how people work and are more focused on spiritual aspects of life rather than material. There appears to be a disconnect. The best way to combat social constructs and navigate systems that are not like minded are to open the doors for communication and encourage discussions about possible change. This can and needs to be done in a peaceful manner so that our children see how soulful living is also peaceful living. Emotional reactivity from parents towards a system of care will not only shut down lines of communication, it will undo what you have attempted to teach your child about openness, appropriate assertiveness, peaceful promotion of new ways of thinking, and how to operate from a deep connection to love and light.

Being academically trained, and having worked several years as a Licensed Marriage and Family Therapist, I see the benefits of psychotherapy. It can be very useful for children when coping with sensitivities, trauma, life changes, emotional or behavioral conditions, or simply to provide a safe place to connect and communicate with someone. Discussing with a therapist beforehand your beliefs about your child's abilities will be important in order to determine whether this person will be a good fit to work with your child. Open and honest evaluation of those who work with our children is important. We want those who can actively participate in your child's H.O.P.E. Tribe. Not only is it important that you are comfortable, but that the therapist or mental health professional is comfortable as well. This doesn't mean we change who our child is to make it fit, it means we have meaningful proactive conversations beforehand with the professional and start the process out from an authentic open space. The therapist, in my opinion, will, at a minimum, need to be open to the idea of your child's extrasensory capabilities (if they have them), curious about how best to help, and comfortable hearing any extrasensory (or "clair" experiences) that your child shares. Discussing beliefs about diagnosis and medications will be helpful as well.

Since mental health therapists are not traditionally trained in extrasensory experiences or from a 'spiritual' lens, it is imperative that the parents, to the best of their abilities, and your child, explain the unique abilities your child possesses. It can be difficult for some people to think of senses beyond our commonly discussed five, however if we think about 'gut' feelings we already know that there is a possibility of more. Think about women's intuition, a mother's knowing, and the "I just had a feeling" feeling.

We already are accepting that our bodies are able to perceive things that are beyond scientific explanation. How many times have we gone down a certain street because of a 'certain feeling' that told us not to? Or, thought we might see someone at the grocery store and then there they were? Or, knew who was calling on the phone before answering? Or, had the feeling that your sister is sick and upon calling her she tells you she isn't feeling well? These are all examples of how our bodies can pick up certain energies, thoughts, vibrations, messages, downloads, and a "knowingness" that informs our thoughts and actions. These "feelings" also influence how we hold energy in our bodies, determining if they transform into physical or emotional symptoms. The way in which this information is given to us, can be through different avenues.

Working with outside professionals, inviting them into our H.O.P.E. Tribe, is vital to our children's success. Regular communication with your child's school, teacher, therapist, Occupational Therapist, Speech Pathologist, best friend's mother, spiritual leader at church, grandmother, uncle, H.O.P.E. Tribe members, Reiki healer, Guardian Angels, Archangel Michael, and so on will help support you in discovering what your child needs to live soulfully. Utilizing the information gathered from all of these avenues helps your child understand the need for a H.O.P.E. Tribe. In addition, it imperative that children of a similar age are also fostered to be active meaningful participants in your child's H.O.P.E. Tribe. Including as many people who share your vision is beneficial. At the heart of this vision is your child's unique soul purpose and gifts.

As a parent at times I feel frozen and unable to create the changes

I want to see for my children. I have started to break these desires for 'bigger change' into more bite size projects. We often ask our children to do something similar with meeting their personal goals. We can also apply deductive strategies to our more global, collective hopes, dreams, wishes, and larger scale changes we wish to see.

For example, my son attended a birthday laser tag party. I mentioned this same event in an earlier chapter. While I wanted my son to participate in the activity to celebrate his friend, I did not agree with how the attendant / staff member described the activity. It was difficult to hear "violent" language being used to describe a laser tag game to 8 year olds. Being an empath myself, language is important because what I hear, see, feel, affects me deeply. When the staff member was talking about 'how to play the game' he used words like 'sniper', 'killing', 'hunting down', and more. These words were actually painful to my body. In light of current situations in which school shootings and violence are on the rise, I believe that our greatest gift to our children is to change our language. We can approach situations and topics with more mindful expression. We must commit to help our children understand how what they watch, hear and think impacts their bodies. What we put in effects what we give out, especially in a negative way if not processed effectively and in a healthy way. Due to my sensitivity to this language, I wrote a letter to the laser tag company. It was peaceful, it was mindful, and it provided examples of what I think could be more sensitive language for our current reality. The letter had no intention of saying that the activity of laser tag should not be allowed for our children, or that the instructor was doing anything wrong. It was simply a way to start a dialogue about the activities are children are engaging in, how language can change meaning of an activity, and how we can, as a society, be more sensitive to issues that are children and their families are facing.

Parents can begin to write letters, in a peaceful way, as a means to initiate these conversations. My neighborhood wrote letters to our HOA because we wanted our children to be able to have basketball hoops in our driveways to promote more outdoor activity, exercise, and community connection. Enough parents wrote and our HOA rules were changed. Now basketball hoops adorn our street and children are outside all the time. If we start to entertain the bigger picture and various alternatives to positively lead change, we find ourselves able to take small steps toward a larger goal. Change is set in motion.

H.O.P.E. Tribe members can begin by simply talking about things! For when we create space, communication begins, and connection occurs. Connection is where true change starts, this is where HOPE in the situation is found. It is all about connecting: Connecting to the idea, connecting to our soul, connecting to other, connecting to Source/God, connecting to the collective, connecting to the greater good! The black hole syndrome is reversed and becomes the White star syndrome, in which creates action based on connected soulful dialogue. (See Chapter 10 for explanations of The Black Hold Syndrome)

To offset current societal perceptions of what our 'kids' can do and can't do, offering 'out of the box' activities for our children can open the eyes and soul's of others in the community. For example, extracurricular activities are wonderful for children, and studies show how children who engage in these activities are more likely to make prosocial choices, navigate peer pressure more effectively, utilize healthy coping strategies. I think it is helpful to dig a little deeper by exploring other ideas and activates.

Imagine for a moment that our children are not only engaged in more traditional extracurricular activities, but also are engaged in soul inspiring ones. Creating these spaces for children not only would allow them to share who they are, it would dispel myths and social stigmas that surround the terms "highly sensitive, empath, spiritual, metaphysical, and intuitive" children. Navigating our current systems and societal social constructs is important, and yet sometimes new routes need to be explored. If we allow for the expansion of ideas, thinking outside the box, and providing 'new route' activities, we are navigating a system by creating a space for that which we want.

When we create the space, we open lines of communication, and then connections can be formed. These connections can be on a person to person level, but also deeper, on a more neurobiological level. For when we engage in an action around our belief, our bodies physically change at a synaptic level and a neurological level. Links, strands, cords, and connective tissue begins to form, changing us, changing our experience, and changing who we are and how we live. So as with positive affirmations and the Law of Attraction, the H.O.P.E. Tribe then becomes a living idea that begins to permeate self and soul causing a ripple effect as we live out our beliefs within our communities.

Part Three

How Do We H.O.P.E.?

Chapter 9

The Action Mindset

How do we live H.O.P.E. and use it in practical ways?

"It's not just about hope and ideas. It's about action."
Shirin Ebadi

According to Louise Hay, "you have to look at the dirt in order to clean the house". With this said, as parents and adults we need to embrace the H.O.P.E. tribe ideals not only for children but for ourselves. We need to see the dirt, all of it; ours, theirs and the collective. What we do with and for children **needs to mirror 'what we do for and with ourselves'.** We can only help our children as much as we are willing to help ourselves. To do this we must start with an action mindset.

To ACT is to <u>A</u>cknowledge, <u>C</u>reate space for the shift (change), and <u>T</u>ake a step in a purposeful and soulful direction. This is a living, life-long idea, a process, just like one would say about parenting. Parenting isn't just an idea that is from biological parent to a child. Parenting is a process of caring for, coaching, teaching, and rearing. This process can be with self as well as with other. Re-parenting occurs in many professions, from teaching to psychotherapy. To re-parent and be re-parented occurs daily without even recognizing it. Re-parenting can be done with self as well, However, re-parenting within relationships offer a reciprocity and dynamic that aids in deeper rewiring and deeper understanding. Even as adults we may have relationships with people who re-parent us in ways; the relationship rewiring us and teaching us about living life.

Parenting is a journey, a journey that requires hope and a tribe. Allow yourself to be on this journey of learning, expanding, growing, and changing **with** and **for** yourself as much as you are doing it for the child. Remember that you are not perfect. Act from a place of self-love and self-compassion. Remain open to your experiences (in body, mind, spirit, and soul) and allow for the process to happen. Adults and parents need to honor what they are going through. Parenting (and re-parenting) is a HARD process to be engaged in! It takes work, discipline, and an ability to 'allow' what is. This will inspire positive interactions and connection, allowing children to see you putting words into action, and living out what you hope for them.

Action Mindset Step 1: Keep an open mind by acknowledging and allowing.

Be open to what emotionally arises for you as you interact with a sensitive child who has empath abilities. What resources or supports might you need or find useful? What changes might be required? What might you need to add into your life?

Remaining open also warrants maintaining a positive attitude. Supporting a child requires an open mind, positivity in your approach, and allowing for **their** experience to shine through. This is easier said than done. I know! I am a parent of a highly sensitive child. Traits of empathic and sensitive children can be challenging to cope with in certain situations. Again, checking in with self can help de-escalate a situation and highlight the deeper meaning behind what is occurring.

Changing our language and the way we perceive a situation is at the basis for 'seeing things differently'. Positive language begets positive thinking. Positive thinking begets positive interaction. Positive interaction begets positive connection. Positive connection begets positive change. Remembering how important 'intent' is, rather than action alone, will create congruence in the relational dynamic between you and the child, allowing for true discovery of each soul in the moment.

Action Step 2: Acknowledge and identify the push and pull.

Taking notice of where a child feels 'pulled' versus 'pushed' is warranted. My son was pushing a chair across the carpet. He found himself struggling, pushing with all his might, and getting nowhere. The chair was catching on the carpet, and frustration started to ensue. His face became red with effort, and then flushed with frustration as he continued more of the same. Then he stopped, took a deep breath and walked to the other side of the chair. He began to pull it. The chair moved with ease. His body used less effort and force. He looked up with a smile, face no longer red, and said, "the pull makes things much easier than the push". We began a dialogue, a 39 year-old and an 8 year-old talking about the push and pulls of life. We were sharing thoughts about this phenomenon. When we feel 'pulled' towards something it 'just seems easier'. When we are pushed 'we lack motivation, can feel frustrated, and as if we are being 'forced' to do something'. How then can we acknowledge this push and pull in our lives and the lives of our children?

Start paying attention to or taking notice of where a child is 'pulled'. Being pulled is being 'soul led', where a child is naturally drawn. This is a feeling of being 'called', inspired by the Divine. Below are a few questions and conversation starters about how to determine the 'pull'.

What brings about an authentic genuine smile?

Where do you see the child's greatest joy being expressed in heart, body, and mind?

What things do they say they 'love'?

What comes naturally for the child?

What are they determined to do even though it looks like it takes a lot of work?

When do they begin dancing just for the fun of it (what happened right before, right after)?

What takes little parenting effort to get them to do? Do they prefer working with their hands?

What 'style of learner' might their teacher say they are? What do they choose to do when given several choices of activities?

Being pushed can be soul hindering. This force rubs against a child's desire and motivation. External motivation is a type of 'push' and is not inherently negative. The intent is the key, where the child will sense the authenticity of the 'push'. Motivating with soulful and positive intent is different than motivating out of fear or control. A sensitive and empathic child will be able to determine where the intent originates; therefore, the level of intrinsic motivation to engage in what is being 'pushed' will present itself accordingly. A child attending school, learning new things, or needing to pass an academic test is of a different nature. These are the 'pushes' in life that a child may or may not want to do or be soul 'led' to do, however find that they need to engage in. Soul stifling 'pushes' are more value based, belief driven, or activities that are forced onto a child from an external source. A child may be made to feel like they 'have to do it for another's benefit or for appearance sake'.

This could sound like statements such as ...

"you need to try every sport at least one time to see if you like it"
"I don't care if you don't want to ...."
"I always liked math growing up and so I am sure you will"
"It's in your genes to be ..."
"I can't believe you don't like ____, everyone in our family likes that"
"Boys don't grow their hair long"
"Girls wear make-up"

and the list can go on.

It is important that we teach our children, and ourselves, the difference between what being 'pulled' and being 'pushed' feels like, looks like. It is critical to recognize the messages we tell ourselves in the midst of each. Identifying in the body and mind where these 'feelings' originate and are held will allow for more rapid identification and less difficulty in realigning self. At times these forces are clear to see and decipher. Other times they seem difficult to tease out. Accessing the spirit realm to decipher 'pulls' and 'pushes' is another means to deciphering the subtleties between these two forces. Spirit will provide signs and symbols. Taking notice of these then becomes our assignment.

A child who is less social by natural desire, can be motivated (or 'pushed') to be more so if they are provided with reasons why it would be beneficial for them to be. Just stating that a child 'should' be more social will not suffice. It is important to allow the child to engage in the process of discovering the need for the desired task to be completed, how that task will aid them in more efficient soulful living, and why the task is important for the greater good. Focusing on the 'pulls' will naturally allow your child to lead a more soulful life. Careful 'pushes' with positive intent can lead to this as well.

Below are a few questions and conversation starters about how to determine the 'push':

Where do they feel forced, restricted, oppositional, angry, or lack joy?

What occurred prior to that negative behavior pattern ('meltdown', temper tantrum, excessive crying)?

What occurred immediately following?

What activities is it most difficult for the child to be motivated to engage in?

What is the child's least favorite subject in school?

When a suggestion is given about an activity or idea what is the child's initial reaction?

How would a friend describe this child?

How would you describe this child?

As a parent (or someone in a 'parenting role' (as defined earlier) where do you feel most frustrated in the parenting of this child?

List three things you 'wish' your child would engage in but the child resists.

What messages did you receive from your family of origin that continue to replay in your mind that prevent you from hearing your child's needs and wants?

Fill in the following statement...

"When my child does _____ I feel
_____. I immediately start to sense _____(physical
sensation)_____ in my body. I begin telling myself (list thoughts
about the situation or your child that come into your mind)___. Once my
mind and body begin this pattern I start to feel _____
and then I begin dishonoring self, my child, and the need for curiosity
about the situation. If someone could look deep inside me they would
see that _____(what is it you believe people would think about
you or your child in that moment) _____ and
this leaves me feeling _____."

In order to recognize the push, and turn it into a time for self-reflection and partnering WITH the child, the adult needs to emotionally detach from the ego-self and find the 'heart and soul' of the issue. It is important to dissect the situation from the angle of self, prior to other, so that it is clear what the push is that needs to happen for the child. Is it a push that is simply being placed upon the child for other psychological reasons?

Much has been written about empathic and intuitive children, but little has been provided regarding actual strategies and hands on tools for raising and fostering their talents and abilities. Here information has been compiled from many different ideas, schools of thought, and modalities into one living and evolving document. Connecting the dots comes from discussion and trying strategies to determine their success for each unique child. The H.O.P.E. Tribe is about digging deeper; deeper within self, deeper within connection, deeper within topics, and deeper within mindsets and worldviews. Hope is the trust, the desire for something to be. When we hope we allow ourselves to seek answers to create change.

Approaching our actions and our children from a heart space, we immediately are "doing something".

Action Step 3: Creating space for action and change through informed acknowledgment.

Holding all parts of ourselves and our connection to them, is an action step to living a HOPE tribe value. This is an important way of honoring our children. Putting pressure on ourselves to do everything 'just right', living in guilt or fear, holding the brick above our head (see diagram below), breeds shame and separation. Acknowledging is where knowledge and know-how is combined. Acknowledging a child's abilities, strengths, talents, sensitivities, and the things that are difficult for you as a parent will create more long term and lasting effects for your child. To remain curious and truly seek understanding is the basis for creating space. Creating space is the openness to search and to allow what is present to unfold and show itself. If what is discovered is carried as a burden, a person becomes fixated on finding a 'solution'. There is a difference between a 'solution' and a 'strategy'. Solutions are typically focused on the 'end-result'. Solutions can often originate from a place of panic, worry, anxiety, fear, scarcity. They can be Ego driven, reactive, and merely aimed to get to a desired outcome. A 'strategy', is a process, an idea that holds variability of outcome, leaves room for further exploration and discovering, and embraces the connection of 'how we get there'. Strategies allow for space to look at how our body feels, reacts, thinks, and listens to how our soul is informing us along the way. Once a strategy is successful in aiding a child to better understand self, integrate, and continue embracing soul gifts, then the result is a possible solution in that present moment. This solution may or may not have the same effect in the future. Utilizing this solution could set in motion a way of coping and dealing with specific needs should a similar situation presents itself. Searching for strategies will not only help find solutions, but will allow children to engage in a process of critical thinking skills. When we sift through alternatives we support a child in developing many coping mechanisms. The process is done from a soulful place rather than just attempting to decrease discomfort or change who they are.

This image comes to mind:

Action Step 4: Take a step forward by creating a HOPE tribe.

To help hold the brick in your heart space, a tribe is needed to provide support, feedback, and growth. Holding the brick up as an individual, means we are depending on only self, our own strength.

Missing the engagement of other, forfeiting reliance on Source and angelic intervention, makes the brick seem even heavier, a burden we have been dealt, rather than an assignment or mission for growth (for both you and the child!). To hold the brick in the center, a person becomes grounded, balanced, with equal energy from bottom to top. This "centered" approach allows for leg muscles to support arm muscles, and back muscles to stabilize. As your 'whole' body supports the brick, the 'whole' (self, other, Spirit Realm, Source/God) of life supports you. Adding others, creating a tribe, and allowing them to help us hold this brick means we are supported even more, freeing up energy and space to find strategies for self and our children, modeling how to do this for themselves. (as a side note: this idea and image can also be used as a strategy or worksheet when discussing a situation/goal/feeling/thought with your child)

The H.O.P.E. Tribe operates from a soulful strategic standpoint where being curious about children, their experiences, and honoring their unique soul is at the forefront.

The H.O.P.E. Tribe uses the motto:

"The Tribe honors open, perceptive, and empathic children. The Tribe holds hope. The Tribe trusts that from our positive collective energy anything is possible and that our children will be provided a place to live their soul blueprint in a safe and creative space. This soulful expression of God inspired talents will create positive change effecting the collective, impacting the greater good of all. Souls will fulfill their purpose while here on Earth, and continued soulful legacies will be left to continue in aiding soulful expansion and evolution of other."

Finding emotional supports for yourself and your child is imperative. This will aid in maintaining the positive attitude just discussed and will provide a sounding board for strategies and other ideas. The H.O.P.E. Tribe is a place for shared storytelling; where past and present meet to inform future; where spiritual matters are kept alive in the face of materialism; where shared resources are genuinely and generously offered and received; where people find more of who they are by connecting with other.

Some children who are gifted with extrasensory perceptions may even have intuitive insights and an ability to predict future events (precognition). When their predictions come true a child can feel a range of emotions, including fear, shame, guilt, hopelessness, just to name a few. This type of ability can also be very frightening or surprising to the people closest to the child. The H.O.P.E. Tribe then becomes the sacred space where these abilities can be shared without judgement, or shame and where emotional support can help redirect any fear. It acts as the ceremonial ground, coming into contact with the essence of a person's soul, where all is accepted based on love, and where a group holds the brick in a heart space for each member. Like-minded and authentic connection with other fuels further soul-connection to self, ultimately syncing soul to Source.

Action Step 5: Take a step by strategizing and implementing!

Carl Jung said, "You are what you do, not what you say you'll do", and if you ask any child who they highly respect, admire, and learn from, they most likely would answer, those who do what they say they will do. Action is an intention put into motion, one that says, "I can say it, but you are worth the extra step and so I **do** it". Children who know they are worth this extra step feel loved, honored, and have increased self-worth. When a person has self-worth they can defend their soul passions without fear. They fully belong to self and belonging to self allows for true belonging amongst others. The H.O.P.E. Tribe wants children to know they are worth the extra step and holds the hope that if we begin to interact with ourselves, each other, our tribes, and the collective from a place of honor and mindfulness we can help our children stay tuned in to their soul purpose. Keeping intuition strong can be done by a few simple and practical strategies. Making the 'intuition' and 'empathic' muscles strong is like any other disciplined endeavor. Creating space for it to occur, engaging in strategies on a consistent basis, and believing that what is being done is beneficial will keep things on track. When intuition is strong our children will believe in themselves, trust themselves, and act in accordance with the greater good.

Chapter 10

The Strategies

How can I build H.O.P.E.?

"And suddenly you know...It's time start something new
and trust the magic of new beginnings."-Anonymous

The remainder of this book will provide strategies in the form of ideas, exercises, activities and tools that foster intuition and empathic abilities in children. While some of these strategies are considered 'in the moment' strategies for coping with acute symptoms, most are viewed as proactive in nature. Proactive parenting and re-parenting involves thinking ahead, utilizing personal creativity, and providing a foundation for what is hoped to be learned or gained. The hope is that the strategies in this book are less about 'things to do' and more about 'the way we do things'; a mindset change around how we interact and connect with and for children.

Essentially, the H.O.P.E. Tribe champions ideas that retrain our minds and bodies in a neurological way. When we perform repetitive practice of a skill, we require more attentional focus in the beginning. The more we practice, the need for focus decreases and our cell memory takes over. It becomes more ingrained, as a part of who we are. To be a mindful and soulful person isn't to set aside only 10 minutes a day and 'be' that, it takes changing who we are from the inside out. This becomes our practice, such as a daily meditation routine. To truly engage in life from a deep H.O.P.E. Tribe mentality, shifts in consciousness and ways of relating must inform all decisions and actions. We become living expressions of our soul rather than people just sharing pieces of our soul.

Adults using these strategies and activities are encouraged to modify the activity to fit the child's needs and abilities. Differentiation of the exercises will provide more connection to the process for the child and therefore, create a stronger integration bond. Integration bond refers to the strength of connection between experience, soul desire, and utilizing an effective strategy for coping. Integration bonds are when our actions become the 'glue', linking the experience to all aspects of self and changing the cellular makeup of our bodies.

Like people who learn from each other, our cells communicate. They talk and share. The energy of one changes that of another. Science has shown how neurons 'fire' and how information is transferred from one to the other. Deep inside our body magical and mysterious things take place every second of every day. Energy jumping gaps, spaces of nothingness, hold the link between one energetic thing to another. The 'jump' in that space creates the meaning and keeps the message traveling. In this way Spirit and Human are separated by 'space', a synaptic gap of sorts, a vast sea of air and untouchable matter. When Spirit provides symbols, signs, downloads, or when people experience extrasensory perceptions, it is energy 'jumping' from one to the other. Dendritic energetic strands between soul self and the Spirit realm are linked and 'fired', allowing for energy to be transmitted and each to be informed. For some this is hard to rationalize and believe as possible. Yet, if this notion works deep within our physical bodies, inspired by the Divine, it makes sense that similar principles and ideas can be used outside of human self and outside of the physical realm.

Interconnectedness of ideas, thoughts, and ways of relating then shine a light on an even larger concept of how we receive such information. Simply put, addressing our mindset, creating energetic bonds with like-minded people, and operating from a strategically soulful place ultimately will lead to a mental and physical change in your body. The strategies in this chapter are here to promote strategic and intentional soulful living. This change will allow for a 'new way of doing things". This change will be interactive and build connections through relating in authentic ways.

The next sections of this book address many facets of a child, and provides multiple methods for communicating, increasing emotional and soul intelligence, aligning self, and coping with discomfort. The exercises will be grouped together according to the self-concept intended to become illuminated. **However**, it should be noted and it is imperative to know, there is crossover for many strategies. Getting creative in the implementation of strategies is recommended.

There are three sections in this chapter. Section one provides a tool to help align all aspects of body, mind and spirit while providing key information. The H.O.P.E chart is a quick reference to identify further areas of inquiry. Section 2 includes nine concepts that are helpful to address when honoring open, empathic and perceptive children. The concepts are as follows: 1) Develop a Ritual for Thinking Through Problems, 2) Connection, 3) Gathering Information and Knowledge, 4) Believe and Trust, 5) Emoting as a way of using Creative Expression and Artistic Outlets, 6) Coping Strategies for Difficult Situations, 7) Setting Boundaries, 8) Healthy Living, 9) Balance and 10) Manifesting Intent. After each concept, strategies will be provided to aid you and your child in learning more about how to address needs within each core concept. Remember, these strategies are versatile and can be used in multiple ways. The idea is to help your child unlock the secrets and power that lies within. Using creative ways of addressing these nine core concepts is the goal so that children feel safe, comfortable and gain a deeper understanding of their soul purpose. Section 3 provides a look into the future of the H.O.P.E. Tribe. The H.O.P.E. Tribe will continue to offer ways to help parents support their highly sensitive, intuitive and empathic children. Please look for members of the H.O.P.E. Tribe in schools, online, in future writing, and as we move forward with ideas to champion our core beliefs.

Section 1: The H.O.P.E. Chart

The following chart is a tool to be used as a streamlined method for finding helpful information. At times people can feel overwhelmed with all the information, strategies, and ideas circulating in the world. Each strategy and idea is valuable and yet, it can be difficult to navigate all that is available. This chart, and this book, is an attempt to put a multitude of helpful information from various modalities into one place as a resource guide. The chart links theory and practice. It provides a starting place for figuring out a child's soul needs and ways to foster their soul gifts.

The most effective way to utilize this chart is up to the user. We all learn differently and operate from different lenses. It is important that we begin to understand how to trust self. Let your own intuitive ability and the knowledge of your child, guide you when using the chart.

For sake of providing some helpful guidance, this chart can be used to pinpoint strategies that address emotional and behavioral concerns or 'symptomology'. Anita Moorjani spoke recently in a podcast of how our 'illness' and 'disease' is our body showing us something. It is our teacher in the moment. It is our body's way of communicating. If we begin to see children's behavior as a way of communicating, then our attachment to external perception of its manifestation becomes less intense and we become less reactive. With this said, one way to use the chart is to look at 'symptoms' the child may be exhibiting to decipher what the child is needing. Looking down the chart you can see where the child's behavior or emotional responses fit and use strategies that focus on that aspect.

Another method of using the chart is to simply have the child start with the first listed chakra and work their way through and down the chart. Each section of the chart can be addressed, giving the child time to engage in different strategies and proactively balance their system. If this method is used, allowing enough time is crucial. In no way is it meant to be an immersion technique in which a child spends all day randomly working through concepts and strategies for hours and hours. Workshops, retreats, and other types of seminars are great for an 'instant reset' for people, however, this chart is designed with a different purpose in mind.

Yet others may simply start with affirmations and putting them up visually for their child. The chart is merely a guide, a compass, and finding what works or is useful is up to you. Adapting, revising, changing, and creating your own chart can be a strategy in and of itself.

Chakra	Color	Stone	Possible Overactive symptoms in children	Concepts/ Strategies	Fragrance	Archangel	Affirmation
Root	Red	Red Jasper	Anxiety; Fear without a threat; irrational	• Grounding/ Earthing • Meditation • Breathing • In the moment techniques • Desensitization • Identifying Coping Strategies • Increasing Emotional Awareness • Self-Soothing Daily Routine • EFT (tapping)	Patchouli	Uriel	"I can leave fear behind" "I can put fear in a box, close it, and think about a strategy" "I am able to defeat fear"
Sacral	Orange	Carnelian	Decreased creativity; Rigid; Lacks connection to other people	• Emote and provide creative outlets • Coping with transitions and change • Balancing self • Create a Tribe • Safe and Sacred places • EFT (tapping)	Ylang-ylang	Gabriel	"I am like a scale and both sides can be equal"

Solar Plexus	Yellow	Citrine	Difficulty emotionally regulating; Lack of empathy or compassion	• Self-awareness • Mindfulness activities Create a Tribe • Safe and Sacred Places • coping strategies • Stone work • Increasing emotional intelligence • Increasing 'gut' awareness • EFT (tapping) • Body scan	Neroli	Jophiel	"I am able to make good choice for myself"
Heart	Green	Malachite	Difficulty in relationships, Suffers from lack of trust and safety, Needs to forgive, Low self-esteem	• Create a Tribe • Safe and Sacred places • Coping strategies • Mindfulness activities Self-soothing daily routine • Assertiveness training • Anti-bullying strategies • EFT (tapping)	Rose	Raphael	"I can trust myself" "I have people I feel safe with" "I can find support"

Throat	Blue	Blue Lace Agate	Act out to communicate thoughts/feeling, Speaks loudly, Difficulty clearly communicating verbally, Trouble saying what they mean	• Mindfulness activities • Provide create outlets for other ways of expression • Body scan	Lavender	Michael	"I say what I mean and I mean what I say"
Third eye	Indigo	Lapis Lazuli	Spacey (not grounded), Living to much outside of themselves Focus or obsess on more spiritual matters, abstract thinking that distracts from daily tasks	• Goal setting and manifestation strategies • Mindfulness activities • Task orienting language and exercises • Routines	Sandalwood	Raziel	"I have a lot of work to do while here on this Earth. I can focus and do what I need to get done"
Crown	Violet-White	Amethyst	(NA) This is the GOAL! Begin self and soul Actualization here!	• Soul Scaping • Meditation • Body scan	Frankincense	Zadkiel	"I share love and light in the world" "I am a creation of God"

Section 2: Concepts and Strategies

The concepts provide the core areas of need that a highly sensitive, intuitive, and empathic child may need to develop further. This is by no means an exhaustive list of core concepts. The ten concepts are starting places for deeper inquiry, which may lead to subsequent, more intimate aspects of growth.

When a child is experiencing or demonstrating a possible "over reactive" symptom, you can identify the concept and a possible strategy on the H.O.P.E. chart. Again, the idea is not to pigeon hole you into one core area or the use of one strategy to address a child's need. Each child is unique, has their own soul purpose, and needs to be the co-creator in their process. The chart provides a starting place. It is then recommended that the parent/adult, review the core concept and peruse the strategies provided. If the concept or strategy does not "fit", move on to another core concept. You are the expert on your child. You will sense a feeling of "rightness" when you come across the right strategy to use with your child. Trust yourself and utilize the tools to help affirm your thinking and feeling. If you are stuck, just pick a core concept and a strategy that most closely aligns with the child's need and go. Often times we can become frozen and take no action. Remember, we must have an Action Mindset in order to support our children. These strategies are beneficial for anyone, so there is no harm in choosing one and giving it a shot. We can only learn from our action, whereas inaction leaves us in stagnant energy.

Some of the strategies are more routine based, things you will want to encourage your intuitive or empathic child, or any child starting at a young age, to engage in on a consistent basis. For example, sticking to a routine at home for school days, journaling (drawing, writing, coloring, tape recording, etc), family discussions about the link between thoughts/feelings/actions (in age appropriate ways), allowing expressive outlets, and exercise.

Before coping strategies and/or other strategies for deciphering if an empathic or intuitive child has picked up on someone else's emotions or bodily sensations, a child needs to first be aware of themselves. This is a difficult task with a child in general, but with highly sensitive and empathic children it is imperative that they begin to learn early on what things feel like in their body, who they are, where they stop and another starts (figuratively and sometimes literally). They must learn how to tell what is their own.

Concept 1: Develop a Ritual for Thinking Through Problems

Rituals are performed often, sometimes without even recognizing it. Rituals help bring our minds back into emotional homeostasis. When we perform rituals we are seeking balance and a sense of "control" over a situation. We reduce anxiety and are able to maintain in a clear, confident and regulated state.

It is human nature to feel anxious and uncertain in multiple scenarios. With rituals we can mitigate the factors that "stress us out" and create imbalance in our lives. Rituals bring awareness to the present moment. They require us to be in the moment, focusing on ourselves, and bring attention to the act we are performing. Rituals insist that we be mindful.

Rituals can breed further action. Certain rituals ask that we think about the current behavior and then set intentions for future behaviors. This conscious purpose moves us into commitments to ourselves and others. When we begin to commit, we are brought into communion with others. Rituals, therefore, can provide for further connection. This connection is built on shared experiences and the production of common meaning within our worlds. Rituals are powerful ways to remind ourselves to be grateful and be intentional about how we want to live a soulful life, connected to our unique talents.

Strategy 1: Guided mediations

1) This meditation is for "In the moment/short/quick refocus".
   Take 3 deep breaths in:
   In through your nose, filling your lungs, hold for 4.3.2.1 then let out
   Repeat for second breath.

On third, imagine a white light entering through the top of your head and then hold after lungs for 4.3.2.1, then let all of the air out imagining it as a dark cloud, or dust leaving your body. Say aloud, "anything that is negative, doesn't feel good, doesn't serve me, or isn't my own now leaves my body".

2) Guided meditation that can take 10-30 minutes:

Start the meditation with at least 3 breaths, deep in through your nose, and out through your mouth. Focusing your thoughts on your breathing. If a child visibly appears, or states that they need additional breaths continue until they are ready or try in a set of 3 (so, 3, or 6, or 9). Why 3? This number reminds us that we carry divinity within, is a spiritual number, and also can be symbolic of past, present, and future all coming together in one moment for inner soul reflection/introspection.

Imagine yourself in a forest. What do you see? Is there a lot of trees, few, or a clearing? A path lies before you. You begin to walk slowly forward. What is the path made of (rock, dirt, paved, gravel, grass, ...) and how does it feel on your feet? As you keep walking, what do you see around you? What animals are around? Are they near, far, or have characteristics that you don't see in your 'waking' life? If so, make note of these. What does it feel like in this forest (is it warm outside, cold, chilly, slight breeze...)? You continue walking noticing and paying attention to what is all around you. The path ends and a large peaceful beautiful clearing is in front of you. Just to the right side is a sacred spot of yours. You created it, it is made out of your favorite things, and perhaps it is a color? What color(s) do you see on, or around this spot? You walk to an opening or a door of this sacred place and you gently knock. You ask yourself if you can enter. You walk in and what do you see? Around you are things you love, types of furniture that you would enjoy having, and you find the most comfortable spot in the place. What does this spot feel like? Look like? Smell like? And where is it in the room? You make yourself comfortable (sitting down, lying down, …) and you take a deep breath. You have found your safe spot. Now, you look beside you to your left and there is a box that is labeled "Not mine" and to your right is a box labeled "mine". Pick up the box labeled "not mine" first and open it. Is it empty? Is it full? If there is 'stuff' inside pay attention to what it is. Did you put it in there (perhaps it is left over from the last time you visited if you are doing this meditation on a consistent basis). State your intention by saying, "the things that arise for me while I scan my body, mind, and spirit, I will know they are 'not my own' and will put them into the box". Now, scan your body, by thinking about each part starting at your feet. If you see, hear, feel, or sense something then put it in the box. When you are done (have reached the top of your head), then close the box. Simply state, "I am done with you for now", then place it to the left side. Then pick up the "mine" box and do the same thing. After you have scanned and placed things in your box, state "These are mine. And the ones that best serve me are….". You close the box and put it back to the right side. There is a pen and paper next to the mine box, if you choose, take the paper and write anything and everything that you hold that is yours and doesn't serve you (negative thoughts, behaviors, etc). Then imagine yourself writing these down (or drawing a picture). When you are done you get up and you walk back outside to the clearing. Just a little way there is a fire ring. It is all ready for your spiritual bonfire. You put the paper in the middle and then watch it burn, releasing it, and letting it go. You stay here as long as you like, and then you walk with only the thought of your positive 'mine box' ideas/images/thoughts/feelings/ etc and you begin back down the same path. You walk slowly, looking at what is around you. What do you see? Is it different? The same? Then you get back to

> where you started. You begin to bring yourself back to the present moment. You wiggle your toes three times, wiggle your fingers three times, and then slowly begin to blink your eyes.

After completing the meditation, a child may want to write, discuss, or draw what they envisioned during it. Remember that changing the words based on your child's age is recommended and shortening the meditation is possible as well. As we know from behavioral science, a child's attention span is about 1 minute for each chronological age. Therefore, a 7-year-old has an attention span in which they can fully be present of about 7 minutes. This can be different for each child, however, it is important to know the typical age span for your child. Some children also are visual and kinesthetic so actually having boxes with these labels and them putting their thoughts/feelings/sensations/etc in the boxes can provide a visual release for them. This meditation can be used in a more typical sense, or adapted to help children walk through their feelings as well as done in a guided way to increase self-awareness. This might mean a child does not have to close their eyes if they don't want. The meditation should be geared towards what will help the child calmly look at their body and emotions, while attempting to decipher what is theirs or someone else's, and what they can use for their higher good.

There are many good guided meditations online. This one I created for my children and I, because of the visual aids provided. The more hands on approach I can use with my children when discussing their thoughts and feelings, the better it seems. You can also create your own personalized guided meditation to use. When creating your own, remember it will be important to bring your child back to a place of grounding. Guiding them back to a place of reality/awareness in a calm and peaceful way will be essential. If not, the information will not be integrated due to a 'jolt' to the energy and nervous system. Staying in a less grounded state for children can create anxiety, and more acting out due to restless or anxious energy. Therefore, remember to help facilitate your child coming back to the present moment in a systematic and mindful way.

<u>Strategy 2: Love is the compass of life chart</u>

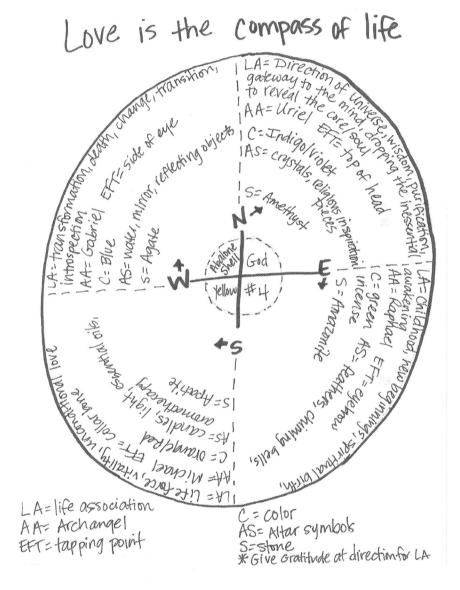

Love is the compass of life

LA= Direction of Universe; wisdom, purification, gateway to the mind; dropping the inessential to reveal the core/soul
AA= Uriel   EFT= top of head
C= Indigo/violet
AS= crystals, religious pieces
S= Amethyst

LA= transformation, death, change, transition, introspection
AA= Gabriel   EFT= side of eye
C= Blue
AS= water, mirror, reflecting objects
S= Agate

LA= Childhood, new beginnings; spiritual awakening, spiritual birth;
AA= Raphael   EFT= eyebrow
C= green   AS= feathers, chiming bells; incense
S= Amazonite

LA= Life force; vitality; essence; unconditional love
AA= Michael   EFT= collar bone
C= Orange/Red   AS= candles, light; aromatherapy
S= Apophite

N ↗
W ↗
Abalone Shell | God
Yellow #4
E ↓
S ↙

LA= life association
AA= Archangel
EFT= tapping point

C = color
AS= Altar symbols
S= stone
* Give Gratitude at direction for LA

This chart is based on the four cardinal directions, North, East, South, and West. With each labeled cardinal direction are the corresponding metaphysical characteristics (association of the cardinal direction with crystals, chakras, colors, Arch Angels). Again, this chart, similar to the H.O.P.E. chart, provides a visual and is used best by allowing one to be intuitively 'led' or 'pulled' in any direction one sees fit. As an example, if you ask a child, "What direction comes to mind for you this morning?" Insist the child answer in a simplistic form, only with North, East, South, or West rather than Northeast, or Northwest. Using the compass, the child can engage in activities that align with the metaphysical characteristics mentioned with that direction. This can be done daily and more consistently, as a way to 'set' the child's body for the day.

Another possible way to utilize the chart is by observing your child's behavior. For example, an adult may recognize that the child is struggling with transitions and therefore locate this on the compass. By locating a need, adults can help pinpoint other strategies to try with their child. As we work through this example, we note that change and transitions are located on the West, therefore, we may want the child to engage with water play, using mirroring strategies, focusing on using the color blue or holding an agate. The Arch Angel associated with this area of the compass is Gabriel. If the child is drawn to it, he/she can engage in the Arch Angel Gabriel meditation or find more information about this Arch Angel. It is important to note is that the child may try 'in the moment' tapping at the side of the eye location. Using this technique prior to, during, or immediately following transitions can be beneficial. This example demonstrates how the 'love is the compass of life' tool can be used, but adapting the tool to benefit the child is of utmost importance.

Strategy 3: Use the S.O.U.L. Acronym

This acronym can be used as a guide in all situations and for each person involved. It is a tool that interrupts the cycle of negative thought patterns, maladaptive behaviors, and can bring a person back to their essence. Using SOUL and practicing it with your child can help individuals make more soulful choices throughout their day. It also can be used in role-playing. Role-playing is an effective strategy for more realistic application and a child can better sense ('see, feel, hear, and experience') what their mind, body, and spirit may be experiencing in the moment. Putting it in action for a child will give it life and make it relevant for them. It is imperative that adults use SOUL as well, discussing how you utilized it in your day can be a 'teachable' moment for the child.

S: self, seek to understand self (what is mine?)
O: other, seek to understand if this is someone else's (is this not mine, how do I know?)
U: uncover any negative thoughts or things you might be telling yourself. What is my self-talk right now?
L: listen to your gut, intuition, your body, your spirit guides/God, what are they telling you to do in this moment; what do I feel in my gut? My core? What signs were given to me from the Spirit realm

Here is a general example of an adult creating a tribe using the SOUL Acronym.
A parent can use the SOUL acronym to aid in soul self-discovery. It might look like the following.
S=get clear about who we are, what we believe, and who we want in our support system.
O=Others influence on me can be positive or negative. I need to have healthy boundaries around who joins the tribe. Some 'suck our energy' and others might be added out of obligation rather than interest. Mindful selection of members will allow for better self-growth. When we receive feedback and support from those who are healthy and positive for us, we in turn learn, grow, and align to our true purpose.
U=we need to consistently check in with ourselves and uncover what we are thinking, feeling, and clearly identify our internal dialogue. What we think, we create. This carries over to our child and their experience of the world as well so it is vital that we uncover these hidden messages.
L= listen to our gut/intuition. Pay attention to signs. Utilize strategies that allow yourself to identify the meaning of my gut reactions. What does my body feel like when my gut response is "no"? when it is "yes"? How do I know I am being guided by the angelic realm and God? What symbols show me I am on my right path?

Here is another general example. This time a child is using the SOUL Acronym to cope with feelings. Let's pretend a child joins a social situation with his peers. He begins to have physical ailments. The child uses the SOUL acronym to investigate the situation and "protect" himself from unwanted problems.

S=Seek and understand where the ownership lies. Is this emotional drain mine? Is this feeling of sadness really my own? I didn't feel sad or upset, frustrated, or unmotivated before I got here. What happened right before I started feeling this way? Think about this more and dig in. Where in my body do I feel it? Is the feeling in my heart or is it in my head? What is my first response or answer to this question?

O=How did I find the others? When I got here he began making jokes 'with me', but they felt like they were more about me. He told me he was mad at his older brother before he came to school. He said his older brother was teasing him. He seems angry. Maybe he is sad. I didn't feel this way before I was around him. Could this be his feelings? What is his body acting like? In my gut, does the feeling rise up or down when I am around him? What is my "gut-o-meter" saying? (See Gut-o-meter under Concept 6: Coping Strategies for difficult situations)

U=I need to uncover my own thoughts. When I woke up this morning, I thought "today is going to be a good day! I have PE at school, a special project in class, and yesterday my friends and I made a plan to play a game I really enjoy at recess". Then I got to school and started talking to 'my friend'. I started thinking, "Why is he saying that stuff to me"? I laugh but I don't really want to laugh. "I don't like it here right now". "Where are my friends?". "I should stay here and talk to him because I just got a good citizenship award and I think that is what that means". "I don't' want to be here right now though". What if I listened to my heart and my gut? Do they say to go do something different? What can I say or do to get myself out of this situation?

L= I need to listen to myself. Being here in this place with him doesn't feel right to me. I feel sad, when I didn't before. My stomach kind of hurts, and I'm squinting my eyes (at least inside I am... I don't know what I look like on the outside), I rolled my eyes two times already, I am starting to feel very 'down' and tired. If I stop and listen to myself, I know I really don't want to be here. I don't want to be talking to him.

He's bringing me down. I am going to tell him I hope he has a good day and go find another friend to be with. I know what is best for me in this situation.

Strategy 4: Remember the "black hole"

When you hear your child say a negative thought help them replace it with a positive one. Sometimes I like to use the analogy of a black hole in space. I call it "the black hole syndrome" with my children. We start down a path of negative thinking, and one thought leads to another, and another and then we are sucked in, and can't get out. Our trajectory is a downward spiral. It is here that we need to teach our children to find a way to spin in reverse, a way to get out of that cycle. How do we interrupt the black hole process? Because it is a black hole we also tend to keep to ourselves in it, allowing our negative thought patterns to isolate us and prevent us from releasing by sharing our feelings and thoughts. We become an endless hole and it becomes difficult for our children to see their way out.

This idea first came to my son and I as we were playing Angry Birds Star wars. In one level your bird gets sent into motion and gets stuck in these circular force fields. My son and I began talking about negative thoughts and patterns that seem like this. Here is a diagram to help facilitate conversations with your child about the "black hole syndrome" and ways to spin out of that cycle.

The BLACK HOLE SYNDROME
This represents our initial negative thought,
Then it is confirmed or validated in our minds, so
Another negative thought ensues, and so on.
But along the way, there are points where we can
Try to get off this trajectory.

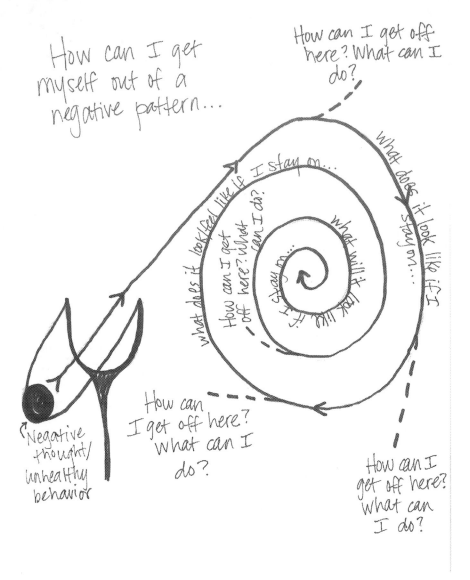

How can I get myself out of a negative pattern...

How can I get off here? What can I do?

What does it look like if I stay on...

How can I get off here? What can I do?

what does it look/feel like if I stay on...

what will it look like if I stay on...

How can I get off here? What can I do?

Negative thought/ unhealthy behavior

How can I get off here? What can I do?

How can I get off here? What can I do?

Strategy 5: Sacred Space

Allow for children to create spaces where they can go to 'dig deeper', sit with self, integrate and realign. I have created different types of safe/sacred spaces for children based on a child's interests and needs. These spaces ranged from indoor rainforests, to 'breathing rooms' with plants all around, to outdoor forts, and plush 'fall' zones. Some example names given to sacred spaces include, Breathing room, Soul Zone, Time out, Taking Space, Clearing room, Mindful Moment, Mindful Retreat, Safety Zone, Ridding Rainforest, Comfy Corner, Calm Corner, ...

Understanding what a child resonates with will be important for creating a space. These spaces are where a child can go to decompress, align self, integrate experiences, and shed anything from their body and mind that is not their own. This can also include things that children want to energetically rid themselves of. These 'sacred/safe spaces' need to be child inspired. A highly intuitive child sometimes knows immediately what they need in a space to feel most comfortable, calm, and soothed. Other children may struggle to know where to begin. Here is a check list of questions to ask when determining what a child most would like in their space.

- Does the child love being indoors or outdoors?
- What is the child's most favorite toy? What does this represent?
- Is the child hands on?
- What textures does the child enjoy? Any that should be avoided?
- Does the child prefer dark, light, and what type of light?
- Does this child get claustrophobic, prefer open space or smaller space?
- Does this child enjoy plants, animals, or natural things? Nature?
- Would this child benefit from a water feature/sound machine?
- What is the temperature of the space? Cold? Hot? Drafty?
- What part of the day is best for your child?
- When do they tend to have the most energy? The least?
- When does your child tend to feel their most frustration? The least?
- Is there an activity that a child strongly dislikes in their daily routine (i.e. bedtime)? If so don't set up a time around bedtime to have conversations.
- Does your child engage more outdoors? Indoors? Open space? Closed space? Comfy chairs such as bean bags, on the bed, or rocking chair?

- Will an object help your child engage more? Blanket? Favorite stuffed animal?
- Music on? Music off?
- Does this child want to be seen while in this space?

And the list goes on and on.

Creating space for deeper conversations is also like setting up a workout routine. It provides time and space for exercising our emotional soul muscles as we prepare ourselves to share, receive, give, and express. It's not always easy for people, so creating a time and place allows for safety and security. In order to create optimal "sacred space" we must be mindful of certain aspects related to our child.

All of these questions, plus others that you create, are important in creating a sacred space for a child. The goal is for your child to feel safe enough to share experiences or thoughts about their day, their feelings, and what they may be picking up from others.

Again, safety is the key! This is not about physical safety but emotional safety. We must not judge what a child shares, only provide guidance towards developing healthy, appropriate affirmations. If a child is expressing that they saw a spirit of someone who has crossed over (passed away), don't deny it and don't make it a bigger deal than it is to the child. Simply state that there is nothing to fear, and ask questions if it feels right to do so. For example, who do they think this person is? What was the experience like? Could you see colors around? Did they talk with this person? Etc. If a child is discussing a possible premonition, help them calm any anxiety. I have heard stories of children telling their parents that a grandparent had passed away, and later that night the grandparent did in fact pass away. Sometimes a child may need to call that person, hear their voice, draw or write. Allowing the child to express him or herself will be important. Anxiety reduction will need to be implemented. Help your child engage in coping strategies that will decrease any fearful feelings, reduce anger, or lessen anxious responses.

Essentially the space needs to be comfortable for the child. This space must be in a place that makes emotional and physical sense. It must allow for the implementation of coping strategies that will help the child integrate their experience within themselves. These mindful retreats can be indoors or outdoors, but most importantly they need to be accessible most of the time. The space can be filled with books, pictures, pillows or soft items, plants (alive!), music, art supplies and other interests a child has. GET CREATIVE!

Strategy 6: Bear Hug Jar

The Bear Hug Jar is about creating rituals around gratitude. Giving thanks for things that happened during the day is a way to foster a positive attitude with kids. As you put them in the jar throughout the day, it promotes mindful practices, intentionally noticing the 'good' and positivity in our lives. If you would like, have a specified day and create a space, even naming that day for reading those 'gratitudes'. You might want to co-create a name for the day as a family. Examples might be 'Sun Salutation Sunday', 'Thankful Thursday', 'Focus on the Good Friday', 'Mindful Monday', etc.

Strategy 7: Family Gratitude Journal

You can create a Family Gratitude Journal or a HOPE tribe guest book. Friends of your child can sign the book and write a note each time they come over to visit. My family created a tree inside the house out of large tree branches that we found on hikes. We put them in a large vase and decorated them with glitter, glued on decorative pom poms, and hung little jewels on them. When my children's friends came over they could add to the HOPE tree. It was a place to put wishes, positives, and hopes for them, their families, or others. The children enjoyed it greatly and it was a unique way for them to express their wishes and hopes in a non-threatening way. I found this ritual to be very powerful.

Strategy 8: Windows of Possibilities

When a child is anticipating an upcoming ev ent, or situation, you can use the window of possibilities to help the child foresee possible, positive outcomes. Use the worksheet to dig deeper into possibilities. You will want your child to fill in or tell you verbally for you to fill in the answers on the worksheet. Discovering the possible positive outcomes of a situation, facing a fear, or an upcoming event can help a child feel more prepared for novel incidents.

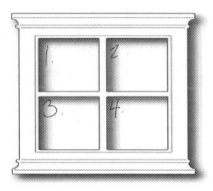

Strategy 9: Balancing the Scales Activity

Using an actual scale (they make some excellent children's scales that teach math and other concepts at educational stores such as Lakeshore Learning) or a drawing of one, choose something that has weight (both literally and figuratively) to represent different aspects of self. The goal of the scale activity is to find balance in a situation, or with a thought, etc. For example, when a somatic/physical complaint appears, look to balance it with more mind or spirit activities, when mind/thought complaint shows up balance it with spirit and body. When a 'spirit' complaint arises (i.e. difficulty concentrating due to clairvoyant messages), add body and mind to balance.

Balance the scales:

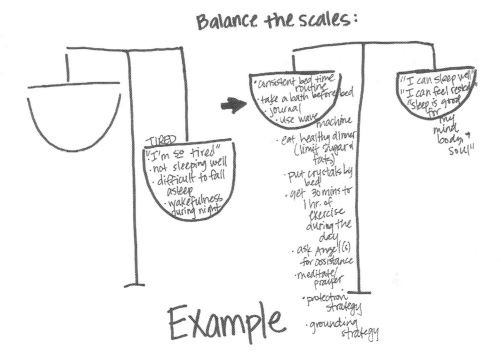

Example

Strategy 10: Smudging

Use clearing and cleansing techniques with your child. One such technique is smudging. You can use sage sticks, incense, crystals, simple sweeping or brushing of their aura, or other rituals that you create with your child on a daily basis to help with empath fatigue. Routinely engaging in this clearing activity before the start of your child's day and at the end of their day, can be helpful in managing their fatigue levels.

Here are some ideas if you choose to use multiple techniques.

- If choosing to use a Sage stick, you would light the end of the sage creating smoke. Carefully wave the sage stick, wafting the smoked around from the front to the back side of your child.
- If you are choosing to use Singing bowls or sound for clearing, you might have this type of music or sound playing as your child engages in their morning or night time routine.

- Incense is another way to clear or cleanse. Incense provides a pleasing scent to your child. The scent also aids in working through certain situations or providing a type of healing. Incense could be burning during morning and night time routine to offer these good qualities.
- Crystal work is another way to help cleanse and clear spaces. Placing certain crystals that were intentionally and mindfully chosen and that match certain goals or anticipated needs (see list in Concept 9: Balancing Systems) in your child's backpack overnight, removing them before school or sending them with them to school could help a child deal with a negative situation at school. Having them carry a crystal that increases vitality, aids in motivation and concentration, and decreasing fatigue could be useful as well.
- Brushing or sweeping your child's aura can be helpful as well. Morning and night, have your child brush or sweep their aura specifically addressing the desire to clear any draining energy. They can simply have someone make a sweeping motion about 1-2 inches away from body and then over their body, or they can sweep it themselves, being sure to go over all parts of the body. You can buy 'dry brushes' or other type of therapeutic brushes online.
- A salt lamp in your child's room or in the home, can also be a terrific cleansing or clearing tool. While current research studies haven't shown effectiveness in salt lamps, at the very least they provide a warm, inviting, and calming ambience to a room. This can aid in better sleep, calming the body, or other possible health benefits.

Concept 2: Strengthen Connection

While it sounds simple, as a mother of two, I know connection isn't always. Staying open and responsive is vital to a child's emotional wellbeing. Engaging in activities and discussions together is a foundational strategy. Connecting strategies create a platform from which to grow emotionally and spiritually. A child will want to engage with a trusted adult if they can share their truest self, feel safe, and when their experience is honored.

Parents may wonder how early to start these deep ways of connecting. The H.O.P.E. tribe members believe it is imperative to begin thinking in untraditional ways when our children are infants. Whether an infant, or even in utero, talking to your child is important. It is essential for brain development, but is also essential for connection. This early connection will breed communication, and began to build a foundation with your child.

While infants cannot speak in words, they definitely can communicate. Talking with your child about our observations, asking them questions (i.e. what do you want to do next? How does that feel? I wonder what you are thinking now?), and setting the stage for soulful expression later on (i.e. I can't wait to see all the things you try, I'm excited to see who you become tomorrow, I love that you are you, you have very special gifts and I can't wait to learn what they are, you are so good at…, oh look how you…,) will serve you and your child well. Connecting with children is the first place of action. Without connecting, really wanting to see, hear, experience, and learn from our children, there is no safety or security. Connection, on all levels, is the 'why' we are here.

If you hold similar beliefs to me, then we share the idea that we are connected to Source. When our connection to Source begins to break down, constrict, be squeezed, suffocated, and/or become severed, we begin to question life, our meaning. This permits other forms of dysfunction to set in. Therefore, connecting with our children is always at the forefront of the action steps. Don't fret if you think you didn't 'begin this process early enough'. And whatever you do, do not go to a place of guilt, shame, or self-blame. We are all a work in process and starting as soon as you are aware is what matters. Life is in fact a process, an Earthly place for us to 'process' and grow.

We must connect, but question, "How do I connect?" The answer to this question is held inside each of us. There is no one way to connect. Connecting looks and feels very different for each person at different stages of development. In infancy, being present and honoring your child's feelings in the moment is essential. For example, if your child falls down and begins to cry, start by trying to talk with them in ways that don't discount their reaction. We truly don't know if someone feels pain or not. I often hear people telling children "that doesn't hurt". This is not only discounting their experience; it is a false sense of control. Our Ego is at work pretending that we know what they are actually experiencing. As a child gets older, different strategies and ideas will help increase the connection, the communication, and the child's ability to explore and share their self at a soul level.

Strategy 1: Have a Sacred Space / Time / Ritual

How does one stay open and responsive? Aside from maintaining a positive attitude, strategically creating space and time for connection is useful. Plan certain times of the day where conversations are routine and make emotional sense. For many, like my family, sitting around the dinner table is a sacred space. It is here that we gather together. Sometimes it's not even at a table, but a picnic set up in the living room, outside for some back porch sitting, at a restaurant, or in front of the television for movie night, **but** it is always a 'talking space' for meaningful conversation before anything else. Our story telling begins, discussing the day, sharing "good" stories and "not so good ones". Assigning terms like 'good' and 'not so good' with emotions like sadness, anger, excitement, love, surprising, joy expands our emotional intelligence and increases emotional vocabulary. Sharing using visual imagery, using "roses, thorns, and dandelions", as favorite part, worst part, and a wish respectively, gives a deeper meaning to the experience and aids in symbolic identification. Taking it a bit further, we state colors that symbolically correspond to the experience which can provide even deeper integration for a person. Allowing children to share their symbols in any form of creative expression may take a family some time to get acquainted to. However, when allowing this type of expression children are tapping into their soul's natural way of communicating and engaging in a more profound creative integrated way. This undefined creativity can include drawing, dancing, creating and singing a song, writing, verbally sharing, psychodrama, or any other form of expression. The key is that they share.

When children share, we have access to more information. This information has many layers and children will often "say" more when using these creative outlets. It allows inside access into their emotional and physical states, their social circles, their deep-rooted sense of self and values, and how aligned their energy centers are. The choice to communicate in any expressive manner integrates the information they are sharing on soul level and allows for connection to their gifts and abilities without parameters.

Strategy 2: Have Ground Rules

During this type of sharing, it is suggested that we create Do's and Don'ts for interacting. These will foster the intended style of connecting. In addition, these Do's and Don'ts provide a foundation for your core beliefs about the child's abilities, your understanding of it, and family responses to it. Post these reminders if needed for yourself and the child. Below are some lists of possibilities for practical thoughts, Do's, Don'ts, and values.

Practical thoughts and insights

- Stay **open**
- Don't judge
- Remember this is who the child 'is', a part of their natural intelligence, their soul blueprint
- Stick to the child's story (don't embellish it, don't discount it)
- **Respond** with love and openness
- **HONOR** by allowing for conversations or healthy self-expression
- Be **strategy-focused** without moving past their experience too quickly, and seek solutions that embrace the child's soul
- **Believe** what they say
- Let your child know that how they perceive the world is not right or wrong, just their perception which makes it right for them
- **Share** your observations in a loving and affirming manner
- Let your child know they are not alone (and believe that for yourself!), and remind them who is in your **HOPE** tribe

Parent Dos and Don'ts

Dos

- Be positive (responsive not reactive)
- Help your child feel safe (find additional support); Help your child find friends and discuss healthy supportive friendships/ relationships
- Be curious: Ask questions, create space for connection, set intentions to build an authentic relationship; Seek to understand; be available and present with the child
- Pay attention to the health of your child (emotional, physical, behavioral, spiritual)
- Support imaginative play
- Allow for creative expression
- Promote healthy eating and exercise (as a sensitive body is more easily affected)
- Boost confidence (engage in extracurricular activities, focus on strengths, provide the child with affirmations)
- Communicate (TALK, TALK TALK!) (always remind them they are not alone)
- Offer to help in find strategies to decrease any discomfort (emotional or physical) but allowing the discomfort to inform soulful decisions
- Remind yourself that you are lucky to have such a beautiful caring sensitive child
- Be proud and be their biggest supporter!
- Be patient with your child and yourself – it is a difficult job!

Don't:

- Laugh, tease, or bully your child (or allow others to)
- Deny their experience
- Ignore what you observe or what they report
- Use harsh punishment or consequences
- Make them join a social situation that causes great distress

- Ask them, "what is wrong with you?", or "every other child does…"
- Raise your voice in aggressive manner (don't hit, spank, or become aggressive); don't neglect to manage your emotional reactivity to situations
- Leave them feeling alone (don't leave in a difficult situation, don't force space if they need you close)
- Tell the child or allow others to imply that the child "takes things too personal" (rather begin discussing emotions and coping strategies for these feelings)
- Force a child to play on sports teams or in activities they do not want to participate in
- Enable fear to dictate their decisions and behaviors (see outside professional help if needed)

Strategy 3: Have a Family Foundation

It is important for children to know limits, boundaries, expectations, and the values of a family. Providing them (and the family as a whole) with identified values or expectations can help create space for talking about difficult things, sharing self with the group, and providing loving containment.

Create a family values chart(s)
In our family we want to (be):
OK to be who we are as individuals and as a family
Nurturing
Have rules that are reasonable and expectations that are reachable
Flexible, fun, but has limits that are known and understood
Have choices and can make choices for ourselves
Receive and give guidance with respect
Allowed to have our feelings and emotions
Tolerant and open minded
Healthy (in mind, body, and spirit)

Create a spiritual one as well:

<u>We believe God (or whatever you call a Higher Power) is:</u>
Love
Safe
Consistent
Light
Source
Has healing power

Create one for soul:
<u>We believe our souls are:</u>
Unique
Love and light
Have a soul blueprint
Contain great strengths, talents and abilities
God breathed and God designed
Make us who we are
Are allowed to drive our life choices
Are infinite with wisdom, hope, peace, and joy
Are a better place to live from than just our Ego self

<u>Strategy 4: The Human Knot</u>

This activity is loved by my children. I first did this activity when I was in high school and on a retreat with other students and friends. It was a team building activity, and one that I have relived over and over again in my mind. It is a powerful way to visualize the way we are all connected to each other, the way we can get entangled in other people's thoughts, feelings, and sensations. When the knot is 'figured out' and we are left still holding hands, connected in a complete circle, the most meaningful space has been created in the middle. The space is what ties us together and yet it allows everyone's experience to be what it is. We can be appreciative of the differences. We don't have to 'hold' each other's 'stuff' to be connected. We can be connected by experience, a shared space. We can create a safe space to hold all that we offer.

How to 'play' the human knot: each person takes a hand of another, and each of your hands needs to be holding the hand of a different person. Once everyone has taken hands, there should be a jumbled mess of hands, a knot, in the center. Without breaking hands, undo the knot until you find yourself holding hands forming a circle. Getting ready to smile, laugh, and have fun. This activity requires bending, moving, shifting and sometimes even jumping over arms to untangle the knot. Laughter is usually a byproduct of this one!

Strategy 5: Ball of Yarn

Choose a ball of yarn. If you want to go deeper then discuss what color of yarn to use to represent either your connection with the person or to symbolize a relationship. This relationship can between you and your child, your child and another, a belief, a thought, etc. Make a large loop in the yarn. The loop should be one that will be able to go around you and your child and allow for you both to take 1-2 large steps away from each other. Then toss the yarn back and forth to each other while having a conversation, discussing a situation, or describing the relationship between your child and another. Spend several minutes doing this, trying to discuss details. Toss the yarn back and forth several times. You may want to set a timer so that tossing the yarn still occurs even if there is a lull in conversation. 5 minutes may be sufficient for the situation. When you are done, you will visibly see the cords that connect the two of you in the moment. Discuss what these cords represent. Some possible questions might be: a) How might we stay attached to these thoughts, feelings, etc? b) What might we be feeling? c) What might we be thinking? Discuss the strands and what they represent in as many details as possible. The strands of yarn may represent energy back and forth that binds us up. After the discussion is finished, have a dialogue about why cutting cords is important. Cutting of the yarn represents letting go of ties to that situation, feeling, sensation, or any negative energy. Possible debriefing questions might be: a) How can letting go of others emotions and feelings free us and not tie us together in a way that keeps negative energy in our own body? B) How are these strands blocking our own energy flow? C) How can cutting them release this energy blockage? You can even try to move together with these strands around you, and discuss how you are not your own person when you take on the other person's thoughts, feelings, sensations. With scissors, when you are both ready, you physically cut the cords practicing affirmations or cord cutting statements like:

*I care about you and your situation but I
don't have to hold them in my body
*I let go of anything that does make me my best person

*Your stuff is yours and mine is mine
*We can care about each other and help each other
but we don't have to be exactly like each other
*If I hold someone else's feelings/thoughts/
sensations then I can't be who I am
*I feel tired when I hold your stuff, so I'm letting
it go so I can have my energy back

Creating your own cord cutting statements with your child will be important. These statements will need to be connected to the thought or situation in order to be effective.

Strategy 6: Create a Tribe

Create a tribe for yourself, and a tribe for the child. The parent's tribe may have members that are also members of their child's tribe. Tribes do not need to be separate, but rather a connecting web of people that support one another. With this said, it is critical that the child identify same age supports and others whom they have a special bond with. This must be a tribe that the child has actively helped create. It will be less effective in helping the child find their place in the world, if parent's simply identify the members of a child's tribe. Ideas of people can help facilitate thought and stimulate the process of children determining key members. Parents must realize that controlling who is a part of the child's tribe simply will not work. I would like to add that it is the prime responsibility as a parent to ensure a child's safety Therefore if your child identifies a member and you question safety, then it is your obligation to act and ensure that your child know why this person is not a member of their tribe. Members of the tribe can be family, friends, family friends, support groups, clubs of like-minded people, medical professionals, mental health counselors, special service providers such as Occupational Therapists, Speech pathologist, teachers, like minded individuals, etc. Do not limit or place boundaries on who can be a member (unless safety is of concern). Some children may identify pets as members of their tribe.

Making a visual for your Tribe can give it more life and be an easy way to access certain people during times of need and support. An example of this may be to draw a large tree on poster board with roots, a thick trunk, and several flowering branches. Make each part of the tree representative of tribal members. The roots can be labeled as 1) ancestors 2) past lives (if your family shares in this idea), 3) family members (grandparents, uncles/aunts, extended family), and so on. The branches can represent the other members. Examples being 1) friends, 2) teachers, 3) therapist, 4) specialists (including doctors, Reiki practitioners, …), 5) church congregation, 6) and the list goes on. The trunk of the tree can symbolize physical self so natural talents, abilities and gifts can be written on there. Other items like inspirational quotes, affirmations, or favorite books that speak to a child's soul can be added to the tree. After labeling the tree a large circle can be drawn all around the tree and one can write Diving, or Creator (whatever your family uses to call the Higher Power) both inside and outside the circle. Floating inside the circle around the tree Angels, Spirit Guides, Spirit Animals, Crystals with meaning for the child, and more can be written in or a picture put on. This poster will be a living document that can be added to, redrawn and continues to inform the family and child about their support system and Tribe.

Strategy 7: Read with one another and be present

Reading and being present with your infant, young child and even older child, are also protective factors for maladaptive behaviors, and increase a child's self-awareness and connection with you as caregiver. Reading to your child can create spaces that allow for relaxation, creating routines in their days, and can begin laying the framework for letting them express themselves through imagination and creative play. Asking your child questions during this time is important, whether they will answer you verbally or not. The type of material you choose to read can play a significant role as well. Reading books that hold intuitive, perceptive, self-love, and self-awareness in high esteem will provide a solid foundation for self-exploration, self-discovery, and soulful living. Please see the children's book list for possible ideas. This is not an exhaustive list, but rather acts as a starting point for connecting through reading.

A few children's books resources:
The 4 Questions for kids: Byron Katie
Bumps: Dr. Wayne Dyer
What to do with a Problem: Kobi Yamada & Mae Besom
What to do with an Idea: Kobi Yamada & Mae Besom
What to do with a Chance: Kobi Yamada & Mae Besom
Gorilla Thumps and Bear Hugs: A tapping solution Children's Story, Nick Ortner
The Tapping Solution for Teenage Girls: Nick Ortner
Crystals R for kids (little Angels Book): Leia Stinnett
Healing with Crystals for kids: Stephanie Tingle
National Geographic Kids Everything Rocks and Minerals: Steve Tomecek
I think, I AM: Louise Hay
The Adventures of Lulu: Louise Hay

Strategy 8: Mindful Scavenger Hunts

My children and I engage in Mindful Scavenger Hunts. This game not only gives my children something to distract them from the physical activity of hikes or walks (because let's face it, they sometimes just don't want to get outside), but helps them become more aware of their surroundings, our connection to nature and each other, and promotes intuitive living. How the scavenger hunt works is simple (but the outcome and results are deep and complex!). All you do is take a piece of paper and have each person write down several things they are expecting to see on the walk/hike, what they hope to see, and one thing that would be extra rare to see. Example of a scavenger hunt my children and I went on:

Mindful Scavenger Hunt
Today's Date: _____

- _____ a yellow butterfly
- _____ a hummingbird drinking nectar
- _____ a lizard
- _____ a leaf in the shape of a heart
- _____ a person walking their dog
- _____ a person exercising (running, riding a bike, etc)
- _____ the word 'love'
- _____ a roadrunner (the actual bird bc where we live it is possible)
- _____ something beautiful
- _____ something that reminds me of myself
- _____ a roly poly
- _____ a STOP sign
- _____ a rock that is a really cool color
- _____ a red flower
- _____ a river/or stream of water
- _____ something purple
- _____ a ladybug

You can leave several spaces for things that catch your attention and fill it in as you go. For example, my children and I saw a name written on the concrete with sidewalk chalk that said Cherish. That was a perfect way to sum up our walk that day. A moment I will cherish.

After your walk/hike is over you get to see what you marked off and what you noticed. It is a great conversation starter and can help children focus on their surroundings, and themselves. Asking questions about what they found that 'reminded them of themselves' and 'what they thought was beautiful' gives insight to you as their parent/caregiver, and also allows them to understand themselves on a deeper level. Strong connections can be built with activities like a Mindful Scavenger Hunt.

Strategy 9: The Sandwich Technique

Some children struggle to complete certain tasks. They may actually have a visceral reaction to a task they must complete. When this is the case, use the sandwich technique with your child. We will want to provide Positives for our children. We will want to give feedback that is uplifting, expect them to continue their work, and then provide more positive feedback. The Sandwich Technique can also be used to sandwich preferred tasks with un-preferred tasks. It might look like the following: Fun activity, chore (task, responsibility), fun activity.

Strategy 10: Chunk Tasks / Chores

Highly sensitive, intuitive and empathic children can become overwhelmed easily. To reduce feelings of being overwhelmed, don't give your child a laundry list of things they need to change/fix/do. Long verbal lists can exacerbate overwhelm, leaving children stuck and practically "frozen". Putting things in writing or having them pull slips of paper with tasks written on them from a jar may be easier to process and digest.

Strategy 11: Sound exercise

Choose a bell, singing bowl, or another tool that vibrates. Have your child, or a group of children, sit down in a comfortable position in a quiet environment. Ring the bell or play the singing bowl, asking the children to be quiet. Instruct them to raise their hand or touch their nose when the sound stops, when they don't hear the vibration any more. Then, for at least 30 seconds after, ask your child what noises they hear. Make a list and see what sounds they took notice of. Was it a high pitched humming, the dog barking two doors down, the dryer running, the hum of the air conditioner, etc?. This raises mindfulness and begins to fine tunes their audio perception.

Strategy 12: Free journaling (also known as free association)

This is a typical journal style, writing or drawing whatever comes to mind each day for a period of time in the morning or at night, or any time in between for additional coping.

Strategy 13: Mindful journaling

Mindful journaling can be keeping record of any dreams, information or messages received throughout the day, what grabbed their attention and what they believe it to mean for themselves or someone else. I know some children that keep a dream journal, and a 'what I noticed today' journal. The type of mindful journal and the amount of journaling will depend on the child and their level of interest.

Strategy 14: Body awareness journaling

Using a journal, or creating your own, draw an outline of a person. Have your child color, using whatever color represents the feeling they are having/or had in their body, the different parts of the body. Next, draw a small picture or symbol next to it. Then have your child write or verbally share any thoughts or feelings about each of the colored areas. This process will encourage understanding in how the body and psyche are linked. It also aids in the integration of multisensory awareness as it pertains to emotions.

Strategy 15: Song journal

If a highly sensitive or intuitive child is passionate about music, then this can be the inspiration for journaling. Have your child listen to a song on repeat and draw or write while it is playing. Keep track of the song and what type of music the song is. Writing what song was listened to will help keep record for your child. This will allow your child to learn how certain music may alter his/her mood. Additionally, it allows for greater understanding and self-awareness about how music can impact moods and interactions.

If certain music creates problems for a highly sensitive child, boundaries around that music, when it might be played or not, can be put in place. This will help a child have a better understanding of appropriate times for his/her body to engage in that activity.

Strategy 16: Animal Journal

Many children can relate to animal or animal imagery. Having a child draw an animal and then write why that animal describes them that day will provide a guided way for them to express internal feelings/thoughts, and other perceptions. My children and I look up different animals we see during the day that we don't typically see. We use a pocket book about spirit animals. It creates a way to have discussions about many different aspects of life, and emotions.

Strategy 17: Check in and check out systems

Check in systems with your child before their day, and/or an activity, can be useful. A check out system, one at the end of the day or after an activity, especially if the situation touches sensitivities, can be just as powerful for a child. This can be done verbally or in written/worksheet form.

Checking in with our children on a consistent basis is imperative to our relationship with them. Checking in is simple in theory but takes mindful practice on the parent's part to not only remember to do it, but to do it in a way that is helpful. Possible check in and check out questions are listed below:

How did you sleep?

Any lingering thoughts or feelings from any dreams?

On a scale from 1-5 (1 being SO TIRED to 5 being NOT TIRED AT ALL) where are you?

Is there anything you can do to help keep yourself on track?

Show/tell me what feeling you are experiencing right now?

What color would you say you are right now?

What does that color mean to you?

What might change that color?

Any sensations in your body? If so, where? Any thoughts about why they are there? Any ideas for ways to cope?

What is your goal today? Mind goal? Body Goal? Soul Goal?

Can you list one (or more) gratitude?

As you can see, the list for check in and check outs can go on and on. The basis of this activity is that we are 'checking in' with our children to try to better understand their experience, identify possible effective coping strategies, and ways we can support them. All of these things build a strong connection between ourselves and our child.

Another idea of taking things deeper is to ask a parent to engage in their own self-monitoring. Checking in and out with yourself will be not only useful to you, but useful to your child. What we do for ourselves, we will do for our children. The more mindful we are, the more mindful they can become. The more we pay attention to our own soul, the more we pay attention to the soul of another. Living your expectation is the best way for your child to meet your expectation!

Strategy 18: Gardening

Gardening with your children can be such a mindful and connecting activity. Not only is it giving and promoting life, it is relaxing and soothing. Planting flowers that attract butterflies or hummingbirds for watching can provide a sense of awe and teachable moments about life cycles, metamorphosis and change. My children and I enjoy watching birds, and we have a bird book that we use daily. We can look up the bird and hear its vocalization. It is very soothing and a wonderful activity for getting the children outside.

Marking off a section in your garden for your child (in my case, two sections) and allowing your child to make his/her own garden, whether it is with plants, fairies, dragons, or other creative items will provide a space for them to have free reign outdoors. They can create this space exactly how they want it, and it can be their garden sanctuary. After all of our gardens are created, we can build stronger connections with one another through observation, conversation and supporting the growth of all.

Strategy 19: Shapes in clouds or stars

One activity my family enjoys doing is laying out a blanket in a field, on grass, or at the beach. We all lay on our backs and get comfortable. We even bring pillows, blankets and snacks or a picnic sometimes. We lay in nature and look at the clouds. We like to find images and share what we see. We create stories with the images we see. It is a great time of connection but also mindful noticing of our environment. This tends to be an activity that carries over to car rides for my children as well, where they will gaze out their windows and tell me what they see in the clouds.

Strategy 20: Go on a spiritual camping trip

When outdoors among nature, pretend that you are going on a camping trip. You can only take things that symbolize being your best self. What would you take? Why? What does it represent? How can we help each other be our best self? What would we eat on this trip? Would any animals join us? If so, which ones? What would we learn from this trip?

Strategy 21: Visit local outdoor sacred spaces

Visit your local outdoor and sacred spaces. These areas might include conserved wildlife refuges, state parks, protected areas and wildlands. See what is around you. Have your children talk about the act of conservation and leaving areas "untouched" by man. Take notice of what you see, what you experience, the people you meet. How do we make our souls one of these sacred spaces (kept how it was intended to be made, created just the way it was)?

Concept 3: Gathering information and knowledge

Reading this, and other books on fostering intuitive and empathic children will help you gather more information and develop a deeper knowledge base for supporting highly sensitive, intuitive, or empathic children. Empathic children require empathic parenting. Loving support of a child will go a long way. This coupled with increasing knowledge will aid in providing soulful and heart based experiences for your child.

Interoception is the signaling and perception of internal bodily sensations. Essentially, it is how a person makes sense of their internal state. Much research is being done on Interoception, Perhaps, in the future, we will see research that can tell us more about highly sensitive, intuitive, and empathic children and their interoceptive abilities, revealing the way in which their brain makes sense of different signals and perceptions.

Interoception is about exploring self through our senses. These activities help a child learn, explore, and determine how their body works for them. Highly sensitive, empathic, and perceptive children can benefit from these type of activities. Preferably we will begin with younger children, the younger the better, not only to increase self-awareness but to create coping strategies that will work for them more effectively. These can only be identified through gathering more information and knowledge about our child.

Helping yourself and your children experience self-discovery and self-exploration as fun will help the process not only have more meaning, but stick. It is important that children find joy in their own journey of self-exploration and diving deeper into their experience. When we are engaged and having fun, we associate or link those positive emotions to what we are doing, what we are learning. So, have fun with your children and they will be more eager to communicate, engage, and dive deeper into self. Having 'too serious' of an approach to soulful living will not only suck the joy out of it, it doesn't teach the true essence of the soul. At our deepest soul level, we are joy, peace, love, and hope. We are and possess all the ingredients to create a joyful and purposeful life! Allowing our children to have fun with self-exploration and soul discovery will ultimately keep them coming back for more!

Strategy 1: Look from different angles

Highly sensitive, intuitive and empathic children may express themselves using various outward expressions and behaviors. You may want to look at areas such as behavior interventions, Function of

Behavior, trauma informed care, cognitive behavioral therapy, asking questions of professionals, etc. Highly sensitive and empathic children can also act out due to their sensory overload, extrasensory perceptions, emotional reactions to information they receive, and how their body stores their own and other emotions and life circumstances. Paying attention to our child's health, physical, emotional, and spiritual needs, is important.

In order to ensure due diligence on behalf of all the highly sensitive and intuitive children in the world, I must reiterate that it is imperative that adults **pay attention to a child's health.** If an empathic, sensitive, or intuitive child is acting out with angry outbursts, is vulnerable to dramatic mood swings, or is suffering from unexplained aches and pains, they may be reacting to the constant inflow of feelings and information from the outside world. Having a child seen by a medical practitioner is also useful in discovering their sensitivities. Don't shy away from talking with other professionals about what you are observing and what the child is reporting or demonstrating. Children who are empaths need to learn how to manage stress, recognize others› emotions without taking them on, and protect their health. By understanding that your child›s symptoms are, you can help him identify effective healthy coping skills. Alternatively, you may find that they are not reacting to outside stressors or experiencing challenges due to empath abilities or sensitivities, which means that medical intervention may be needed to address the situation.

Strategy 2: Make a list from your child's perspective

Write a list of your child's strengths, interests, and talents. Write this from your child's perspective. Pretend you are your child. Do your best to channel your child and filter your own ideas. Have your child do the same. If you child is not old enough to write them down, have them verbally tell you as you record. Don't censor your child's thoughts about himself/herself. Make the experience positive, not allowing them or yourself to note limitations, difficulties, or perceived short comings. Then ask your child to write down different times throughout their day they can engage in these strengths, talents, abilities. Share the lists out loud. Then ask your child to identify any 'friends' or students that they recognize as having similar strengths or interests. If they have difficulty identifying other peers, you can suggest a child you may be aware of, or you can ask your child's teacher if they know of any students who may have some similarities or things in common with your child. Ask more questions about how they may be able to engage around some of these peers. Also, finding clubs or extracurricular activities that your child enjoys can help build a positive support network while increasing self-esteem and boost self-confidence. This activity can provide you with so much information regarding the way you perceive your child as well as how they perceive themselves. In addition, asking more questions helps you identify possible tribe members to support your child's tribe, be aware of social aspects of your child's experience and much more. As stated at the beginning of this chapter, this activity may also be used to address concept 1 building connections.

Strategy 3: Declutter self and home

Questions for Decluttering Self: Ask your child about thoughts, physical body sensations, fears, feelings/emotions/ actions/behaviors, people in their life, …

- What thoughts are unnecessary that need to be 'shelved', put in the recycle bin, or completely trashed.
    - o Shelved: What are the thoughts that I don't need to worry about now but I will need to take care of later?
    - o Recycled: What thoughts could be useful in the future so I need to hold onto it?
    - o Completely trashed: Does this thought bring me down? Does this support me with my goals? Does this help me be the person I want to be? If this is a negative thought and does not support me, I need to completely trash it.

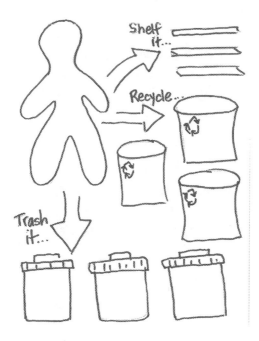

Questions to Declutter home/space/room: Ask your child questions about the things they surround themselves with

- Do I need this item? Do I want this item? What is the difference between a want and a need?
- Do I USE this item?
- How does this item make me feel? When I feel that way, what thoughts do I have? What sensations are expressed in my body? What do I want to do? What action do I want to take?
- Have I played with/taken notice of/used this in the last 6 months? Why or why not?
- Could someone else get more use out of this if I am unsure if I need/want it?
- Do I use this item for its intended purpose?
- If I don't need/want this item, but find it difficult to part with it, what can I do? Draw a picture, take a picture and put it in a photo book, write about it, perform a ceremony for letting it go, meditate about it, find a 'good home' for it (outside the home), …
- What other questions can you think of?

Strategy 4: Be Present

One of the best ways to gather information and increase knowledge is to simply be present. Be mindful of your surroundings on a consistent basis. Ask your child questions about what they see, hear, feel, smell, sense.

Strategy 5: Best gift I ever received was and why?

Ask your child(ren) to answer the question, "What is the best gift I have ever received and why?" This helps shape attitudes of gratitude and helps parents identify children's mental associations with certain items or activities.

Strategy 6: Waves

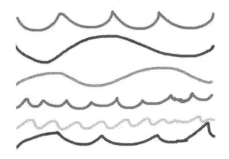

What wave are you on today?
What does your wave look like today?
Is the water smooth or rough?
Is the water moving up and down, or is it flat?
What color is the water?
Trace the wave with the color of your wave?
Did the attributes of the wave change throughout the day, or did it stay the same?
What was happening when it began to change?
When was the wave at its highest point? Lowest point?
If the color changed, what color did it change to, why do you think it changed & when did it changed?

Why might my wave look fast, as if there are many smaller waves inside the big one?

Why might my wave look as if it is going slower, with long spaces in between the ups and downs?

Get creative and use this metaphor with your child to find out more about how they felt, what their behavior was, what their thoughts where, who was with them, and what changed 'in their waves' as their days and weeks proceed.

Strategy 7: What is all around me?

In order to gather as much information about what our child is experiencing, it is helpful to increase self-awareness, mindfulness, and perceptibility by using all of our senses.

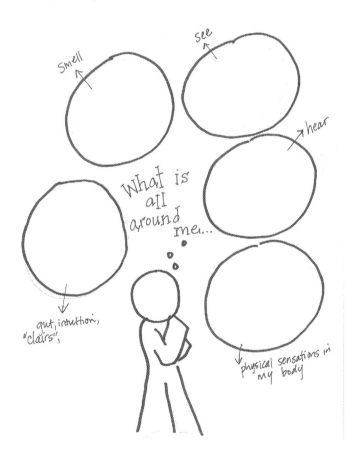

Strategy 8: Train Exercises

Imagine you are a train…what baggage do you carry? What provides the fuel (Love, God's divine light is our soul's fuel)? What is the baggage you need to drop off? Where can you drop baggage off? What color is your baggage? Are you carrying someone else's baggage?

For younger children, you might even use a train set with tracks. Have stations where the train stops to 'drop off' different types of baggage. You can have pictures or even write words/colors to represent certain feelings, somatic complaints, or stressors. Then play with your child, but mindfully engage in emotional regulation skills, social skills, and recognizing what is our own and what is others.

Strategy 9: Pros and Cons

Sometimes empathic children don't really know what they want in the moment. They may wait to see or hear what another person chooses before they make their choice. Try to allow for time for them to think, process, and not 'be given the answer'. Also, when a child is having a difficult time deciding something (whether it's to go to the park with friends or not, which toy to choose for spending their chore money, or what to pack in their lunch), a quick pros/cons list either on paper or out loud can help them see that a choice is just a choice. This can help them see that there are positives to every choice. Every choice can be a good one if you make it a good one! Color coding different choices in a particular situation can also provide a visual for a child.

Situation: _____

Choice 1:_____

Choice 2:_____

Choice 3:_____

Pros/Cons

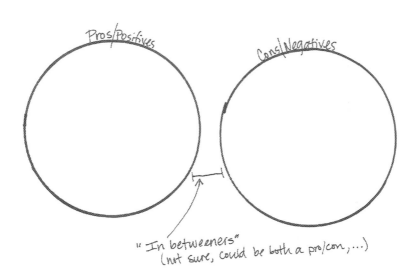

Pros/Positives

Cons/Negatives

" In betweeners"
(not sure, could be both a pro/con, ...)

<u>Strategy 10: Body scan</u>

Body scans help us increase self-awareness and boost mindful living. Practicing and engaging in activities that help our children become more aware of themselves will help them make less irrational decisions, increase connection to others by understanding how they relate to self, and increase their ability to focus. The first example is one that focuses on just one part of the body and is geared more for younger children with less of an attention span. The second example is a lengthy body scan for older children. Mark Bertin wrote an article in Mindful Magazine online which highlighted mindful parenting for ADHD. Mindful Magazine can be another tool for accessing strategies.

Example 1:

1) Have your child get comfortable either standing or sitting and remove their shoes (many times children feel more relaxed and comfortable with no shoes on. My son calls his shoes 'feet traps'!)
2) Take 3 deep breaths (can use hand to belly breathing technique)

3) Have your child (if comfortable with it) close their eyes

4) Have your child then focus on his/her feet (you can choose other body parts as well, but we will use feet for the grounding element they provide). Have them push them against the ground (softly, no need to put a lot of force or pressure) and keep them their for a few moments with soles touching the ground. (this can be done outside for additional grounding (Earthing) benefits). Ask your child mindful questions… how does this feel to them? Is the ground soft or hard? Do they feel any pain or sensations in their feet? Are they wearing socks or no socks? How does that feel? Anything that makes their feet feel uncomfortable? Can they shift and change the position of their foot to increase comfort? Are their feet ticklish? Do they feel their toes (as one large entity, or all separate pieces)? When they wiggle their toes what to do they feel (other sensations) in their foot or other parts of their body? What muscles are being used when they wiggle their toes? Do they like the feeling of light pressure or would they prefer hard? Allow them to sit and discover what they are experiencing.

5) Have them tap on each toe three times. Tap, Tap, Tap on big toe, and son on to pinky toe, and then back through ending on their big toe.

6) Now have them just sit and be in the experience. What do they feel? What are they thinking? Can they only think about their toes or feet? How hard or easy is it to keep this focus? Does it bring anything up for them emotionally (sadness, anxiety, restlessness)?

7) Have your child now focus on what is holding their body (floor, chair, earth). What is their posture like? Do they feel comfortable or do they need to change their posture? Can your child fully allow them to be held by the chair/ground/floor as much as possible? What do they feel, sense, think?

8) The exercise can be short or longer in duration. It can be used daily as a daily meditation practice, or in the moment for grounding or calming body. Ask your child when this exercise could be helpful to them. What did they notice about their body/

mood/thoughts from when they started to now as it is ending? Help them identify situations where they could use this and practice it. It may even be helpful as part of a bedtime routine for self-soothing, calming thoughts and body, for ease at relaxing into sleep.

Example 2:

1) Have your child lie down, on their back (if able to) and rest their arms comfortably to theirs sides. Allow them to get comfortable, shifting and rearranging their body and then ask if they are comfortable with closing their eyes. If so, encourage this as decreased stimulation will allow for decreased need to filter and aid in deeper relaxation and mindfulness.

2) Have your child take 3 deep breaths (using hand to belly breathing technique if needed)

3) Tell your child that now you will start to focus on different parts of their body. This is just the 'art of noticing' and there is no pressure for your child to feel or experience anything than what they take notice of in their own body. You will start with their fee. Do their feet feel restless, tired, achy, or no feeling? Are your feet cold, warm, sweaty, dry? Is something over your feet (socks, blanket) or are they bare, open to the air? What are your feet touching (carpet, tile, bed, earth)? Tell your child that if they begin to think about something else, to just allow that thought to float away and bring themselves back to the part of the body they are focusing on.

4) Move up the body to the legs. Asking similar questions that come to your mind. Think 'outside the box'…and questions can be creative. Allow for time at each spot of the body. Younger children, or children who have shorter attention spans will require less time at each spot. However, trying to build up your child's mindfulness muscle will serve them well. So, each time you engage in this activity you might want to add a second or two to each spot. Notice if there seems to be a pattern with your child. For example, every time your child is 'focusing on their

legs' they seem to be the most distracted, trouble settling in to it, or distracted. Is there something going on with their legs? Are the legs symbolic of something they are needing to pay attention to? Have them focus on smaller parts of each 'spot' of the body. So with legs, focus on front of knee, back of knee, thigh, calf, etc.

5) Make sure your child is breathing – adequate effective breathing!

6) Move up from legs to belly. Engage in Mindful questioning. At belly ask about emotions or sensations in their 'gut'

7) Move up to chest. Engage in mindful questions. How is the chest rising? Do you feel your heart beat? What does that feel like? Fast, slow, some skips?

8) Move to your hands. Engage in mindful questions as you did with feet.

9) Move to your arms. Engage in mindful questioning.

10) Move to your lower back. Is it supported? Aches, pains? How does it move with each breath? Engage in mindful questioning.

11) Move to your neck and shoulders. What do you sense here? Where in your body do you hold tension? Are your neck or shoulders tight? Tense these muscles, holding for count of 3, then release. What do you feel, notice, experience? Engage in mindful questioning.

12) Move to your face. Engage in mindful questioning. Ask about facial expressions or muscles that are tight (jaw, checks, and around the eyes). If someone was looking at your right now what would they guess you were feeling based on what your face looks like? Take a deep breath in through your nose, and feel the air travel and then exhale and feel the air leave.

13) Haver your child take 3 deep breaths

14) Now focus attention on whole body. What do they feel? Sense? Are they different than when they started, how?Allow them time to just be here and relax into the experience and the moment, taking notice of any part of their body their mind is drawn to. What is this part of their body telling them?

15) When they are ready have them take 3 deep breaths.

16) Blink their eyes slowly, and come back to current awareness. Have your child take their time getting up, breathing effectively

and deeply prior to, and making sure that they are fully back into their body before standing.

Strategy 11: Candy Exercise

You will need M&Ms, skittles, starburst, sixlets, or any kind of candy that has several colors. Each color will represent at part of their body, a situation, social skill, or other topic to increase mindfulness, emotional regulation and the like. Using M&Ms as an example, the following are ways of learning more about your child.

General feelings/thoughts

Blue: Something positive I can tell myself…

Red: When I feel angry I can …

Orange: When I am feeling out of balance, or overwhelmed with something I need to do I can ….

Brown: A good way for me to connect with nature today is…

Yellow: I know I am made from God's love because…

Green: A person I can go to and feel safe with is…

Each child is given a bag (that is not see through) of M&Ms and they reach in a pull one out. Depending on what color they draw out, that is what they will share with you. This activity can be altered for discussing nearly anything and everything, so get creative!

Strategy 12: Feeling Chart

Make and use a feeling chart with your children. Create an emotions list that extends beyond the typical emotions and feelings we normally discuss. Make it as exhaustive as you can. It can be a family project based on feeling identification and increasing emotional intelligence. In our home we had magnets that had actual pictures of children expressing certain emotions. This was beneficial in social skills training, mirroring, feeling identification, as well as expanding feelings. This expansion and growth will help your child learn how others may react to a certain expression of an emotion we are having.

Strategy 13: My Body Cues

Prepare an outline of a child. Have the child draw, write, or use symbols to indicate where in their body they feel certain things. This is another visual and tangible way for parents and children to communicate about how they are feeling in a situation. We must remember to ask them about what they notice within a situation as well. Parent and child can start to record and understand what areas of the body are affected for the child when they may be experiencing extrasensory things. This can feel like they are both on different channels, not fully able to tune into one another.

For example, my son will complain of headaches, or being too hot. When this happens, I know that he may be experiencing something more aligned with his intuitive, psychic side. Now, with this said, every time my child says he has a headache or is hot, he is not always responding to spirit or having a psychic download. I must also check in with myself, the situation, and ask curious questions to determine how to best help my son get his needs met. This can be with discussing his body cues, asking about where in his body he feels certain things and at what level of intensity. I may also ask him about what he was thinking prior to the headache or being too hot was noticed.

Strategy 14: Have a silly face contest

Now, this might sound ridiculous (well, it is, but that is the point!), but this activity can actually help children with more than just having a good laugh. While just laughing is fun, it can also help them understand what they look like to others, as well as how they perceive others. This activity is also useful in seeing how your child reacts to different facial expressions, interprets body movements, adjusts to behavior, or even changes their facial expression. These can all be signs to you as a parent on how the child might be receiving an expression. It can also be very useful to discuss feelings and associate a facial expression with this activity. This can help with feeling identification (for self and others), can help with early discussion about empathic reactions to different facial expressions associated with feelings, and can help a highly sensitive child form a protective boundary (i.e. your child can keep smiling while you share a sad expression). These types of activities are building blocks for future strategies.

Strategy 15: Mirroring

Similarly, like the strategy shared above, mirroring can be very beneficial. Sit face to face with your child and copy one another's facial expressions. Try to imitate the other person. Talk about what you are doing and why. How are you changing your body, what does it change internally (do you physically feel different, have different thoughts running through your mind, see images and if so, what are they, do you have any urges or behaviors you want to engage in?)?

This will help a child begin to identify visually how we can unknowingly take on other people's energy. When we change our facial expression and body language to match that of another, we can begin to change on a deeper level. This can occur the other way around as well. We start thinking the same thought as another, body language changes, and then feelings and behaviors can align. It can be a powerful and non-threatening way to show how energetically we can be connected to others.

Strategy 16: Hot Air Balloon Activity

Draw a hot air balloon or better yet, have your child draw it! There are many ways to use this visual, however, I believe it can be a powerful way to gather information and learn more about our children. What are the People/Places/Thoughts/Things that 'raise us up'? What gives us air and are healthy positive supports in our lives? These can be written in the balloon part. What are the People/Places/Thoughts/Things that 'weigh us down'? What bring us down emotionally, physically, or spiritually? The possibilities are endless, so get creative and remember that visuals can provide another depth for children to talk about what they are experiencing and provide a kid friendly language for discussing these topics!

<u>Strategy 17: Onion Exercise</u>

Peeling back the layers. Talk with your child about the layers of being human or the layers of a certain situation. Sometimes to really understand a situation, emotion, or thought we need to peel back the layers. The center will be our soul (or truest self). This activity can be modified to fit your child's age, cognitive ability, and the situation they find themselves in. It is a strategy that involves discussion, navigating different aspects of a situation and helps a child visualize the different layers that extend out from an aspect of self. Use a real onion if you would like, or simply draw one.

Concept 4: Believe and Trust

As stated several times before, believing in a child and trusting what they say, will help them believe and trust in themselves. While this is simple to write, it is difficult to put into practice at times. This requires mindful intervention and authentic attempts to connect with the child. This is very hard work and necessitates an open-minded and self-less approach. The adult must be willing to engage in introspective techniques and be prepared to meet a child where they are at emotionally and behaviorally. The adult's ego must be 'in check'. Most importantly, a soulful approach is needed.

While listening to Hay House radio, Anita Moorjani and David Hamilton spoke regarding 'Mind, Body, and the Placebo Effect'. As the universe has done so many times before, the timing of this was perfect. They spoke of topics directly related to the H.O.P.E Tribe. They expressed ideas regarding trust and safe spaces. When we are connecting with children, trusting and believing in their experiences will promote increased connection, increased self-awareness, and their ability to trust themselves. This not only helps them cope with everyday stressors, but also allows them to listen to their bodies for intuitive messages about situations and people. David Hamilton mentioned how as a child his 'mother would kiss his hurt away' and how effective it was. When his mother kissed an injured part of his body he didn't feel the pain anymore. His physical pain response was actually interrupted and dissipated. A discussion ensued. Research and medical studies regarding the effectiveness of the placebo effect were shared. As shown in brain imaging scans, the brain is activated even with a placebo said to reduce pain.

This clearly shows that positive interaction, which embraces ideals of trust, faith, honor, and believing in children, can decrease their emotional and physical pain by simply being heard and attended to in a soulful manner. This decreases emotional reactivity, decreases pain, and increases the space for soul connection and integration. The space left from this process is then available for the true soul identity to cope and create strategies that are soul-inspired. When energy, whether recognized as our own or someone else's gets stored, similar to effects of generational trauma being stored in the body, our focus becomes more on symptomology and alleviating what our body feels, rather than living from our soul purpose.

Our bodies and our souls, when blocked with energy that doesn't serve us, are suffocated. Literally our body can negatively respond physically and emotionally. When a child is not allowed to live from an authentic place, the soul is constricted. This restriction can cause somatic complaints, emotional difficulties, and behavioral challenges. Thus, believing and trusting children, empowering them to share soul self is what creates the foundation for soul and self-actualized living. The H.O.P.E. Tribe needs to adopt the belief that expressing the true soul self is the key to not only healthy living, but also the ability to change current societal ideas that keep children stuck and blocked energetically. To be 'stuck' is stagnation, soul-stalled, and mind and body become frozen and unable to act in accordance with soul intent. Belief and trust in another releases this block, circulating energy and provides space to authentically express and 'be' soul self.

Thoughts are energy. What we think, believe and put our trust in will come to fruition and multiply. What can we do as parents to help our children begin participating in their life in a mindful way that promotes multiplying the good, the positive, and utilizing the power of their minds/thoughts/feelings? How can we help them believe and trust?

Strategy 1: The 3 C's (Connection, Communication, Create Space)

Changing your language to a more positive connotation can begin to shift thoughts and responses to situations. Being mindful of language and how we define our experiences changes the core of who we are. When we choose positivity, our core becomes positive, viewing life and all its circumstances from a more loving and light filled place. This in turn keeps us connected to Source, God in Heaven who created us with purpose and loving intent. Here are a few simple ways to be mindful about your positive outlook:

- Pay attention to your language. Is it positive? Negative? What are the phrases you tend to use the most?)
- Is it congruent with your behavior? Does it match? Does it send a mixed message to self or other?
- Does the tone of your voice reflect your internal state? How does the inflection of your voice altar the meaning of what you are saying?
- Is there a time of day where your language is more positive or negative than other times? Are you a 'morning' person? Night person? What does this look like? How does it impact your relationships?
- Does the child use any of your phrases or favorite sayings? If so, is the meaning behind them positive, negative, sarcastic, etc.?
- When expressing your thoughts feelings do you use "I statements"? An example is I feel frustrated when I have to ask you several times to get ready for school.
- Do you attempt to stay away from blaming or shaming language?
- If you rated yourself on a scale from 1-5, 1 being not at all positive and 5 being always positive, where would you put yourself? Where would others rate you? Ask and receive feedback from trusted others to ensure you are aware of your level of

positivity. This feedback could help you take it to the next level of understanding. Where does the child place themselves on the scale? Where would others place this child?

These questions are a start to becoming a more mindful person. When adults become more mindful and model the practices associate with such living, it can lead to a child engaging in mindful questioning of self and other.

Language is an aspect of thought. What we think we tend to express verbally or using other methods, such as facial expressions, gestures, tone, volume, and our behavior. Our thoughts, and all that ensues, create our experience. The Law of Attraction is just that; we attract what we put out into the world. The Law of Attraction shows us how energy, whether from thought or action, becomes what we see, what we experience, consistently bringing back to us what we put out into the world. The H.O.P.E. Tribe needs to operate from this mentality; thoughts are energy and the H.O.P.E. tribe is a spiritual, physical, emotional, and thought energy system that is being put in place. How we think about the H.O.P.E. tribe, what we believe it is, will manifest itself for us and our children. The H.O.P.E. tribe needs to help children connect to the idea of The Law of Attraction not only for the betterment of the child's life but for the effectiveness of the Tribe. The power we possess will help extend its reach, changing mindsets and amending worldviews.

Adding more to the above aspects of positive language, the 3 Cs flow to and from each other in a fluid motion. For when we create a space to have open and positive conversation/communication, a connection develops. Connection to our children is the key to their success and the key to them understanding self in their world. In order for a deeper a connection to be formed there must be a space for the connection to be held; a container of sorts, sometimes physically and sometimes emotionally, that fosters true belonging.

How does one create space for connection and communication? The use of metaphors, and visuals can create wonderful launching points for deeper conversations. Asking questions of each other creates the space for more soulful connections. Using symbols when we communicate can create a deeper meaning, providing a child a more tangible way to weave it into their senses. Symbols can help children assimilate information they receive from extrasensory perceptions and logically make sense of how they receive this information, whether emotionally, physically, and mentally. As with the example earlier, using the symbol of a rose to represent their 'favorite part of the day' combined with assigning a color deepens the connectivity between what is said, felt, heard, and seen.

Shared experiences and rituals bring people closer together. These points of connectivity are what provide deeper emotional meaning to the relationship. Allowing senses to have shared experiences can create stronger connection and integration. Stronger connection creates stronger belief and trust in that connection. Linking the senses together for one experience provides depth, soulful understanding, and an ability to draw upon that experience in the future with more clarity and trust.

These exercises create a safe place to talk about things that sometimes leave children speechless or not sure how to share. Rather than "hitting the end of the day wall", characterized by children being "in the mood to share about their day', you can create a fun, creative, positive space by using symbolic representations. This opening of the space for creative expression brings new life to the process and can be a mitigating factor. Communicating to connect is the goal!

Symbolic representations can be anything the child feels connected to and personally represents the idea or concept that is being discussed. Allowing children to co-create these symbols is very powerful. A sports team, animals (see animal imagery worksheets in Chapter 10), colors, fragrances, foods, and more, are all great tools for creating meaningful symbols. The possibilities are endless. The key is to keep the symbol meaningful for the child. This will increase the connection and make creating space for communication easier.

It has become commonplace for me to be referred to as 'the hawk lady'. This began when I found myself looking for "signs" that I was on the right path in my life. I would frequently see a hawk. It often looked as though it was following me, sending me a very clear message. I would shout out with excitement and gratitude, "Look! It is my hawk!". Now it has become a family "sign" of sorts. My family is always on the lookout for 'the hawk'. This not only keeps us mindful and present, it is an enjoyable way to connect. When 'the hawk' shows up it sparks jubilation and conversation. This is a great offering by the Universe, a chance to check in with self, one another, have common experiences and share stories. These shared experiences build connection.

These interesting signs and symbols are ways that Spirit can intervene and send messages throughout the day. Connecting these dots to the Universe, spirit, self, other, and the collective whole brings us in touch with our soul, our true essence. This is vital to the HOPE tribe. This allows us to Honor all aspects of life, seen and unseen.

Strategy 2: Affirmations

Have your children come up with age appropriate affirmations that mean something to them. The trick here is not to put your affirmations on the, but for them to be actively engaged in the process of forming their own affirmations. Esther Hicks, in a dialogue with Dr. Wayne Dyer, stated "that you can say the words but the feeling must match for there to be manifestation." Our children may need to say the words over and over again to evoke the feeling. Then, once the feeling and words match, manifestation will begin. Below are examples of some affirmations. Again, remember your child needs to create their own meaningful affirmations.

Example Affirmations:

- I am a wonderful, special, and a unique person.
- I have everything I need to make today a great day.
- I will spend my time with friends and people who let me be myself and don't put me down.
- I belong, not just "fit in"
- I will share my joy today. Give a smile, help someone, say something kind, think a kind thought about someone else, or laugh with a friend.
- I am right where I am supposed to be.
- In math, I'm good at the level I find myself.
- In reading, I'm good at the level I find myself.
- In science, I'm good at the level I find myself.
- In PE, I'm good at the level I find myself.

- In writing, I'm good at the level I find myself.
- I will keep working hard and my hard work will continue to pay off.
- I can do whatever I put my mind to.
- I am powerful.

Posting these affirmations for each person in the family and reading them before you leave for the day as a routine, is a good way to consistently teach a child to tell themselves positive thoughts. If adults engage in this activity too, the results will multiply as well.

Strategy 3: Stuffed Animal Positives

Choose a stuffed animal and have your child say, or write, everything positive they can think of about that stuffed animal. They might write: You are soft. I love you. You are cute. You help me sleep better. You are comfy. I like your eyes. You have a smile. Let your child go on as long as they can, recording positive attributes. Then have them list all the positive attributes they can think of about themselves. If they get stuck, ask them if they can change any of the ones that they mentioned about the stuffed animal and make them fit for themselves.

Strategy 4: Pendulum Exercise

One of the most important tasks of being a parent is to help our children feel comfortable in their own skin, to be confident, to have self-esteem, and to know what is 'right' and 'wrong'. We all come with an internal pendulum, a guiding force deep within our soul. Some call it a 'gut feeling' other's intuition, and even others 'soul wisdom'. While people tend to access this only in times of great distress or danger, or in times of pure excitement and joy, it is available to us at all times. Our 'gut' really does speak and hold answers for us. While the idea of 'soul wisdom' seems abstract, there are places in our body where we can recognize it, if we pay attention. Helping our children understand their bodies, what their 'gut' is telling them, and using it to guide their choices is imperative.

Where does this "feeling/energy" start? It begins in our Solar Plexus area. This is the point of centering, where we come to 'stillness', right behind soft cartilage at the bottom of the breastbone. When we check in with our inner-selves and get the sense "No. Don't do that. I shouldn't be here. I don't want to be here", the feeling/energy moves from solar plexus down into the gut. When we sense a "Yes. I love this. This is the right thing. This is fantastic", the feeling moves from solar plexus up into the heart.

When we talk with our children about recognizing the feelings, sensing energy within ourselves, it can be helpful to recall situations where they know that something didn't feel right or those times when they felt joy. We can ask them "truths" to see where they feel it in their body and how it is sensed or perceived. The same is important to determine for those things that may not be "truth" or "good for us". In order to truly decipher these "feelings and sensations" we must do the following:

1. Create the space by calming the body, revisiting those times and having them verbally share, draw/color, or write down what they felt in their body, thought in their mind, when they knew "truth" or something that was "right".

2. Pay attention to your body. What is your inner pendulum saying? Is this situation "good for you"? Is this "right"? Does it ring "true"? How do you know? Where do you feel it in your body? When you sense it here in your body, you can say that it is "good for you" or "truth".

3. Ask them to do the same for a time they felt something was not "right" or felt untrue for them. Again ask probing questions. When you sense it here Iyour body, you can say that it is "not good for you" or it is not true.

Teaching this skill will take some practice, and it is a skill that us as parents need to learn how to do prior to trying to teach our children. We must practice using it, and then engage in the process with our children. When we start to use this on a consistent basis of checking in with self, and with 'gut', we gain clarity for ourselves. We can start to truly believe and trust in our "gut". We can search for answers to hard questions deep within. (The Complete Guide to Crystal Chakra Healing, Permutt, page 20).

There are two other ways to use the idea of a pendulum. This will be based on your own comfort level as a parent and your own belief system. For people who are comfortable or have had practice using an actual crystal pendulum they can utilize it to show a child how energy works. Holding the pendulum in your hand you can dangle it over your other. You can ask it a question and see how the pendulum moves in a different direction to 'answer your question' or represent energy associated with that thought. Remember to begin with "primer" questions. These questions are ones that are simple and have clear answers, but a "yes" and a "no". It is important to ask these simple questions to understand how the pendulum will react. This allows you to determine how to "read" the pendulum.

Another example is to use a typical pendulum found on many office desks. They usually have several balls on it. When one end is hit the energy moves through the balls and makes the one on the other end move. Not only can this be mesmerizing and calming for children (can be used as a mindfulness or stress reduction activity) it shows clearly in a visual way how energy moves through and out. Using this as a way to discuss thoughts and energy can be very useful for children. They tend to be more visual, hands on, and learn through experience. Say an affirmation and then pull back the ball on the left side. Have the energy move through, ending and being pushed out on the right side. This is symbolic of forward movement, spiritual expansion, meeting goals, or manifesting hopes.

The parent can give an example of a negative thought and pull the right end of the ball and have the energy move to the left and out. This can be how a negative thought holds us back and can 'block' us from forward movement. Next the child can say a positive affirmation. Do the same as before, pulling the ball from the left side and watching it move the ball on the right. Sandwich this activity with positive thought, negative thought, positive thought. Beginning this demonstration with a positive will set an intention. It puts the law of attraction into motion. By ending the exercise with a positive, it will keep that positive energy flowing.

Strategy 5: Gut-o-meter

When we have the confidence to go deep within ourselves, trust and believe that we hold the answers, we can manifest greatness in our lives. The Gut-o-meter is a way to begin to help the child identify how they feel about a situation. Have the child engage in self priming technique prior to. This technique is as follows:

*Have the child stand up. Standing tall have the child make only true concrete factual statements.

Examples: I live at _____.
I am _____ years old.

When making these statements as the child to discuss, write down, or use stickers that they place on their physical bodies, to show where and how they feel these statements to be true. Have several statements so that there is credibility and reliability of their physical and emotional response.

Using the same technique, have the child say outlandish false statements.

Once this has been done have the child write down where in their body they feel these statements, starting with true and then the false. What sensations do they feel in their body? What thoughts do they think? Where in their body do they feel it the most? What emotions are brought to the surface?

Practicing the Gut-o-meter. Then using a situation, have the child make a statement about the situation or a person involved. Ask the child to pay attention and focus on their body when making the statement to see what it most closely matches...true or false? Have them use their emotional and body intelligence to point them in the direction that best serves their soul. For younger children, you can use an already created diagram called the Gut-o-meter. This exercise acts in the same way, however, labels for the child where they will feel it in their body and provide a framework for them to use. If the sensation they have in their 'gut' (aka stomach, abdomen) sinks low or moves down then it can represent a false or untruth. If the sensation moves upward towards the heart it can represent a true or truth for them. Be mindful of the child's age, cognitive abilities, current emotional intelligence, and ability to decipher bodily sensations to determine which aspect of this activity would be most useful. As with a continuum, as the child practices more and more mindfulness techniques the child can move from the gut-o-meter framework into more free form self-inquiry. Using a simple drawing of a child's body can deepen the experience and create a stronger integration bond for what is 'discovered'.

Strategy 6: Replacement Thought Activity

Teaching a child how to replace negative or disserving thoughts with ones that are more 'hopeful' and reframed positively, can aid them in avoiding any 'black holes. This technique serves everyone, no matter age, well. Replacement thoughts are affirmations in action. An affirmation may be something you say routinely or on a daily basis but when affirmations truly come alive, lived out, is when we can catch ourselves in the moment and change our way of thinking in the present. With practice this then becomes our way of thinking and we are less likely to edge towards the slippery slope of negative thought patterns.

Child's thought:	Replacement thought:
I'm not good at that.	I am not good at this YET.
_____ is better than me at running.	_____ is great at running.
I will never get that toy I want.	I have what it takes to save money for that toy if I want it bad enough.

Strategy 7: Muscle Testing

Muscle testing is an in the moment way to see how your body reacts to a thought, situation, or when making a decision. Your child will need a partner to do this, so be available to practice muscle testing. It is quick and informative! Steps for muscle testing are as follows.

1) Face each other.
2) Child will stand with one arm outstretched to the side parallel with the ground.
3) The other arm will rest comfortably at their side.
4) The statement/decision to be made/situation will be said out loud by your child.
5) You will push down with your hand on the forearm of the outstretched arm.
6) The amount of resistance will indicate the subconscious belief in that statement. The greater the resistance the more the statement resonates. The less resistance, the less it resonates.

Muscle testing can be done with just self as well. My son does this instinctually. He actually showed me this process before I even knew about it! Paying attention to our children can help us tremendously, too! They are often our teachers. (https://www.healerslibrary.com/muscle-testing https://www.healerslibrary.com/muscle-testing)

Strategy 8: The Ring-in-Ring Test

The Ring-in-Ring test is another way to gain concrete evidence to build trust in ourselves. Follow the steps listed. Using pointer fingers or middle fingers, form rings by placing them on your thumbs. Interlock the two rings together. Say the statement, the thought, the decision that needs to be made and then simply try to pull your rings apart. Notice the resistance. The rings that remain together, more resistant or more difficult to pull apart, is an answer affirming the original statement. Less resistance, or the rings coming apart easily is indicative of a negative response.

Concept 5: Emoting as a way of Using Creative Expression and Artistic outlets

Creative expression, as referred to in my home as 'emoting', is defined by gratefulness.org in the following way: Creative expression is "one of the most potent forces in the world. It is creativity that points to new paths, new ways of seeing and solving, and which offers us inspiration from the inside and outside. Creative expression is rooted in the capacities for observation, discovery, imagination, and courage. It wakes us up, challenges us, and enriches all of life. Those who dive deeply into a commitment to creative expression make their whole lives a canvas, a blank page, onto which their hearts are poured….and our world is made better because of it." (2017)

This definition of creative expression sums up the importance of engaging in and creating space for such soulful discovery. I am grateful for such an all-encompassing way of looking at creative expression.

To emote, according to Wikipedia, is to "portray emotion in a theatrical manner" (2018). Similarly, Merriam Webster dictionary states that emoting is to "give expression to emotion especially in acting" (2018). These definitions are interesting and call us to focus on the 'acting' or theatrical description. If God, our Source, created us, and breathed in our soul space the blueprint of our life, wouldn't it makes sense that we are 'acting' in His show? We are created with purpose and the Earth is where our soul purpose is to be lived and acted out. To emote then is a birthright, to creatively express with no parameters. We are called to allow our soul to demonstrate the unique light, love, and intent that fills the space within.

The free fall feeling, one of butterflies in the stomach, we get when we express our soul self in this way, is the moment when we are reconnecting to the energy of life. Releasing creative energy allows for integration, assimilation, and connection to true passions and desires. When children 'emote' they are called to live out their soul blueprint in that moment. Creating more and more of these moments in their day is when we will be allowing them to truly show up as they were intended to. Imagination is a release of internal source light and energy moving from Source, through body, to world.

On another level, creative expression can provide an outlet for children to release blocked energy. This may be energy that is not their own. It provides a physical flow for the energy to move out of them and into another energetic creation. The art form can hold the feelings, sensations, and thoughts. The child can move freely from other to soul-self more quickly and with less interruptions or refractions.

Art and creative outlets are communication platforms, a place for children to share with adults and others their unique experiences. Similar to adults, many children find it difficult to share at a deep level for many reasons. Fearful of another's response, unsure of what they have actually experienced, lacking clarity, may leave a child unable or unwilling to communicate. Creativity allows children a safe place to communicate using various modalities that are socially acceptable. Creative expression and the use of the imagination is viewed as a positive, sometimes even "safe". The risk of being labeled different or odd is minimized.

A child's experience, shared or not, is valid and meaningful. Children are required to navigate social situations that prove difficult. Stigmas, peer pressure, and bullying are present and are powerful forces in our children's lives. These negative forces can keep children from expressing who they are. Creative expression allows for this to flow in a way that can feel safe and freeing. Emoting builds self-confidence as the empathic and sensitive child starts to understand how their experience and the essence of who they are at their core can create a masterpiece. This is exactly what we want H.O.P.E tribe children to experience...the creation of their own masterpiece!

The goal of creative expression for the child is to shed, integrate, and express themselves. Remembering this will help the parent allow for pure creativity and let go of their own expectations. Many parents engage in their ego-self urge to make the art project more about what they want it to be. They may attempt to "control" what their child creates, ensuring it is what they want the world to see. When parents, consciously or subconsciously do this, the act of creating is less about 'emoting'. Soulful creative expression is about letting out whatever we have inside. It is a way to energetically let go of what is being held. The goal is to give meaning to the emotional energy, and allow for integration of mind, body, spirit and soul with no judgement.

Strategy 1: One liner drawings

As a family (or a pair) simply get a white piece of paper and a few pens (no pencils—no erasing). One person starts by drawing a single line on the paper, then passes it to the next person, and so on. After a certain amount of time, or when the group determines the activity is over, you all get to see what the final picture is. What was created? Sometimes an undeniable image will emerge and everyone agrees on what it is. Other times, each person will see something different in the artistic creation. Then as a roundtable discussion you can talk about what you see, any symbolism or meaning associated with it, and the project can be repeated as many times as you like. This is a good activity for when you go out to eat with your children at a restaurant.

Strategy 2: Dress up!

Allowing children to dress up in costumes, clothes, or even turning other items into wearables (lampshades for hats, pillow cases for capes, boxes for shoes, …), provides space to be silly, imaginative, creative, and to express themselves. Paying attention to your young child when doing this can tell us so much about where they may feel things in their body, what parts of their body may be 'bothering' them, and more.

For example, my son would constantly dress up and make himself into a robot. He would turn boxes into his robotic armor and he literally would be covered head to toe in cardboard. The best part was when he wore it outside to play with the neighborhood kids. Despite not being able to move freely, he tried his hardest to keep on his robot costume and engage. This became a metaphor for us discussing situations.
What are the ways you felt robotic? Were you being seen and not heard?

How do you feel different from other kids your age?

Why do you need robotic protection? What types of things are you shielding yourself from?

Could you keep some protection but have a different type of material that allowed for more 'free' moving, and was less disruptive to his joy factor?

Strategy 3: Weekly or Daily drawing exercise

Have your child use artistic expression to express thoughts and utilize the Law of Attraction. This can be done daily or weekly. Have your child draw a picture of what they hope the day (or week) to look like, feel like, or what they wish to manifest. They can draw pictures in a story line to depict the start of a week to the end. They can draw a self-portrait of how they want to feel at the end of the day. They can draw a picture of something they hope occurs for them.

Please talk with your child about manifestation and its purpose. A child may see the goal as making a wish for a gaming system to magically appear by the end of the week, however, this is about a deeper more spiritual experience. We want to help our children see outside the material and into the spiritual. I encourage continued reading about the Law of Attraction at lawofattraction.com and other useful websites, books, and articles.

Strategy 4: Scrapbooking

This really doesn't require much explanation. Scrapbooking materials can be found at most places that carry any form of art supplies. Allowing your child to pick a scrapbook out (i.e. one they are drawn to because of it's color, it's image on the front, etc) will give the book more meaning. Then allow your child to scrapbook pages weekly, monthly, or as a coping strategy. These books are not only useful for creating and expressing, but they tell a story later that provides a baseline for the child to go back and visually see where they were and where they are.

Strategy 5: Mandalas

This exercise of creating patterns or coloring different mandalas can provide peace, calm, and foster self-expression. Depending on the child and the type of image being used, have the child pick a color and color the mandala with all different shades of that particular color. To take it a step further you can link that color to a chakra or an emotion. You can ask your child, "What feeling do you think of when you use that color"? You can look up chakras and the colors associated with them. This can help increase the possibility discern what a child might be experiencing. For example, the color blue relates to the throat chakra. It is important to remember that listening to the child is first and foremost. The H.O.P.E. Chart located in Section one of this chapter might be a helpful tool.

Strategy 6: Rainbow Loom/crochet/sewing

Again creating with your hands allows for a project to take on the energy that is needing to be expelled. It can provide a sense of accomplishment, relaxation, and can provide a holder of emotion for an intuitive and empathic child.

Strategy 7: Heart Based Drawings

Have your child, only using the heart shape, to make an entire picture. Name the picture "Love". Allow them to draw whatever they would like using only the shape of the heart. Frame this activity with the essential guiding questions: What can be created with love?

Strategy 8: Out of this World Rocket Ship

If you could do anything for this world, an out of this world idea, what would it be and why? Have the child draw their rocket ship, decorating it however they feel led.

Strategy 9: Sand art

Using different colored sand and a jar that a child chooses, allow them to pour in the different colors that represent the layers of their feelings that day. For example, if the bottom of the jar was symbolic of the space closest to their heart and soul, then they would put a color that represents that space. See what colors they choose, what the layers look like, what the colors represent (their thoughts or feelings), and seal the jar for their keeping. They can label the jar with glass markers or stickers that have affirmations, coping skills, or simply name the feeling/thought that corresponds with each color.

Strategy 10: Affirmations pillow

You will need a pillow that attracts your child's attention and fabric markers. Your child will write 3 affirmations on the pillow. This pillow can be kept in their sacred space, in their room, or taken with them when they go to new places. The pillow project offers a way to integrate multiple senses into one activity. The mind is incorporated through the affirmations. The pillow helps with emotional regulation and can be used as a self-soothing tool. The body is incorporated by sense of touch. Your child can scream into it, hug it, or rub and stroke it if it has a pleasing texture. The spirit is incorporated by creating affirmations connected to the Spirit realm and Source. When we have a calm body, we have a calm mind. When our mind is calm, our spirit can calm. This is when our SOUL SPACE can be accessed and we can manifest our dreams.

Strategy 11: Dance party

Believe it or not, a really hyperactive dance party can be good at shedding energy and letting go of things (thoughts, sensations, emotions) that are not our own. It gives the negative energy somewhere to go, like when we engage in a creative arts project. My son will say that "the music takes over his mind and he just dances however he feels compelled to". It is great to watch. Totally uninhibited dancing is so fun to be a part of. This also will help them dispel any anxious energy or constriction in their body while allowing for movement of energetic blockages emotionally, spiritually, and/or physically. Some schools incorporate GoNoodle, and brain breaks that utilize some of these strategies.

Strategy 12: Red water balloons

A way to work with your child's anger is the use of something fun and enticing like water balloons. If your child associates the color red with anger, then choose red balloons. Fill them up with water. Have your child talk about what they feel angry about while throwing the water balloons at a safe target. You can even write or put a picture up of what they are feeling angry about on the target. Let's be mindful here that putting a picture of a person would not fit in with the HOPE tribe's mentality and core values. It is the situation with, the feelings that arise from, or what your child sees in that person where the anger originates. Digging deeper is essential. You can also you darts or throwing paper, socks, etc.

Strategy 13: Anger Altar

Allowing your child to create an anger alter, or using any other emotion will provide a 'space' physically and emotionally to cope with anger (or any feeling that needs further exploration). Activities geared to develop emotional regulation, awareness, and even possibly forgiveness, when the child is ready, can be performed or referenced at this anger alter.

Strategy 14: Using our Imagination to play in nature

One aspect of childhood that seems to be disappearing or, lying dormant, is creative play, and using the imagination. Our lives are so fast paced these days that we forget to just let our children be creative, using whatever they can find in nature to imagine a storyline. If you are a believer in Earthing, where you simply connect to the earth by different ways, most commonly standing bare foot on the ground outside, you know the benefits to connecting in both an emotional and physical way to nature and its elements. Allowing children to play outdoors with sticks, dirt, and rocks not only is helping them exercise their imagination, it is connecting them to Source, the creator of everything.

Painting or decorating rocks can be another way to hold elements of nature in your hand and connect to loving, pure, Source energy. Have your child build a fort using materials from the outdoors. Camping trips, or pretend camping trips in the backyard can help with connecting to nature. Skipping rocks in a river or lake, watching the ocean waves or jumping in them can not only be calming and fun, but also elementally and energetically cleansing.

Another idea is to make a stepping stone path in your back or front yard (or indoors if you don't have outside space). Find rocks from outdoor places near your home, or purchase rocks for your stepping path. These rocks can have different textures, be different sizes and heights, and create a natural balance beam of sorts. If outdoors these rocks will naturally shift and change with the elements, making them hotter on sunnier summer days, and cooler in the fall. Walking the path barefoot can provide sensory input for a child, can be soothing, and can just be fun! You can also have the child walk the path as a goal manifestation technique:

Start at rock one which represents a current place/situation/thought/ feeling. Along the way, as they walk the path, ask questions that will help them reach their goal or desired outcome. These questions can include:

- o Who can support you in this?
- o How will you know you are getting close?
- o Where in your body do you feel that?
- o What obstacles/challenges might you face?
- o What positive thoughts can you tell yourself?
- o What affirmations or 'gratitudes' can you send out to the universe about this?
- o What practical steps can you take/ or to do list can you make?
- o How much time/ how long will it take?
- o Is this goal attainable? How do I know?
- o When I get there I will feel? I will think? My body will...? My soul will...?

These ideas all have powerful effects on children. Both their emotional and physical state are touched through this imaginative play in nature. Connecting to nature and integrating imaginative play can have profound positive effects for children. Emoting can take many forms.

Of course, being out in nature is best (hiking, walking, relaxing, enjoying an outdoor activity), but this isn't always possible. Bring the outdoors in. Have plants, water features, and outdoor scenes indoors to aid in relaxation and soothing effects. Some children love the outdoors but our living spaces don't allow for large backyard forts or retreats for these children. Bringing some elements inside can be helpful. Water features are very relaxing, plants can be nurtured like a pet (the reciprocity between caregiving and being cared for with a pet or a plant is profound for children), and their bedroom can have serene pictures of calming outdoor scenes if they prefer (mountains, ocean, forest, …). I have provided young girls with fake flowers that they put all over their room, some in pots, some hanging from the walls, and then they could reorganize the different flowers whenever they wanted to. Changing out the colors in certain place, putting a few away for a while before letting them make another appearance, whatever comes to mind, keeps things fresh and children feeling more "alive" indoors. Simply decorating in new ways is a great tool for emoting and engaging in creative outlets.

More ideas for using our imagination to play in nature are:

1) Create a Rock garden. Decorate rocks with pictures, affirmations, or soulful ideas and put them outside in the garden. Visit them daily and read them as a part of a mindful activity or meditation routine.

2) As a family, go out in nature and draw what you see. To save on things you need to bring, color or paint the drawings when you get back home. Then set up an "art gallery" and have each family member share their picture and talk about what they experienced while out in nature. HOPE tribe children's meeting can do this as well, then friends and family can come view the 'art gallery'

3) Nature Art. Allow your children to walk around in nature, collecting things they find (dirt, rocks, sticks, leaves, flowers, etc) and then provide them with materials like poster board, glue, markers, jewels, beads, and so on. Let them make their own nature scene using nature. You will be impressed with what they create!

4) Dirty Soup: Allow your child to get a large bucket of water and use whatever they find in nature to make their own soup. They can tell you what ingredients they added, what the soup would be good for, how it helps your body work at its best, what the soup when eaten (don't really eat! ☺) can inspire, and create your own questions or 'mindful nature restaurant' to continue this activity!

<u>Strategy 15: The use of Color</u>

According to The Angel Bible by Hazel Raven,

> "color is a universal language that bypasses the logical mind and speaks directly to the soul. Colored rays affect our physical bodies, emotions, moods, mental faculties, and spiritual nature. We all have an intimate and person relationship with color." (pg 103)

Using color in a mindful and intuitive way, can help with behaviors, mood, sleep, eating habits, helping children make sense of their world. Mindful color choices can add to the balance and quality of our lives from the inside out. Using color in our strategies with our children, or having our children associate certain colors with emotions, can help deepen their experience as well as our understanding of their experience. There are 7 visible colors, each one linked to one of our 7 energy centers, and they are said to have therapeutic qualities. I don't know about you, but I certainly have found myself saying things like, "I need a little more color in my life", or "oh I am going to wear that sunshine yellow shirt tomorrow so I smile more", or "oh I feel so blue", or "They were so sick, their face looked green". We associate color to certain feelings, sometimes even experiences and people in our lives. The following are some ideas where color can be used to make a difference in our children's day to day lives.

- painting children's rooms certain soothing colors
- allowing children to pick out their clothes for the day
- asking for colors when discussing a situation

- allowing for different colored light bulbs if your child likes the way it 'makes them feel' or it changes their mood
- colored sand timers can add a depth to the activity (as well as colored kinetic sand, play dough, using food coloring in water, or with rice sensory tables)
- offering many different shades of the same color can also help with articulating certain aspects of emotions (like sad being one shade of blue, disappointment being another, loneliness another, and so on) – you may even ask them to do an entire art project just using 'one color' but all the different shades and hues of that color.
- using hyper color silly putty
- using mood rings as a fun way to open up communication
- using color to help express emotion;
- creating color cards that correspond with your child's emotions that they can post as a way to communicate (not verbally) how they are feeling in the moment

Concept 6: Coping Strategies for difficult situations

When we discuss coping strategies, it is essential to remind ourselves how our bodies, minds and spirit react to something stressful. For our purposes, I would like to talk about stress in a new way. Stress is when something does not happen the way we would like it to happen; when we have an expectation and it is not met. Stress may be as simple as the coffee pot not being turned on the night before, and now our "get up and go juice" is not ready as it is every morning. Stress may also be related to bigger, more significant events that occur. Levels of stress fall on a continuum, however often times our bodies, minds and spirit react in a similar manner, not able to distinguish between lower level, less threatening stress, and higher level, more threatening stress. What happens is we perceive stress and then we become "fearful". Our bodies react from a place of fear and danger, even if there is no "real" danger present. When we are fearful, we come from a place of restriction and constriction, our thinking becomes limited and resources seem limited.

When an empathic child is coping with stress, a sensation that is uncomfortable, and/or a situation that is effecting his body and mind, it is difficult to access soul and core self when choosing a reaction. The H.O.P.E. Tribe wants to help our children begin to think ahead, be proactive, and enter situations with soulful resources by remaining connected to their God given talents, strengths, and abilities. Then they are more likely to act in accordance with who they truly are rather than simply reacting to alleviate discomfort. This is why conversations and connecting with our children is so imperative, because it is in these times that they discover, create, and access their own abilities to tackle tough situations.

Strategy 1: The Finger Technique

Whenever we discuss coping strategies it is critical to think about resources. What will the child have at their "fingertips" in order to help them deal with a challenging situation? For this coping strategy, the only thing your child needs is their own fingertips. Your child's hand is with them at all times. They can easily visualize the steps for coping by spreading out their hand. By counting and labeling each finger with a possible thing they can do, children are able to provide alternatives. When faced with a situation that 'doesn't feel right', 'they want out of', or in response to a feeling they might be experiencing, they carry with them at least 10 possibilities. Examples of possible actions your child can take include, "walk away", "buddy up (find a friend to hang with)", "tell an adult", "take three deep breaths to clear the mind", "focus on your gut feeling", etc.

Strategy 2: Co-regulation of Breathing

When reacting to an emotional stressor, a sensitivity that has been triggered, or extrasensory information that is difficult to understand, children can begin to breath faster and more shallow. This breathing affects sensations in their bodies suffocating the flow of positive and useful energy. This can lead to negative thinking, exacerbating the symptoms. When we are in this place we tend to act from a place of scarcity, fear, doubt, and sensory overload. Helping our children cope in the moment, come back to a soul/heart space of calm and less constricted being, they are able to access deep capabilities to handle the situation more effectively.

Sometimes breathing 'for' and 'with' our children in the moment helps calm them down. They notice our breaths, begin mirroring us, and then they slow down their own breathing. Parents can breathe in the moment when a child is emotionally heightened. Parents must model the breathing. Therefore, it must be heard. Breathe in through the nose, inflating the lungs, holding it for 3 seconds, counting 1 2 3, and then out through the mouth with audible expression for the count of 3. Children feed off of the energy of others and therefore, can respond positively to their parents breathing and behavior during stressful times.

Purposefully making the act of exhaling longer than the act of inhalation is key. Exhaling provides the body with the release and the relaxation it seeks during stress. Inhaling without sufficient exhaling can cause increased anxiety. If the body doesn't have time to take in and let out deep breaths, sufficient oxygen will not be taken to the brain, the place for higher order thinking. The body will neglect the necessary release of "toxins". Shallow breathing can lead to more reactive responses, increased fear, and increased anxiety. Teaching our children how to mindfully breathe allows them to then receive the positive influx of energy and release the negative energy. When done in a mindful and intentional way, breathing allows for more creative, self-aligned, effective strategies for coping.

Parents can also utilize an app called My calm beat. It is an app that you can download on your phone and have access to in the moment. It aids in visual breathing. It utilizes the principles of meditative breathing to help children practice as well as return their breathing rates to a more productive pattern, one that encourages relaxation and problem solving.

Strategy 3: Yawning

Another in the moment technique to calm the autonomic nervous system is yawning. Even forced yawning can do this. If you notice your child needing to self-soothe, calm their body, or ground themselves, you can begin the act of yawning. The act itself is said to be contagious.

Empathic children, like empathic adults, are thought to engage in yawning when they see another yawn. Your empathic child will 'catch' your yawn and reap the physical, emotional, and spiritual benefits.

The yawning mechanism and using it as a tool has been around for hundreds of years. Yawning is thought to "cool the brain" through the flexing and stretching of our muscles. This provides oxygen to the brain. When our brain has more oxygen we can think clearer and handle more challenging situations. Yawning is good for flushing out toxins in the brain. It is thought that this flushing can also create stronger neural pathways and build connections within our brains. This is critical when we are working with stress patterns. When we can calm ourselves, change our pattern of reacting, think of a new alternative and choose a different solution, we are rewiring our brains. This rewiring, when practiced and encouraged, helps us deal with stress, whether deemed "real" or perceived by others, in more productive ways. So keep yawning and encourage your children to yawn. We often hear that yawning is rude, yet yawning is a sign of self-love and, given its contagious nature, a way of reminding others to "cool their brains" as well. It works wonders in our household!

Strategy 4: Poster of Positives

Sensitive, highly sensitive, empathic, and intuitive children can have a lot of fears. Since they perceive people and the world in a different way, they are forced to sort through and integrate a lot of information at any given moment. Some children see spirit and experience apparitions (seeing spirit) and premonitions (knowing what will happen in the future), which can lead to fear. These experiences can include heavy emotions and information. For example, emotional-laden information such as how someone crossed over and even the pain that person felt in that very moment. Some children realize they are "different". They begin trying to make sense of what is happening for them and why it is not happening to others. This can leave them feeling afraid of social situations, darkness, certain places, etc.

In order to cope with such intense feelings, you might have your child create a Poster of Positives. This will help dispel thoughts and feelings associated with fear. Example: My son created his own mantra, "Dark or light, I will have no fright" to tackle his fear of the dark.

This personal motto or mantra can be written on a notecard to carry with your child, hung up as a poster in a highly visible place or be placed in a "sacred space" as a reminder. My son has an intense fear of the dark. He has difficulty falling asleep on his own at night. He created his own poster, which included his mantra, to help him face this fear. He now uses this in times of need. As his parent, now I have a tool to direct him to. He is reminded of this daily because it is posted in his room.

Strategy 5: Systematic Desensitization

My son was terrified to go up the stairs by himself. His love for video games and 'beating levels' prompted an idea for him to explore going upstairs alone. This video game perspective helped him create ways of becoming successful at conquering his stress. I made signs that stated Level 1 – 10, and each day he went up the stairs just a little bit to reach the next level. Once he got to the level marker each time we had a small celebration. When he reached level 10 (being upstairs by himself for 3 minutes), we had a 'huge tackling your fear celebration'. Chunking the task into smaller, more manageable goals to help children face their fears makes it attainable. Talking with them along the way about their experience, and not rushing them through the process is key. Allow for 'setbacks', which are really just additional time to integrate what is being learned at that stage. Try to monitor your own feelings, perceptions, and frustrations with the process. It is a process, and it is in the process where the learning takes place.

Strategy 6: Name it

Give an image and name to the fear. What does it look like? Draw it on paper if your child needs to. What color is it? Where do you feel it in your body? What does it make your body want to do? What does it say to you or make you say to yourself? Is it inside, outside, or both? Describe it in as depth as much as possible, integrating aspects of the mind, body, and soul. After you have a detailed image of the fear, then look at the opposite. Is there an opposite for your child?

Do they have an image of what it means to be fearless? Do the same process for this but make sure this component of the process is even more detailed. Use solid concrete imagery, understanding of how it is perceived in thoughts and physical sensations and feelings. You want to make this part "larger than life" and super positive because we want to outshine the fearful image. Draw attention and focus to the 'fearless' image and make it 'bigger' than the fearful one.

> Example: My son had become afraid of going upstairs in our home. My daughter latched onto this idea after seeing her brother struggle with it for quite some time. I had both of my children sit down and talk about what their fear looks like. My son said his was a huge pink elephant. He said it was so big, heavy, weighing him down, and it told him over and over again to be afraid of not being close to someone and not to be alone in the house. He felt it primarily in his chest, on his shoulders, and his head. His body felt as though there was an elephant sitting on him. This feeling made him feel frozen, like he couldn't move. Behaviors that followed were crying, sitting down or staying still, and becoming frozen in his fear. His 'fearless' image was a green sea spider. He shared that his green sea spider was tiny and would tell him in a soft voice to not be afraid. He didn't know where he felt his 'fearlessness' in his body. He drew them both. Then I simply facilitated a discussion about how we can change this. I didn't tell him what he should do or even give him the idea of how to change it, just asked the question. This is important because it leaves him with the power, the control to change his thoughts and behaviors in a way that helps him live the life he wants to live. He shared with me that he wanted to have some "shrink rays" to shrink the elephant. These special rays could then make his sea spider huge. So we acted out this idea and shrunk the elephant until it was 9 inches tall. Using the same imagery and theatrical activity, he grew his sea spider until it was 50 feet tall. Then we wrote down the things his sea

spider could tell him and how to listen more to his sea spider in times of fear.

We also, because safety and honoring our fear is always important, discussed that feeling afraid can be a helpful by provided a warning to us and our bodies. We shared situations and reasons when fear was useful. We talked about deciphering between "helpful" fear and "unhelpful" fear. We practiced recognizing when to let fear inform our decisions.

Talking to our children is always the best way to help them understand themselves, the situations they face, and strategies for coping with different emotions. My daughter's 'fearful' and 'fearless' images were so different. To her, 'fearful' was a white big ball on her right shoulder, and fearless was a pink ball on her left shoulder. She wanted to catch her fearful ball and put it up high in a box. We searched the house and found just the right size of box. I let her lead this and by doing so she gained a sense of power and control over her fear. I allowed her to share with me the size and characteristics of her fearful thoughts. Then we acted out catching her white fearful ball. We put it up high in the chosen spot.

This strategy is useful in containing our fears and helping give a child control over their situation. It can help your child feel empowered. They can choose different actions, thoughts, and emotional reaction to fears. Helping children see the connection between their thoughts, feelings, and actions allows them to interrupt the process and live more aligned and in tune to their truest self even in the midst of challenging emotions.

Strategy 7: Emoji awareness

Printing out or drawing emoji expressions and asking your child to use them to describe their feelings can be a great way to speak their language and increase their self-awareness. For younger children, I have hung these up, maybe around the house or classroom. When we see one we stop to share something that made us feel that way.

Strategy 8: Ladder exercise

This exercise can be used for many purposes. One way the ladder technique can be used is to incorporate mind, body, and spirit as a way of coping or working through a difficult situation. Think about how you can help your child use the visual of a ladder in order to increase self-awareness, decrease fear or anxiety,

Strategy 9: Elevator Grounding Technique

Draw a large picture of or use a door to represent an elevator. Create buttons numbered 1 through 7. Next, have your child stand in front of the "elevator". Using the child's imagination, start up at the top floor, level 7, and say out loud an affirmation, or a calming statement (i.e. I am able to calm down, I don't have to be afraid, I know exactly where I am, I am okay, I can relax) a total of 3 times. Then press number 6, repeating the same mindful statement 3 times. Then, press button 5, repeating the statement 3 times, and so on until you reach floor or button number 1.

When your child has reached the number 1 have him/her sit on the floor and close their eyes taking 3 deep breaths. Breathe in and out, noticing the breath and the rise and fall of the chest. Allow your child to sit in calmness for a few minutes. Again, follow your child's lead. If longer is needed, then allow more time if possible. This technique provides the space for calming down, and/or coping with a situation before asking questions, or trying to create solutions. This is critical. We cannot solve problems or deal with challenging situations productively if we are not calm and regulated.

Strategy 10: Coping Skill Checklist

Things that I can do if I am anxious, angry, fearful, upset, etc. are:

_____	take deep breaths
_____	listen to music
_____	go for a walk/run - get some exercise
_____	silly putty, playdough, stress ball, etc
_____	play an instrument
_____	write, draw, color, create

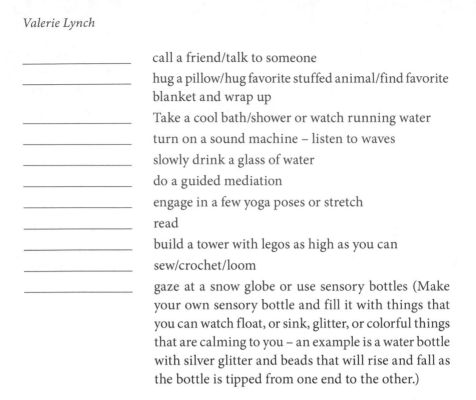

_____	call a friend/talk to someone
_____	hug a pillow/hug favorite stuffed animal/find favorite blanket and wrap up
_____	Take a cool bath/shower or watch running water
_____	turn on a sound machine – listen to waves
_____	slowly drink a glass of water
_____	do a guided mediation
_____	engage in a few yoga poses or stretch
_____	read
_____	build a tower with legos as high as you can
_____	sew/crochet/loom
_____	gaze at a snow globe or use sensory bottles (Make your own sensory bottle and fill it with things that you can watch float, or sink, glitter, or colorful things that are calming to you – an example is a water bottle with silver glitter and beads that will rise and fall as the bottle is tipped from one end to the other.)

The key is finding what is soothing to your child and what will help reduce/calm any anxiety. All children are different and what one finds soothing another may find agitating (i.e. trying to build with Legos while anxious may create frustration rather than peace, so keeping notes about what works and what doesn't will be helpful).

Create a tool box with your child. This tool box contains coping strategies that work well for him/her when feeling a specific emotion. Specify where this will be kept in order to be used as soon as anxiety/fear (or other emotions) are recognized.

Strategy 11: Blowing bubbles

Blowing bubbles is an excellent coping strategy and it is an excellent way to focus back on breath. Empathic children may experience anxiety, some of which may not be their own. By focusing on their breathing they can decrease anxiety. Blowing the bubble can be symbolic of releasing the emotion that isn't their own. Some might question, "How do you know if it is their emotion they are 'blowing away' or someone else's?"

The quick answer is that it doesn't matter necessarily as long as your child is able to release, focus on breath, integrate, and realign himself/herself. You can ask if they 'saw anything, or felt anything' as they blew the bubble and watched it float away, but this is not imperative. What is critical, however, is that the child is offered a way to calm their system and release whatever needs to be released.

Strategy 12: Worry stone

Buying or creating a worry stone for your child can be useful for reducing anxiety or symptoms associated with fears. You can buy worry stones at metaphysical stores, or online. When creating one, you will want your child to search for their stone, this increases the connection to it and the likelihood of it being used effectively. Ensure that your child finds a stone that has the following attributes:
a) able to fit in their own hand, b) texture of the rock is pleasing (typically smooth is best), c) aesthetically pleasing (they enjoy the look of it), etc. They can hold the rock, carrying it with them in their pocket, pulling it out when they are worried and rubbing it to release their emotional energy. The rock holds the worry, stress, fear, etc. for them. The actual rubbing of the worry stone when feeling anxious is a great mindful way of self-soothing and a physical way to de-stress. If your child would like to, they can paint the rock, put words on it, or collage it with magazine clippings. If your child gravitates toward larger rocks, they can be decorated as well and left at home or in the car to help with fears, anxieties, or as a reminder for affirmations.

Strategy 13: Swinging or Rocking

For many children, the act of swinging or rocking can be soothing. While just a rocking chair will do the trick, sometimes it is nice to have the elements of nature around to provide natural healing remedies that we can't package, bottle, or create. The sounds of nature, such as wind blowing through trees, birds chirping, rivers running, bees buzzing, even road noise, can be soothing. A hammock or a UFO swing that a child can relax in can be beneficial to provide a regulating motion with a relaxed body position. In these types of items, as with other therapy swings, a child can fully relax. Their entire body can be put into a position of their choice, sometimes contorted in ways that seem quite uncomfortable to onlookers. Finding times during a child's day when they can rock, swing, or sway, can be useful for integrating, aligning, shedding, and soothing. It can help calm the body, stimulate healthy prosocial critical thinking and provide a way for a child to decompress in the moment.

Strategy 14: Journaling Exercises

Another tool for coping with difficult situations or feelings, is to allow your child to write, draw, or journal on a daily basis. Some children take to this without any prompting, while some may need to be asked if they want to engage in such an activity. It's helpful if a child also sees a parent journaling, writing thoughts, or engaging in mindful activities. They will assign meaning to the act more readily if they see it in practice by a trusted adult. Journaling (whether its written pages, drawings, painted pictures, or recorded voice) is a way to allow our thoughts and experiences to physically leave our body. Not only does it help with self-soothing, it can aid in releasing any emotions or physical sensations that a highly intuitive and empathic child picks up throughout the day. Some of the feelings and thoughts that come up for a child are those that belong to others. Without an activity to rid themselves of these, their mind and body will continue to hold on. This holding on limits your child and often leaves them confused about their experiences and their feelings.

Concept 7: Setting Boundaries

When discussing physical boundaries, it is essential that we explore our core beliefs about physical touch and personal space. My belief is that physical contact is ALWAYS a choice. I have heard parents, grandparents, and others say things like, "Well, where is my hug?" or "You can open your presents after I get my hug". We must know our children. We must remember that some children may not be comfortable with hugging or just may not want one in that moment. On another level, some children may choose not to have physical contact for reasons beyond our understanding or what may be visible at that time. Respecting our children's space, and their needs/wants regarding physical touch is important. It builds safety, trust, connection, and ultimately honors their experience.

We must also help our children learn how to set emotional boundaries. This can be a difficult task for highly sensitive, intuitive and empathic children. The way in which we learn to set psychological and energetic boundaries, is closely related to our self-esteem and self-worth. It is said that, "we teach people how to treat us". As parents it is imperative that we dig deeper into our own boundary setting so that we can help our children. Setting clear emotional boundaries allows for the development of healthy relationships, in which mutual respect, support and love can truly flourish.

Strategy 1: "You are in my Bubble" exercise

You will need different sizes of hula hoops for this activity. Have your child pick up the smallest hula hoop and put it around their waist. Have them circle it around them demonstrating how much space is around them. Tell them that this smallest hula hoop represents their "bubble" or personal space. This space can be bigger with strangers or other people, or even a bit smaller with certain people.

Use the various hula hoop sizes to demonstrate visually space between self and others. Discuss, from an emotional perspective, how to keep emotional space between ourselves and others. During this time, identify people that might require different personal space to be used. It is important to determine how much space your child needs in order to feel comfortable around others. This exercise can be as deep as you see fit for your child at the time. Depending on many factors, this activity may remain at a superficial level until further understanding evolves. The "You are in my Bubble" activity can also be an exercise that deepens over time. This means that the first time your child is exposed to the activity, keep it simple and non-threatening. The next time, go deeper with sharing names of people who might require more space and why.

Subsequent times may call you to go deeper still. This may require child and parent to discuss how to uphold emotional boundaries, as well as ways to conquer taking on feelings/sensations that are not our own.

Strategy 2: Bubble of Protection

Guide your child in imagining a bubble around themselves. Have them visualize all aspects of this bubble, the color, how thick it is, etc.? This bubble is their protection and symbolizes what is let in and what is kept out. Imagine this bubble surrounding your entire body. It can surround your home, your classroom, your school, a group of friends, whatever it needs to surround in this moment or for this day. The bubble only lets in good and positive things. As you go throughout your day, allow this bubble to fully surround you, allowing only good to enter.

Another way to use the Bubble of Protection is to cut out several copies of bubbles or draw your own bubbles to pop. or blow bubbles and as you pop a bubble engage in this exercise. Each bubble will represent a way to protect or shield yourself from negative things. It can be coping strategies, names of supportive people, positive thoughts or affirmations, and activities that help you stay focused on or feeling positive. Write down different strategies that help your child feel empowered to be who they truly are and express themselves.

Strategy 3: Spiritual Shield Exercise

This activity can be utilized when coping with a certain stressor or as a general protection strategy. It can help you build strong emotional, energetic or physical boundaries as needed.

If used for a specific situation, write the situation with as many details as possible. Then in the shield color, draw, or write things that can help with that situation. For example: A child is being teased by another student at school.

Example Situation: Robert is calling me names, pushing me, holding me down on the black top, and taking my food at lunch recess every Tuesday and Thursday. He only does this when I am alone or with one other friend. I have tried telling him to stop but he won't. My teacher knows about it, and has told Robert to stop as well. It keeps happening.

Outside the shield (the situation): The child colored blue because he felt sad about the situation. He felt like he didn't have a voice to fix the problem. His school color is blue so this makes sense as well. The child then drew Robert pushing him. He wrote the names Robert was calling him which included stupid, dumb, crazy, weird, cry baby.

Inside the shield (His protection strategies): He wrote down 3 new ideas (one he has not tried yet) to deal with the situation. These included: 1) Ask a friend to find him and sit with him every Tuesday and Thursday, 2) Have his mother contact his teacher, 3) Use a self-defense karate move -- not intended to hurt Robert but get him to let go of him when he holds him down on the blacktop. He colored the inside of the shield Red because he stated that it is a 'powerful color'. He said it will help him use a stern and angry voice as well as help him have a fire inside. He wanted to ignite a fire in order to do something and face his fear of sticking up for himself. He then chose to draw a fire (like a campfire).

Then discuss this shield with your child. Look at the situation from as many angles as possible, discussing what your child perceives and what your child perceives as possible solutions. This activity can be used for many different types of situations or in different ways with your child. Another example, is helping your child face a fear of the dark. Draw a protective shield and hang it up in your child's room or on their door.

Strategy 4: Role playing or psychodrama

Role playing is an activity that can be modified for any type of situation, even helping a child discuss emotions. Role playing can also be very effective for discussing and teaching boundaries. The term boundaries ranges from boundaries with others, to boundaries with self. Use Role Playing or Psychodrama to teach social skills, coping with bullying or teasing, and more. All of these topics are actually related to the topic of boundaries. Understanding self is in fact rooted in boundary setting. In order to operate in the world effectively, knowing self is the greatest tool for exercising the use of healthy boundaries.

According to psychcentral.com, there are several ways to better build better boundaries. The following are a few quick ways: 1) knowing and naming your limits, 2) pay attention to your feelings, 3) communicate directly and openly, 4) asking for support, 5) learning how to be assertive, and 6) self-care. (10 ways to build and preserve better boundaries by Margarita Tartakovsky, M.S. updated May 2018) This is what H.O.P.E. Tribe does for our children. Helping them learn these skills will allow them to act in accordance with their true self out in the world and internally. Role playing then can help 'teach' and act these skills out in a way that is meaningful for your child. Use different situations from the past or present to 'act out' healthy boundaries. Remember that good boundary setting begins with knowing self (abilities, talents, and limits). Use role playing to address all aspects of creating boundaries.

An example of role playing that our family did with our son demonstrates how understanding self can help create appropriate and healthy boundaries that aid in healthy, expressive, and joyful living. He was invited to a laser tag birthday party. He often becomes agitated, emotional (crying), has difficulty emotionally regulating when noises are too loud, and becomes anxious and afraid in the dark. Laser tag activity combines two of his greatest sensory dislikes. In order for him to participate, we purchased noise cancelling headphones. We let him try these out at home and turned the television up as loud as it would go to help desensitize him to it. We then role played a situation where he put the headphones on and a child whom he did not know who was attending the birthday party approached him. In our acting, this child made a facial expression and said, "What are those?". We helped our son think of some quick responses. Then the other child questioned, "Why do you need those?" We helped our son with responses to this question, one of which was "I have super-sonic hearing". Then the other child said, "Those are weird". As a family we came up with things my son could say in response to that comment, like "Thank you", and "I know, it's great!", "these things come in many different colors", "you should see how brighter the colors are if you aren't needing to hear it all, too". We played this situation out until we couldn't think of any more comments the other child could make.

This was to give our son increased confidence in his ability to cope and engage in the party, which he desperately wanted to attend. It also helped him not change who he was, what he wanted to do, and he could remain himself yet understand his own limits. He was creating boundaries around what he needed to enjoy the activity. He needed to know how to not absorb any negative thoughts or feelings that might arise from other's perceptions of his needs.

When we role play the tough situations of life, we help our children not only navigate the circumstance, but we create the tribe for them. We are honoring what they need in the moment, supporting them, and they know they are not alone in their struggle. I love my super-sonic hearer! Boundaries start with self-awareness, so role playing emotional reactions to situations can increase self-confidence around setting healthy boundaries with others.

Concept 8: Promoting a Healthy Vessel

Viewing our physical bodies as vessels, a "container" for the soul, allows for people to see the importance of taking care of their body. Being a good steward of our body, is being a good steward of our soul. Our time on this Earth is within this body. For us to live out our soul purpose, we need our bodies to be as healthy as possible. Promoting a healthy vessel allows our soul's work to occur 'through' us and 'for' us. How do we promote a healthy vessel?

Strategy 1: Daily Movement

Encourage daily exercise based on age appropriate recommendations and your child's ability. According to the CDC, the following are recommended for children around the age of five to adolescence.

- Aerobic Activity = 60 minutes per day of activity (activities at school count towards the 60 minutes)
- Muscle and Bone Strengthening= ensuring the child participates in exercises that promote muscle strengthening 3 days per week.

Strategy 2: Hydrate

Drink lots of water and stay hydrated. Water is not only vital to life it can help us feel our best self. Connecting to water, connects us to source, to life. When we are hydrated our bodies work at their best. Water can be a powerful cleaning and soothing tool, whether its drinking it, soaking in it, or running hands through it. Symbolically, water helps us connect to the 'flow of life'.

Strategy 3: Tech Time-outs

Take technology time-outs. Give your child an opportunity to sit in his or her own body, mind, and soul self without being stimulated or inundated with electronic energy. Help your child, especially if they are wired to obsess about electronic usage, understand how the mind needs time to regroup. The mind needs to quiet itself, and recharge from stimulation. This helps us stay connected to reality and ourselves in a mindful, intentional way.

Strategy 4: Mindful Meal

My family's mantra is "Eat Alive Feel Alive". When talking to your child about eating habits and choosing foods, allow them to participate in meal planning, in the act of grocery shopping, and in finding out more about what foods do for and to our bodies and minds. Help them better understand the connection to what we put in our bodies and how we feel. Don't stop with just food, but also our thoughts when we eat certain things. How does the food we choose make us feel? When we feel a certain way, who do we choose to spend time with? What is the energy that we bring into our bodies and our lives?

One activity is to create and eat a mindful meal as a family. Look up different foods that are thought to boost immune support, be good energy sources, support intuition, or support clarity of mind. Then shop for the ingredients. I recommend, if possible, going to an outdoor Farmers Market for the shopping experience. This can make the experience even more meaningful by being outdoors and with local farmers. Next, make the meal together. Sit down for a "mindful meal". If you don't have time to do this full activity, you can also ask your child to draw a mindful meal, and color it with the colors symbolizing for them the different aspects of self. Next, they can share the mindful meal with you. It is suggested that you make one as well and share it with them.

Strategy 5: Managing Fatigue Exercises

When managing empath fatigue, remember to see it from the child's perspective. Empath fatigue is a 'real thing' and people must master the art of managing it. Children need practical tools to help them manage their fatigue. Empathy fatigue can lead to burnout and depressive symptoms if not managed effectively. Children, due to feeling physically and emotionally drained, can display anxious reactivity. This anxiety can manifest as feeling 'stuck', disengaging (literally not wanting to leave home), and creating a negative feedback loop of thoughts and actions. This negative feedback loop creates a cycle that the child begins to become accustomed to and soon they perceive it as a 'normal' way of living. What this loop does however, is remain surface level, never checking in with soul. The loop is focused on aspects of ego self that are informing the child. Empath fatigue is a response to overstimulation and difficulty separating self from other. To effectively combat this, the child will have to begin to understand different sensations in the body and mind that allow him/her to interrupt the loop and take a detour to their soul space. In this space then they can begin to recognize the degree of their fatigue, the source of their fatigue, and then ultimately how to manage it.

One way to combat fatigue is to ensure that your child gets adequate sleep. This will be essential to their emotional and physical health. While this is true for all children, it is vital to empathic and intuitive children because they can become more tired, drained, or taxed due to integrating, receiving, shedding, and shielding themselves from so much energy they pick up throughout their day. Having a routine, a bed time schedule, and having your child fall asleep at roughly the same time each night can help aid in better sleep, and better rest habits.

In my home our bedtime routine consists of bath, brushing teeth, oracle card (my son prefers to use his oracle deck at night and pick for the following day), writing chosen card on his calendar (he uses

Dragon oracle cards and he has a yearly calendar with dragon pictures), journaling thoughts if he would like, then reading for at least 15 minutes prior to bed. Lights out is at 8:30 (he is 8 years old) and he is asleep by 8:45.

The morning routine helps the night time routine and vice versa. They are cyclical and each informs the other. Putting routines in place help with predictability, consistency, creating safe spaces, promotes connection and helps children with fatigue symptoms.

Another way to help with fatigue is to allow your child to take a nap if they state they are tired. If a nap is not possible, offer a relaxing space to read, write, or listen to soft music. Sometimes sleep is what our children's body needs to regroup and rejuvenate (literally and figuratively). As my son says, "sleep is what gets our aura ready for the next day".

I am sure we have all heard the saying, "a body in motion stays in motion". For children who are empathic and intuitive, they can feel tired much of the time. This might feel like something is weighing them down and they can't articulate what it is. Exercise and physical activity can actually help them shed this energy, returning more lively and uplifting energy that provides motivation and drive to continue with tasks and/or activities. Another way to combat empath fatigue is regular exercise or movement. I am lucky, my children's public school has one of the best Running Clubs in the nation. The children work towards individual, class, and school goals with regards to walking/running and physical exercise. My children are given ample opportunities, based on their age and interest, to engage in physical activity daily. It not only helps them in the academic sector, it helps them emotionally, socially, and energetically. On a soul level they are provided an opportunity to expend any unwanted energy, cleanse their soul by natural internal processes (physically and mentally), are allowed a time of deep connection to self by being outdoors in natural elements, and are replenishing their body with healthy energy for the day. Exercise does aid in better sleep, and when a child sleeps better their body can rejuvenate in its intended way leading to better outcomes in all facets of life (including but not limited to physically, mentally, socially, academically, intuitively, and soulfully).

Strategy 6: Use Tapping/ EFT

EFT stands for Emotional Freedom Techniques. Tapping is a psychological acupressure technique that can help with a person's emotional wellbeing. It can remove negative emotions, reduce or eliminate pain, help with manifesting goals, and manage fatigue. Tapping, with your fingers, puts "kinetic energy onto specific meridians" of the body. While you are thinking about the specific situation/feeling/problem, you tap in certain patterns. Eventually you add positive affirmations.

Emotional blocks are short circuited and balance can then be returned to your system. Nick Ortner has written "The Tapping Solution" and you can watch videos and even download word for word tapping sessions. One video that comes to mind is on exhaustion. When I think about empathic children who take on all the 'stuff' of the world and the energy around them, they can quickly become depleted and enter into a state of soul exhaustion.

This technique can also be utilized in the moment. Just the other day my children were arguing, and it went on and on with no change from my 'interventions'. I could feel myself becoming overwhelmed, impatient, and starting to feel tension in my body. My heart began to race and my breathing became more and more shallow. Out loud I said, so they could hear me, "I am feeling overwhelmed with all this arguing. I am going to tap". I began tapping on the current emotional state I was in due to the situation. The first 20 seconds they kept arguing. I kept tapping. Then they started laughing, saying, "you look silly mom". I continued the tapping process. Soon they sat watching me. I tapped for 3 minutes. I ended my tapping with the affirmation "My body can be calm, and I don't have to feel overwhelmed". Amazingly, (well, and not so!) both of my children and I sat quietly for several seconds after that. Their arguing ceased. Some might say the change was caused by the mere fact that I was tapping and it created a distraction. I would say, "Awesome" because the goal was ultimately to help them stop the negative interaction. However, my personal belief, based on how I feel after tapping, is that tapping in that moment not only helped me calm my body, mind, and helped me act from a soul/heart space moving forward, but provided an example. It was an example for my children to mirror (subconsciously in the moment) in order for their body to begin to calm, soothe, change an emotional pattern they were stuck in with each other. Ultimately, we were able to move forward. I encourage parents to try tapping for themselves and with their children. There are even videos of tapping in the classroom – a possible H.O.P.E. Tribe meeting discussion for parents! (https://www.thetappingsolution.com)

Strategy 7: Circulate positive energy

Make a list of things that help invigorate or 'circulate positive energy' for your child. This list can be kept on a notecard in their backpack, pocket, in the car, in their room (or all of these places) for ease of using. Be creative...use a color, an image of them doing something they love, a goal they are working towards, etc.

Strategy 8: Mine vs. Theirs

This activity might help your child to begin to notice the difference between their "stuff" and the "stuff" of others.

- I feel tired/drained/taxed/exhausted/sleepy. When I am feeling tired I am more likely to think..... to feel..... to do....
- I know it is mine because (...example: I went to bed late last night, had weird dreams that kept me up all night, and I woke up so tired this morning)
- I know it is not mine because (....example: I slept great last night, I woke up feeling "ready to go", I was excited about my day, then I started hanging out with _____ and I began to feel different. My right shoulder began to hurt a little, my eyes felt like they were straining and then I just started feeling really tired...like I didn't really have energy to do anything)
- 3 things I can do so I can cope with this feeling and still have energy for my day and for ME!

Strategy 9: Kirtan Kriya (see also EFT/tapping exercises)

In her workbook, 101 Trauma Informed Interventions, Linda Curran writes about a technique called Kirtan Kriya. Kundalini is a style of yoga where this technique originated. It combines somatic movements with meditation and is said to aid in prefrontal cortex functioning (pg. 154). The steps are:

1) Have your child sit comfortably, with good posture (if their body allows) and their eyes closed (if they are comfortable with this).
2) Begin deep breathing (see techniques to ensure deep breathing is occurring)
3) While continuing to breath, have your child do the following movements with their hand. (a child may be in a situation where they do not feel comfortable chanting out loud. If so, this can be done in their mind. This technique can be used at school or somewhere wher they can use their hands in a discrete manner (if they are concerned about the impact of this activity on social relations)
   *Touch index finger to thumb and chant Saaaaaaaaaaaaaaahh.
   *Touch middle finger to thumb and chant Taaaaaaaaaaaaaaahh.
   *Touch ring finger to thumb and chant Naaaaaaaaaaaaaaahh.
   *Touch pinky finger to thumb and chant Maaaaaaaaaaaaaaahh.

Strategy 10: Yoga

Finding a family or kid friendly yoga video can provide great exercise and a relaxation routine for empathic and intuitive children. It is a way for them to integrate through body movements while being in a relaxed state. Even having them chant a simple word or phrase, can help them calm their body, center themselves, and allow emotions to be processed.

Strategy 11: Earthing

Allowing children to ground themselves by stepping barefoot outside in the morning, at night, or in a moment of need can help them instantly feel more grounded. Grounding can help your child feel more connected to self and earth. It can raise awareness inside and outside of the body. You may want to ask questions during this process. What do you feel on your feet? Hot, cold? Gritty, smooth? Provide them with questions and allow them to ask their own.

Strategy 12: Sensory Strategies

Children use their five senses, and in our case their "extra" senses, to make sense and meaning of the world around them. Not only is sensory "play" beneficial for brain development it is critical for spiritual development. As we grow we rely more and more on our experiences to make truth. We learn through using our senses to build a foundation of understanding. When we fully integrate our senses with our experiences we have access to vital information. If we are not integrated, we are not allowed to explore all of our senses, our world becomes fragmented and compartmentalized. When this happens, confusion, imbalance, and a lack of trust ensues. If children continue to live their lives from this place of "separateness", they do not have a healthy vessel in which to grow and learn. The vessel, the container for our soul, is left disconnected, unfocused and unable to live from a soulful place. We must provide opportunities for our children to explore their senses and make sense of their world.

One way to offer these types of opportunities is through the use of sand sifting activities or sand timers. Sometimes children just love to watch sand fall through an hourglass. Its soothing, its mindful, and it is methodical in nature. This means they can picture themselves slipping back down into their own body if they have been experiencing extrasensory perceptions, being provided downloads from spirit, are not feeling grounded, or are taking on another's emotions. Time in general for highly intuitive and empathic children can be somewhat of a mystery. Since they see the oneness and interconnectedness, they typically operate on their own time table. They may see life in slow motion, or as if it is rapidly flying past. Time and space have different meaning to them. An hourglass, sand timer, can slow them down and ground them in a way that provides feedback from their senses so that they can understand and integrate.

Sensory tables, often created using water, rice, beans, play dough, kinetic sand, floral beads, shaving cream, and many other materials, can be a very helpful tool to help students integrate and support the maintenance of a healthy vessel. Sensory tables not only help highly sensitive children, but they help empathic children as well. When a child engages in different sensory experiences their brain is receiving the input and integrating it. It can help with children understanding more about their own body, increasing body awareness, increasing coping with uncomfortable feelings, and integrating self-soothing when faced with sensory overload from an external source. Using imaginative play during this time can also help children. Sometimes 'imaginary friends' show up as well. This can be a very special time for you to see how your child handles any extrasensory perceptions, and the presence of spirit if in fact your child has this ability.

Another way to integrate the senses is to take a soothing bath or wade in water. Some children love the feeling of the 'float'. Sometimes they can visualize floating on a cloud, but being in water can provide a soothing sensation. Floating can help with relaxation, time for just 'floating'. Floating can be used to go deep within allowing for a time to relax into the full integration of information, perceptions and emotions. Water also can be energetically cleansing and 'wash away any negative emotions'. Many children are mesmerized by water trickling, making their own rivers, or waterfalls. This visualization can help them shed or let go of any negative energy or situations. It can also be a great time of self-realization and self-exploration.

The sense of smell is extremely powerful. Aromatherapy strategies and using smell can be extremely helpful for your child. Pleasing smells and aromas can help soothe and calm a child's mind and body. Practice self-awareness and what smells children like and dislike. To learn more about the aromas your child prefers you can engage your child in smelling foods at the dinner table, or in grocery stores. Ask mindful questions like, what do you think of when you smell that? Do you like the smell? Do you not like it? What color do you see when you smell that? Does an image or a memory pop into your mind when you smell that?

Essential oils can also be used, however it is important to research what oils are good to use with children and which ones are not recommended. Understanding essential oils, their uses, and how to safely use them around children can be done through online research, reading books, and through finding an essential oil distributor. There are also some new theories about essential oils helping release negative patterns. It can also be as simple as finding a very pleasing relaxing smell, like lemons, and having them smell it to soothe or go inward to a more mindful or soulful place. Please see essential oils book resource list for more information.

My son loves to eat peppermints and enjoys the smell of peppermint. He will randomly, what appears as random but typically is followed up by something that happened at school that worried him, ask for a peppermint to help sooth himself. While eating a peppermint might seem to only use the sense of smell and taste, it is possible to take this and address all senses. An example might be:

- o Taste and smell: suck on a peppermint (the act of sucking is also soothing to some children – even those who have outgrown sucking their thumbs)
- o Touch: he can sit in his bean bag chair (his comfy spot) and be wrapped up in his favorite blanket.
- o Sound: relax to music, turn on singing bowl music or some other music that is relaxing for your child
- o See: what do you see when you are eating the peppermint?

Another sensory strategy and way to promote a healthy vessel, is full body brushing or brushing hair. Full body brushing is helpful for lymphatic flushing and sensory integration. It is also calming and a soothing exercise. This method can also support managing fatigue for you or your child.

In order to help children, heighten their sense of touch you can create feeling boxes. Sometimes you will see these at science or other learning centers. Inside the box there can be different types of textured objects (sandpaper, feather, cotton balls, etc). Without looking with their eyes have your child (or a group of children) feel the object, talk about what they feel, and then guess what the item is.

Sound therapy is an ancient idea that focuses on vibrational frequencies and resonance, how things naturally make a sound based on their vibration. Since everything is energy, energy is not stagnant, therefore the movement creates a sound wave. Singing bowls are increasing in popularity and are inverted bells essentially. When they are struck with a mallet or the rim is brushed they make a musical note. They are used for meditation, vibrational medicine, healing and relaxation.

It is thought by sound therapists and singing bowl therapies that it has many benefits. According to yogayoga.com these include:

- Decreased stress
- Decreased anxiety
- Increased circulation and blood flow
- Increased relaxation
- Decrease pain (used for pain relief)
- Can balance chakras
- Increase mental and emotional clarity
- Stimulates the immune system
- Promotes stillness and mindfulness

These benefits come as we are moved from a place of imbalance to one of balance. Different forms of sound can provide benefits as well. These include things like chanting, saying mantras, listening to music, chiming bells, signing bowls, and more. Allowing children to experiment with sound is not only fun, but can provide great benefits to their inner being. If your child is drawn to music or other auditory input (i.e. enjoys the sound of birds chirping, running water, waves at the ocean, or trains running on tracks, etc) you may want to consider more research into sound therapy and activities that can be conducted at home for relaxation and grounding.

Using sound machines can also be very useful in helping a child calm their mind and body and either relax or engage in a time of self-reflection (soul searching). Some machines have different sounds to choose from (waves, rain, forest, etc). Rain sticks can also be a great tool for children who enjoy sound. Turning over a rain stick a few times to let their "thoughts" sift and fall through them can be useful in calming down prior to making a choice, decision, or in response to emotional reactivity.

The uses of these sensory integration activities, builds on the child 's ability to maintain health. The body is the vessel for the soul. Without a healthy body our soul will suffer. Our focus will, by necessity turn to symptomology of our body, leaving our soul untapped and unfulfilled.

Strategy 13: Hand to belly breathing

Have your child place his/her hand over her belly, and feel how it moves up with each inhale and down with each exhale. Teach them the art of mindful breathing. Inhaling through their nose, holding it for a few seconds, and then releasing it through their mouth. They can naturally make a noise if they feel like it. Talking with your children about effective and mindful breathing is essential. All too often, myself included, our shallow breathing can create somatic and emotional complaints because our body is reacting to ineffective breathing. To stop, breath in and out in a mindful way. This slows the body down, gives it what it needs from the breath, creates the internal space to have soul thoughts, perceptions and be open to flow. The energy in the body is allowed to move completely through when we are engaged in mindful breathing. Shallow breathing can lead to more anxiety, unclear thinking, and scattered thoughts, and acting out of fear rather than Source (love). Children holding stuffed animals or other comforting transitional objects can be helpful in this activity as well.

Strategy 14: Heartbeat

Have your child take your pulse or listen to your heart. hen engage in an exercise like jumping jacks, sit ups, or push-ups, and have them repeat the method. Discuss the differences they notice? Talk about speed, pressure or how they feel it ("bumping harder", "throbbing"), and other observations. Use this information to talk about situations or things that happen during our days that make our heartbeats change to slower (calming down for bed, taking a relaxing bath, listening to calm music) or to faster (running late for school, anxiety about speaking in front of the class, dance party, karate class, mom and dad upset with me). To take this a step further, use this to talk about changes they may notice in their heartbeat if they are picking up someone else's feelings. Use this to help them decipher between theirs and others (did the feeling just come on with no apparent thought or antecedent). You can also share with some children (as appropriate) that when spirit is present with them they can have a physical change or reaction in their body. Sometimes this can be felt as a change in temperature, change in heart palpitations, etc.

<u>Strategy 15: Raise your Joy Factor</u>

When we talk about creating a healthy vessel to house our Spirit driven soul, I am brought to the joy factor! I often would be caught saying, 'let's keep our joy factor up', or 'what is your joy factor right now?" This was a simple way of checking in and also trying to live from a joyful place. Now, with this said, when our child is angry, sad, or upset stating "let's keep our joy factor up" is not an appropriate use of this idea. If we attempt to use this when our child is dysregulated, upset or in a state of fear, we could unintentionally discount their current experience. From our previous reading, we know this is not how we help our children cope, integrate, regulate, and move forward. This idea is more of a norm, something we say at the beginning of the day in hopes to set an intention for joyful and grateful living. We can check in periodically throughout the day or week and ask, "what is your joy factor" (not when a child is in distress, frustrated, or experiencing a visible emotional reaction). We can help find ways to raise it if it needs to be.

Joy factor

1-joy bubble was popped – not joyful at all!

2-

3-

4-

5-bursting with joy!

Concept 9: Investing in Balance

Finding balance can come from personal strength or strategies that we put in place. The H.O.P.E. Tribe also encourages the balance that can be granted from the Divine and the sprit realm. Opening and creating space to allow for Divine intervention, orchestration of events by the Universe, and seeking guidance from other realms or modalities aligns the body from the inside out. Other less spiritual based strategies, are using what is in the physical realm to inform the change from the outside in. Some may see this as reverse. They may ask, "If it is my personal strength why wouldn't that be considered inside out?". Inside we are all created by the Divine, we are a piece of the Divine. Allowing Divine and spirit to work for and through us is living inside out; listening to the call, the pulls, and using personal strength that is rooted in the Divine's love. Finding balance in this way may mean the use of crystals, nature, and spirit. Calling on assistance of Angels, Angel Guides, and conversations with Higher Self and the Divine can help us find balance between our soul and our physical body.

Strategy 1: Crystal field trip

Take your child to a stone shop, or look through a crystal book. Allow them to pick out three stones or crystals they are first drawn to. Start by asking, "Which ones do you love? Next, allow them to choose three they don't prefer or like the look of. Reading about the stones and their metaphysical healing properties can help your child and you understand more about what they may be experiencing or needing. Having them choose ones they don't like is a way to explore more of what they may be actually needing emotionally. Sometimes children, adults as well, push or repel that which they actually need. I tried this with my sister and my son and I was amazed at the results. It seemed to fit their circumstances.

Strategy 2: Placing or laying of stones on body

Using a guide (or you can purchase a crystal chakra set) find stones that your child can positively associate with each energy center. Make sure that the stone chose is from a list of ones that match that chakra.

Have your child lay down flat on their back or stomach and place each stone either on the body at that chakra site, or next to the body. Meditate or sit with calming music for 5-10 minutes. Remember that child attention spans must be taken into account. A general rule of thumb is that a child's attention span is one minute per chronological year. For example, a five-year old child can reasonably attend or focus for five minutes when interested. It is critical to know your child and their specific needs. Some children will have longer attention spans than others. Engage your child in breathing deeply and relaxing allowing the stones and the body to become one, taking in and letting out what needs to. If your child isn't comfortable with this, then drawing an outline of him on a poster board and placing the stones can also work. This outlined self can be used for many different activities and strategies of self-awareness.

Strategy 3: Use of crystals in everyday life

Your child may want to carry a stone or crystal in their pocket, sleep with one under their pillow, close to bedside, or on an altar created in bedroom. They may feel drawn to hold the stone or crystal for 5-10 minutes during meditations or an unpleasant activity. Some children carry stones or crystals that work with certain goals (i.e. increase communication skills, relationship building, decreasing anxiety or restlessness). For more information, see the examples that follow. According to several websites, the highlighted stones and crystals are noted as being great for children.

Below is a quick reference for some crystals and gems. This is not an exhaustive list.

Calcite
Energy amplifier, can be used for clearing and cleansing

Aquamarine
Increasing courage, intellect, and protection; assists in spiritual awareness and actualization

Agate
Balancing ying-yang energy; stabilizes the aura; promotes strength, increases courage; fosters creativity

Amethyst
Soothes; enhances spirituality; increases stability, strength, and peace; excellent for use with mediations; enhances psychic abilities and awareness

Apache Tear
Fosters forgiveness, aids in grieving; excellent to use with children with trauma of any kind; breaks down barriers to soulful and more aligned living

Onyx
Fosters centering; increases self-control and decrease impulsivity; promotes intuitive guidance

Carnelian
Builds confidence

Celestite
Fosters hope and harmony; increases communication; excellent stone choice to have near while journaling or resting on top of journal; Enhances dream recall

Citrine
Increases positive energy; Fosters warmth, joy, and optimism

Rhodochrosite
Increases love energy; promotes well-roundedness and balance in all areas

Hematite

Excellent grounding stone; decreases restlessness and can be useful to use by bedside for children who have difficulty settling down at night

Jade
Promotes compassion and 'teamwork'; aids in reduction of colic and growing pains in children

Petrified Wood
Provides strength, promotes transformation; excellent stone for grounding

Obsidian
Decreases negativity; excellent stone for grounding, healing, and protecting; Increases clarity of self, including self-awareness of flaws and areas of growth; fosters taking responsibility for self

Smoky Quartz
Promotes more peaceful sleep and decreases nightmares; Reduces anxiety by decreasing irrational fears; promotes grounding, balance, and increases positivity; excellent to use with meditation

Rose Quartz
Aids in addressing issues surrounding emotions, thoughts, and behaviors resulting from abandonment (perceived abandonment as well)

Turquoise
Increases spiritual attunement and alignment; excellent stone for strength, grounding and protection; excellent for astral travel

Pyrite
Protecting and shielding from negative energy; enhances intellect and memory; symbol of the sun and can increase positive energy and bring love and light

Kyanite

Stone that aligns all chakras; promotes tranquility; increases communication; raises psychic awareness; excellent stone to use for mediation; aids in dream recall and a good stone to keep near bedside or a dream journal

Lapis Lazuli
Increases wisdom; stone of protection; enhances creative expression (excellent stone to use as your child engages in artistic expression or have near when utilizing artistic outlets)

Lepidolite
Provides stability, hope, and acceptance; reduces anxiety around change and transitions; increases honesty and emotional integrity; Enhances astral travel.

Strategy 4: Rock path exercise:

Put the stones on the floor in order from base chakra associated stone up to crown chakra. Have your child, while standing upright, engage in a quick visual meditation. Facilitate your child imagining their body having roots out of their feet. These roots go deep into the earth. Now, draw their attention to a white light coming in to the top of their head (their crown chakra). After three deep breaths with this visual in their mind, have your child walk barefoot stepping on each stone saying an affirmation that goes with that chakra. Work your way up, then back down again, ending at the feet. At the feet, facilitate a quick grounding meditation where the child visualizes (as they stand upright) roots going from bottom of their feet deep into the Earth, providing a strong foundation and bringing them back into grounded awareness.

Strategy 5: Crystal Grid Making

Crystal grids are thought to combine power of the crystals with the power of thoughts, or intentions, and manifest goals more quickly. While there are many crystal grid resources, and some crystal grids are quite extensive to make, the power here is coming from your child's intention and the process in making it. It combines law of attraction, the power of our thoughts, and then is enhanced by the natural energies of the stones.

How do I make a crystal grid?

1. Find a piece of paper, cloth, or something to put your grid on (it will need to be something that can be used for a period of time, like several days).
2. Find a place in your child's room or your home (it can be near or by their sacred space, anger altar, angel altar, or emotion altar if they have created one). The place should be fairly out of the way so that the grid can rest in its position without being messed up by accidental bumping, or if friends visit, these kinds of situations.

3. Write on a piece of paper your goal or what you are hoping for (be as specific as you can)
4. Choose stones that align with your intention (see list from above); allow your child to trust their intuition on what stones they are drawn to for their intention.
5. Choose a center stone that will be where all the others originate, and point, towards.
6. Clear the space where you will put the grid. Clear by smudging, singing bowls, or other forms of clearing (you can also just set an intention that the space be cleared).
7. Read your intention, goal, hope and then fold the paper, placing it in the center of the paper, cloth, or other item.
8. Take 3 deep breaths in and out thinking of, or saying aloud your intention
9. Begin to place the other stones around the center one, starting outside to in. Finishing by placing the center stone in the middle either near, on top of, or under the written intention.
10. Use a quartz crystal, and draw an invisible line staring on the outside between each stone to energetically connect them (like you are doing a dot to dot and each stone is a dot), ending in the center.
11. The grid can stay out as long as your child would like, continuing to check in with your child about their intention and where things are in the process for them. This is a good conversation starter!

Strategy 6: Use of Oracle Cards

Using child friendly oracle cards, engage your child in this unique process. Again, connection to the cards will be key. In order for children to remain enthusiastic and curious, they must feel connected to the tools they use. This helps children establish relevance and meaning in their lives. My son uses Dragon Oracle Cards by Diana Cooper. My daughter is drawn to "cute" fairies and animals, so naturally prefers these types of sets. Don't forget you may want to get your own set! Oracle cards can be used daily, which can consist of starting your day by pulling a card from the deck. Then by reading about what that card means, you are able to set intentions or simply be reminded of what you might want to be aware of during the day. Discussions at the end of the day about the card and how it "showed" up throughout the day can be powerful. This is a way to create space for connection and communication.

Cards can also be used in the moment to create a positive distraction for a child. Pulling a card during a difficult situation (only if the situation fits such an intervention) can provide another angle in which to approach the situation. This can allow for emotional detachment, which may afford the child needed space to feel and think through the situation from a different perspective. Again the adult must know their child and the situation. An in the moment judgement call about the appropriateness of such an "intervention" may be necessary.

The following are possible ideas for Oracle Cards. There are many offered through Hay House, found online and even found in local bookstores.

- Cherub Angel Cards: Doreen Virtue
- Children's Spirit Animal Cards: Dr. Steven Farmer
- Magical Unicorns: Doreen Virtue
- Flower Therapy: Doreen Virtue & Robert Reeves
- Native Spirit Oracle Cards: Denise Linn

Strategy 7: Angel Meditations and Seeking Angelic Assistance

Asking for assistance from the Spirit realm, as stated above, can provide support. This support often comes in a distinct type of 'balancing'. Some people express an 'unknowingness' of how to access spirit or receive assistance in this way. Here this myth is debunked.

We all have access to the Spirit realm. We all come from the Creator, Source love and light, and therefore we are connected always to the spirit realm. Disallowing this connection, often done by resisting "what is", is where the breakdown occurs. Prayers, meditations, journaling, and other forms of widely accepted forms of connection to 'Spirit' are just a few ways to open up the channels for guidance, inspiration, and support. Another way is through guided meditations. Guided meditations can access different Archangels, a higher self, your Spirit Guides, or other souls with whom you had a connection but have crossed over. Those who have left the Earth realm and now reside in the Spirit realm, can be powerful "assistors" for our time here on Earth. With the following meditations, you may also consider energy work, such as Reiki healing sessions, Mindfulness classes, cord cutting, etc. Another consideration is meeting with an intuitive or psychic medium for some guidance. Remaining open, paying attention to signs, and following your intuition is key to accessing the Spirit realm for assistance. This assistance can guide you and your child to a higher, more purposeful, intentional life.

One resource that I have found extremely helpful has been "The Angel Bible" by Hazel Raven. (2006)

The following are recommended mediations and information from this resource.

- Angelic Temple Meditation   Page 159-160
- Archangel Michael Meditation   Page 162
- Archangel Uriel Meditation   Page 164
- reference for inner child and past abuse Page 349

Strategy 8: Angel worksheets

Begin all meditations for these worksheets with the following:

1) Find a comfortable place to sit, or lay down
2) Take 3 deep breaths in
   i. Inhale through nose, filling up lungs, holding for count of 3, then deep exhalation through your mouth for at least 3.
   ii. A child may benefit from hand to belly breathing (see strategy) to ensure most effective breathing to calm their body
3) Breath as much as you would like until you feel your body is calm
4) Begin meditation that is matched with the Archangel for the situation/feeling/thought/goal/etc
5) Finish each meditation in same way: When you come back to the place you started take 3 deep breaths in (the same way you

started), then begin to wiggle your fingers and your toes slowly bringing yourself back to the present, your current awareness. Write down, or tell someone who will write down, anything that you would like to remember from this experience.

ArchAngel Uriel: "Fire of God" (RED)

Associations: Increase courage, give yourself a boost, let's put it into action.

List 3-6 things that "ignite my fire" (boost my will to do something, motivate me, increase my joy) These things are...

1._____
2._____
3._____
4._____
5._____
6._____

Guided Bonfire Meditation: Feeling how relaxed your body is now, in your mind's eye (or you can use the term imagination) see a path. What does this path look like to you? Dirt, paved, even, uneven? What is beside this path? Trees, sand, ocean, dessert landscape? You begin walking slowly taking notice (can say looking around at what you see) of what is around you. What do you hear? What do you smell? What colors do you notice? Any numbers represented? (4 birds flying by, 3 tall trees, etc). You follow this path and you come upon a bonfire. Here there sits many different tree stumps and large rocks for sitting (or a bench, or comfy chairs). You pick one. What does it look like? What does it feel like? You get comfortable. Then other people begin to join you. Who are they? Friends? Family? Angels? People you haven't met yet? They take their places. You are all connected together. In the middle sits a fire ring (small stones making a circle where a fire will be lit). Say out loud or in your mind something you would like to see happen or that you are working towards. These people (Angels, animals, etc) share their talents and strengths with you, and you with them. Think now of all the things you are good at. What are they? Do you get a chance to use them often? Would you like to use them more? Is there something you would like to be better at? Is there someone here who can share that with you? What do you really like? What makes you feel motivated? In front of you there are several sticks, fuel for this bonfire that is about to be lit. Pick up a stick and say out loud or in your head something that you are good at. Then put the stick in the middle. Pick up another stick and say out loud or in your head something that really makes you feel joy. Put it in the middle. Then another stick, doing the same for something that helps you get motivated. Then another, for something that you can do to help you get to the outcome you are wanting. Do this with as many sticks as you want/need. On your final stick, ask for help with something. Maybe it is a strength you wish you had, some attribute you might need to help you reach your outcome, something you would like to learn, something you would like to improve on. Toss the final stick in and then watch as God ignites the fire. As the fire is ignited with Source love you are filled with passion, motivation, and the willingness to do what it takes to try to reach your goal. Sit as long as you would like at this bonfire. Feel the warmth of the flames. Feel the warmth of everyone and everything around you. Be connected to them, to your goal, to your strengths, and to your desires. When you are ready to leave, simply say "thank you" and rise. Begin slowly walking back down the path you came. Is the path the same? Anything change? What is around you? Still the same? Different? How does your body feel? Same, different? Any sensations you feel in your body? Any thoughts you are having along this walk back? …End meditation with universal ending (see outline above)

Activity: Draw an image of fire with sticks at base. Write on the sticks answers to the same questions in the guided meditation. Then your child can color the fire to add extra depth to it. Their fire need not be traditionally colored – remember creative expression!!!

ArchAngel Gabriel: "Creativity and dissolving fear" (ORANGE)

Associations: can call on Archangel Gabriel for grief/loss, increasing optimism, joy, and when observing signs/symptoms of prolonged sadness (depression)

Guided meditation: Painting a work of art

Begin meditation with universal beginning... You are completely calm and relaxed. Pay attention to your breath. In your mind's eye (or imagination) you turn around and in front of you is a blank canvas, the biggest piece of paper on the wall you have ever seen. You notice that you have as many colors and items to use for decorating this picture. Begin by picking up your first tool. Is it a paint brush? A sponge? A Q-tip? Pencil? Marker? And start working on a beautiful creation of who you are and who you want to be. What colors are you using? Are you using the same tool or switching it up? Are you creating textures, or is it all smooth? Is it bright or dull? Does it cover the whole wall or is it smaller? How are you feeling as you paint this? Sad, mad, empty, open, excited, worried, lost, hopeful, happy? Think now of the person you are. Pick up a color and a tool that would represent you? What is it? Why did you choose that? Think about what you would draw on this blank canvas to symbolize or show others who you are. Begin your drawing. What is it? An animal? A list of words? You doing something? A self-portrait? A scene? Just colors? Spend as much time as you would like here. Then think about who you want to be. Is it the same as what you have already created? Want to add more? What colors? What words come to mind? What images do you see? What do you hear? Put them all on the canvas. Spend as much time here. Creating, expressing, discovering, and finding you. Then when you are done. Take a step back. Look and marvel in amazement at your creation. It's beautiful. It's perfectly imperfect. It's you! Is there anything you would like to add? If so, add it. Just remember there is no getting frustrated in this moment about any 'mistakes', things you don't like, or things you would change...only adding. For who we are is because of those things, too. Now take a deep breath. On the inhale say, "I am a beautiful creation of God (or Source/Universe/Love)" and on the exhale say, "I let go of any negative thoughts or things. I accept who I am in the moment and where I find myself". Then look at your creation again. Really see it. Get a mental picture. Image that you are taking a picture of it with a camera. Click. Capture it. Then, when you are ready, end the meditation by using the universal meditation ending.

Activity: Try to recreate what you made in your meditation.

Activity: Draw and image of a painter's palette. Use this to identify ways to increase creativity, increase joy, or cope with loss (what does each color represent to the child?)

Archangel Jophiel: "Goal Manifestation" (YELLOW)

Associations: Increases concentration, focus, self-control, courage, self-esteem, enhances learning.

Guided meditation: Book (start to finish – end is the goal, chapters are the steps you need to take to get there and Angelic support along the way) Begin meditation with universal beginning. Find yourself holding a book. This is a book about you. It is a book that contains answers, strategies, and ideas for a situation or a problem that you are trying to solve (it can be a goal they are trying to reach as well). Is the book big? Small? What color is it? Is it rough? Smooth? How thick is the book? Is it heavy or light? Flip the book over. The back of the book has a situation/a problem/a goal/ or something you are working towards written on it (or a picture depicting this). Take note of what it says. Then flipping the book back over to the front, the front is your current place (where you find yourself in the situation, the problem). (Again it can be a picture depicting this or simply your name). You take note of where you are. What do you feel? Are you frustrated? Are you worried you won't get to the end of the book (ie. The goal/the outcome/solve the problem)? Are you sad? Are you giving up? Once you are aware of where you find yourself, you open the page. This book has as many pages as you would like it to have, but at least 3. The pages are blank and they are waiting to be written on. These pages represent ideas, thoughts, or strategies for getting to the end of this book, and reaching the goal (or finding resolution to a situation or problem). Look at the first blank page and think about where you are headed. What is one thing you can do to help get yourself there. Write in on the page in your mind's eye. When you have it, reread it, then turn the page. Another blank page awaits. Here write the name of someone that can help you or assist you in your pursuit. When you have imagined writing that name down, reread the name, then turn the page. Fill in as many blank pages of this book as you can with people, places, thoughts, ideas, strategies that will help you reach your end page. When you have reached your final page (can't think of any more) then close your book. Flip your book so you are holding it with the back facing up (your goal/outcome/result facing up). Put your hand on top of the book and say, either out loud or in your head, "I will try my best to get here." "I will look for others who can help me get here" "I ask for God and the Angels to help me reach this if it is for my greater good". "I can do this" "show me signs along the way that help me know I am doing what is right in this situation". Then say "thank you" and flip the book back over. Finding your current place, begin the universal meditation ending.

Activity: Draw an image of a book. Each part of the 'story' represents some aspect of the child. Front cover=current place

Back cover=end result/goal/outcome (you can also use an actual paper book that is inexpensive at craft stores).

Pages= 3-6 steps to take (the action to get there)

Archangel Raphael: "Healing and Harmony" (GREEN)

Associations: increases intuition, aids in healthy relationships, soothes all senses, stabilizes nervous system, decreases restriction.

Guided meditation: Pieces of the puzzle. Begin universal meditation beginning. Imagine you see puzzle pieces spread out before you. Does this puzzle have many pieces (like a 1000 pieces) few pieces (like 25), is it difficult/challenging, seem like it is going to be easy? You sit with the puzzle pieces. Finding one that grabs your attention first. You look at it. What do you see? What color is it? Why did it grab your attention? Does it have writing on it? A picture? Part of a picture? What do you think this puzzle piece is telling you about the end puzzle picture. You place the puzzle piece down. Your mind is drawn to another piece that fits just perfectly with the one before. What does this one look like? You sit, holding this piece. What are you feeling while you hold it? Satisfied, hopeful, like you might have the answer, worried, unsure? You put it down and connect it to the other....it fits! Then the puzzle pieces begin to move themselves and connect to others. You sit watching this puzzle come together before your very eyes. You may want to help with a few pieces, or just watch as the puzzle is completed. How do you feel watching? Is it hard to let the puzzle come together? Easy? Do you want more control? At what point do you know what the final puzzle picture is. When the last piece is added, you step back so you can see the entire thing. You take notice of it, as you know this will help you in some way, it is holding an answer for you. Just let whatever you see be what you are supposed to see. Is it just abstract shapes? Is it clear or is it blurry? Is it a picture with words? Is it an animal, a nature scene, or something else? Do your best to see as many details as you can. Take your time and sit with your puzzle. When you are done and have had time with your answer, slowly begin doing the universal meditation ending. After your child is back in their body and current state of awareness, they can write/draw/or verbally share their experience if they feel compelled to.

Draw an image of a puzzle, paint over an old puzzle, or purchase a 'make your own puzzle'.

Symbolically removing some pieces will represent 'missing pieces' to a situation. Discussing, or writing on the pieces action steps, thoughts, or ways to 'complete the puzzle' will provide action items for the child and provide some closure to a situation.

What are 3 (or more) things I can do to help this situation that do not compromise myself (Ex: how can I handle this problem with my peer)

1._____

2._____

3._____

Archangel Michael: "communication" (BLUE)

Associations: increase communication, able to speak truth, calms the mind, thinking made clearer

Guided meditation: Begin with the universal meditation beginning. In your mind's eye see yourself standing in the middle of a white room. The walls are pure white, the floor is pure white, the ceiling is pure white. It is like you are in a cloud room. While you have never been in a place like this before you feel completely comfortable. You are free to be yourself and have whatever thoughts you would like. You begin to imagine a situation that you don't like/don't feel safe in/are uncomfortable with/or someone you are having difficulty expressing yourself to. Picture this situation with as many details as possible. Pay attention to where in your body you feel the tension related to this situation. Are your shoulders tense? Jaw clinched? Stomach hurting or in a knot? Headache? Tightening muscles? Grinding your teeth? What feelings does this situation bring up? Sad, angry, frustrated, confused, scared, uncomfortable, worried? What thoughts do you tell yourself when you think about this situation? Sit with the situation for several seconds, noticing who you are when you are in the midst of this circumstance. Now a bright white light begins glowing over the top of your head. It is white like the walls, like the floor, and like the ceiling. This light is being sent to you from God/Source, and it is the light of wisdom and protection. This light is flowing down to you, through the top of your head, through your body, and out of your feet. It is giving information and grounding you. This wisdom holds the answers, holds ideas that you can use to deal with this situation. What is the light telling you? Do you hear it saying something? Do you feel your body being filled up with strength, courage, or an ability you thought was lost? Do you feel sensations in your body? Do see any images or pictures from this light source? Focus on what is being sent to you. What answers are being offered. Now this white light takes a shape. It surrounds you and it is in the shape of a spiritual shield, one of great protection. When you are in this shield you have the universe and God on your side. You hold healthy and helpful answers to your problem. Is the shield thick? Thin? Is it white or do you want to give it another color? Does it have anything written or drawn on it? Are you holding it or do you prefer to be completely engulfed (surrounded) by it? When you hold this shield you know your own power, your own strength, you feel brave and courageous, you know you can face your fear, you know who to ask for help and support, you are a spiritual warrior on a quest to conquer your situation in a peaceful and healthy way. Stand proud in or with your shield for several seconds. Feel it in your body, feel it in your soul. Say to yourself "I am strong" "I can do this" "I am protected" "I know my Truth and I can stand proud in it". Then slowly begin to watch as the white light comes up from the ground, moving in an upward motion out the top of your head and out through the top of the ceiling. The light is gone but God/Source is still with you, and you have your shield. Then begin focusing on your breathing. Do universal meditation ending. Coming back to your current awareness grounded with love, light, and protection going forward.

(See Shield Activity: Concept 7 Strategy 3)

Archangel Raziel: "The secret of God" (Intuition/Insight) (INDIGO)

Associations: increases focus and attention to deeper personal issues, promotes self-awareness and self-understanding, aids in emotional stability, clears negative thought patterns.

Guided meditation: Begin meditation with universal beginning. Allow your child to really rest into the moment, get calm, sink into themselves. Aloud say that this meditation is for you to discover your greatest secret soul self. What may come up may be a deep personal issue, soulful strengths, some greater understanding to a situation, ways for you to feel emotionally balance in your day to day life, … Pause and allow your child to really let his/her intuition guide her to what this meditation will be for them. Once they have it in their mind (is it a situation they are dealing with, an emotion they are coping with, discovering soul truths) then have them picture in their minds eye a big crown. What does it look like? Siver? Gold? Some other color or material? Get a good visual image of this. This crown represents you as king/queen over yourself. You hold the answers. You can create change. You can make new rules for the way you want to live your life. These rules are healthy, conscious, mindful, and for your greatest good. Each point of the crown holds a jewel. The jewels are different colors. Start at one of the jewels, what color is it? What do you hear when you look at this jewel? What is God/Source/Angels trying to tell you? What is the 'answer'? Move to the next jewel and do the same questioning. Then to the next, and the next … Do this for as many jewels as they see on their crown. Then have them put the crown on their head. Breath deeply, feeling your body fill up with renewed and rejuvenating air, feel how the crown lifts upward to the sky being infused with Source power, love and light. Do this as many times as you would like. Then in your minds eye see yourself staring in a mirror. You see yourself wearing this crown. Look, see, and say, "I have what it takes!" "I am love, and light!"

"I am a part of God, God breathed, God inspired, God created, and I am ready to live my God given life and purpose!". Then end the meditation with the universal meditation ending. Your child can draw a crown, or the image they saw, and then recreate the colors and write on it what information they were given during the meditation.

Activity: draw an image of a crown or have the child make their own crown. Have the child decorate the crown to represent self or what they experienced during the meditation. The jewels represent 'when I know something is right for me in my gut'... what do I think? Body sensations I have? How do I feel? What am I being told from God/Source or my Angels?

Archangel Zadkiel: "Self-transformation" "Cosmic awareness"

Associations: increases inspiration, creativity, and frees imagination, helps with putting 'bigger ideas' into practical actions, decreases addictive behaviors or addictive patterns

Guided Meditation: Begin with universal meditation beginning. In your mind's eye imagine yourself in a rocket ship or some sort of space travel machine. What does it look like? Does it represent you in any way? Does it look like a space shuttle you would see on television? You board this space shuttle as you are today? You get on, push button that says, "out of this world" and you relax, sit back in a seat, and get ready for the journey. You have no fear. You are completely relaxed. What is the seat like that you sit in? Feel it? Soft, fluffy, smooth, cushioned, textured, feel like your bed, a favorite chair, or a chair at school? This mission is to see the 'world' from a different perspective, to see the big picture, and to see how you can play a part in the good of the earth. Then the countdown begins. It is a completely relaxing countdown. 10.9.8.7.6.5.4.3.2.1 Beyond the Earth you find yourself. What do you see? Earth below, to the right, left, in front? How far away are you from Earth? Is it dark where your are? Light? Space as you would see in a science book? Or different? From here you 'get it', and you see what you would like the world to know. What is it? World peace? Helping animals? Saving our planet from climate change? Nothing is right or wrong, too big or too small. What comes to your mind? Say it out loud or to yourself. Now floating here, imagine how your world might be different when this occurs. How would you know it was happening? What changes would you participate in, see, or hear about? Would things change for you in your day to day routine? Would you see anything different in people? Sit with that and relax into the idea as it plays out in front of you. See the world in exactly the way you wish it to be. Now think about 3 things you might be able to do once you return to Earth to start this change. You don't have to bear all of it, the change will come from people like you starting things. Allow yourself to feel excited about possibilities, not overcome or heavy with a large task. What are 3 smaller things you can do to help your world look more like this one. Say them to yourself, or out loud. Maybe you see an image of you doing/thinking the task or the thing it is that you can do. Then once you have explored this, and have your three smaller things (remember these are exciting things you want to do, nothing too heavy, nothing that you feel pressure to do), you get ready to press your button "back to Earth". Breath in deep 3 times. Press it. 10.9.8.7.6.5.4.3.2.1. You land gently, softly back on Earth. Where did you land? Your bedroom, your house, a pool, a lake, the forest, a dessert, on top of a mountain, at a geological site, your school, …? Now you say to yourself the three things that you can do. You hold them in your heart. They are light. They are just what ifs, not too heavy. They are filled with passion and love. You begin to tuck those inside a place in your heart. You do not have to do them right now, or even tomorrow, but you set an intention that you will in fact do them if you continue to feel led to do so. Now begin breathing slowly, deeply. End meditation with universal ending. Have your child talk about or draw their experience. Helping your child put their 'bigger goals' on paper and finding 'smaller strategies' will not only empower them, but will show them how change is a process. It will allow them to take small steps and release any heavy emotions they have attached to the bigger picture.

Activity: Draw (allow child to draw it if possible) a simple rocket ship. This can depict Earth in the distance and can be entitled, 'out of this world' rocket ship activity. Allow the child to write, draw, color or in some creative manner express their ideal world.

Concept 10: Manifesting Intent (Goal setting and manifesting dreams)

In order to manifest your dreams and goals a person needs to be aware of who they are, but it must be a deep, soulful awareness. Using strategies from Concept # (Emoting) can help a child begin to demystify the idea of 'soul' and align with it in an age appropriate way. Here is an example. Using a strategy like "soulful self-portrait" can allow the child to express him or herself in a way that is 'their own'. This portrait can be hung up in their room or in a sacred space. It will serve as a reminder of who they are at a soul level. As parents we need not judge it, or even truly understand it. It holds meaning for them on a level we may never be fully aware. Remaining curious however, can give parents grounding for helping their child navigate their goals.

<u>Strategy 1: Soulful Self</u>

Paint a picture of you, the you only you know. Not what people think you are, or what you think people want you to be. Just paint YOU. Discuss what their soulful portrait looks like – is it even a person? Is it doing a certain job? Does it have physical characteristics like the child who painted it? What colors were used and why? Was it a difficult thing to do or easy? Are there hard lines or soft lines? Does it flow? What can they tell you about their painting? How does it represent them? What do you see? What would be different in their life if they lived from this soulful self rather than the one they do?

This activity is the originating place for manifesting intent. After engaging in this activity then all other strategies for manifesting intent can be implemented. All are brought back to this place for reference and discussion. Referencing or even having the soulful self portrait out during goal setting strategies can be useful. Goal setting needs to be engaging for children. Too often, when we say "let's make a goal", we as parents get the eye roll, the sigh. Our children often believe that goal setting is just about a lengthy conversation about what "they have to do". Keeping goal setting fun, and creative will engage your child in the process and ultimately connect them to their goal. They need to care, get some personal benefit from it, and enjoy the process for the goal to be a priority and achieved. So, when it comes to goal setting and helping our children manifest, GET CREATIVE AND HAVE FUN!

Strategy 2: Rainbow Bridge

Draw a rainbow on a piece of paper (see one attached) with two clouds, one at each end. This will represent a current situation and a goal. The first cloud, located to the left, which is significant because in English we read left to right, is the child's current state. Where do they find themselves today? What is "showing up" for them? The cloud on the right, located at the end of the rainbow is the goal. This is where they want to be, their desired outcome. The three spaces of the Rainbow are for Spirit, Mind, and Body. Write what can be used in those three areas to help them manifest their goal. Specificity is important. The clearer we are about our intention, or goal, and the tools or steps we will take to get there, the more likely we will find ourselves at the end of the rainbow.

In general, understanding the body is the easiest for children. The concreteness of the physical can be helpful in initiating this activity. Make a list of action items that are related to this area. Due to the abstract nature of the Mind and Spirit, more discussion and more time may be needed.

Spirit: Ask Spirit, God, Angels, Source, and other realms to help orchestrate things (perhaps visualize a puppeteer) to help me achieve my goal. At the end of each day, you may wish to Say thanks, give gratitude or praise for what has been offered.

Mind: Doing positive affirmations every day before leaving for school. At night, I may want to Communicate about the day with my mom and dad. I may wish to journal daily. I may want to listen to a favorite song, one that uplifts me and makes me feel energized to get things done.

Body: I might take a relaxing bath every night or get at least 30 mins of exercise every day. I might set the intention to do my homework or read 20 minutes a night.

Coloring this can also add a layer of depth for a child. Ascribing a color to Spirit, Mind, and Body can be useful when discussing how their day was. If your child always considers body to be blue...you can say something like, "How did your blue go today? Have you got your blue stuff done?". It makes it kid friendlier and easier to discuss, especially for certain ages.

Hanging these up can also spark communication between family members, and create a tribal mentality, one in which everyone is helping one another to reach their goal cloud.

For younger children, especially for my 5-year-old daughter, I have found, that when a goal is reached we need to celebrate. Creativity in our celebrating makes the event very special. You might use cotton balls or coffee filters to throw up in the air, watching them fall like clouds from the sky. This represents the clouds and reaching the goal linked by the rainbow. Celebrating their success and their journey (even if something has not fully come to fruition yet) is a positive way to encourage mindful living.

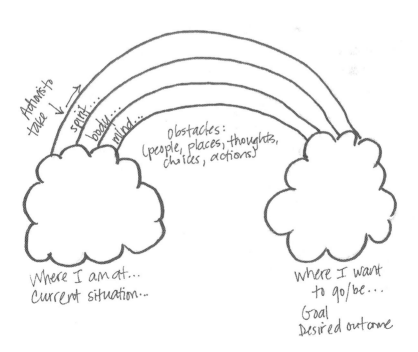

Rainbow Bridge

Support:
(people, places, thoughts, choices, actions, ways to connect to source)

Actions to take

spirit...
body...
mind...

Obstacles:
(people, places, thoughts, choices, actions)

Where I am at...
Current situation...

Where I want to go/be...
Goal
Desired outcome

Strategy 3: Water Manifestation technique

Depending on your child's environment, assess whether it is more open to spiritual concepts or intuitive living or if a child will be put in a difficult situation or teased for certain beliefs, you can have your child write what they hope to manifest on a post it note and tape it to their water bottle for the day. This can be written, a symbol used (for example I have drawn an Angel on my before to represent what I was trying to manifest), or a picture drawn. Then have your child fill the water bottle up for that day. Have them state either to themselves or out loud what they hope to manifest (*or a goal to reach), and then put the post it notes on the bottle. Tell them that as they drink their water to think positively about what they hope to see happen in their life that day. By the end of the day have the water bottle be drank entirely. They may want to journal about this at the end of the day, and if their goal wasn't reached that day, sometimes it will manifest later. Having them record their thoughts/hopes/goals can help them see their own progress and how positive thinking can help them get to where they want to go.

Strategy 4: Goal!

Helping your child have fun while discussing topics like setting goal is a great way to move from thinking about wanting something to using action to make it happen. A fun way for high energy children or those who like to be constantly going, is to utilize random materials, incorporate movement, and think outside of the box.

One way to do this is to use a small trash can. Write the goal your child is trying to reach on it or post it above the can. On pieces of paper, write down the identifiable steps needed or the strengths, abilities, and talents they have to help them reach this goal. Once you have several pieces of paper filled with strategies, helpful steps or attributes, crumble the paper into paper balls. Create a 'stand behind line' which must be based on your child's age and capabilities. Have them keep throwing the balls into the trash can until they all make it in the basket. The line can be moved based on how hard the child believes the goal will be to achieve. Use the line as a teaching tool. If it is a long-term goal, push the 'stand behind line' out further. If the goal will take several steps to achieve, there can be multiple 'stand behind lines'.

Strategy 5: Grounding Dreams

Our physical home layout contains two levels and an overhang with open space below. This has been the most perfect space for having seasonal celebrations. We have used fake leaves falling to celebrate the new season of fall, coffee filters to celebrate winter, fake flowers for spring, and summer colored construction paper for summer. We simply take turns taking up the materials and tossing them over the railing. We watch as they fall, float, twirl, and make their way to the ground.

Using seasons can be a great way to discuss change, manifestation, and 'seasons of life' with children. It has also been a great way to discuss setting goals, believing in lofty dreams, and identifying hopes. My children enjoy this exercise because it helps their "ideas" become grounded. It has been beneficial in figuring out age appropriate action steps for them to take to make their dreams come true.

My children take coffee filters and write or draw a picture of a wish, hope, or goal. Then we throw it over the railing (this can be done outside as well), and watch as it hits the ground. The interesting part is that to some it appears to be the opposite of what we want to be doing. So often we hear, "throw it out to the universe", or "make a wish" and "get it out there". While this activity does these things, it also helps with understanding how mindful energy and purposeful living can aid in creating the life you want. For after it hits the ground, representing it coming to Earth from the "energy" realm to the "physical" realm, we talk about things that might need to happen on the way down for it to become a reality to us. Some of these questions include: What steps would your child need to take? What thoughts would be necessary? What kind of support would they need? The physical exercise becomes a mindful and a spiritual one as well. Their hope becomes not only their own. It is expressed to the universe, shared with me as their mother, and becomes then a thoughtful energy that has been sent into motion. They can realize their own power in the manifestation of their dream, while allowing other entities to support its journey to becoming a reality.

The above-mentioned concepts and strategies are starting points. Getting creative with how they are utilized will provide a deeper connection to the activity and between the child and adult (as well as the child and The Divine). Again, the goal of the strategies is to help children become living expressions of their soul rather than people merely sharing only pieces or fragments of it. The H.O.P.E tribe hopes to be the greatest champion of this cause.

Future HOPEs and possible directions:

The H.O.P.E tribe is a 'living idea', meaning it is an idea that is expected to be put into practice, thoughts turned into actions, and actions creating beliefs that then keep the cycle going. My hope is that this book will generate discussions across all demographics, all ages, and all schools of thought. Beyond more subset goals, my greatest HOPE is that this book provides some insight and strategies so that our children feel safer, securer, and are invited to be their truest soul selves.

This handbook is just the tip of the iceberg, a small glimpse at the many ways we can help our children foster and stretch their soul muscle. There are endless possibilities and directions for the people who choose to participate in the H.O.P.E. Tribe. The H.O.P.E. Tribe is as strong as its members

A future direction of this work is to create more worksheets and useful tools based on different age groups (i.e. 0-5 (yes, there are things we can do with our infants that foster more spiritual and intuitive children), 6-10, and ages 11-16). Each age group comes with a set of 'typical' developmental milestones within developmental stages. Providing parents with tools that extend beyond behavioral control to deeper more meaningful connection to soul self, other, collective, and Source, allows for more integrated soulful living from the onset rather than trying to play catch up later on in life. Soulful living is to be done from the first moment we are here on Earth. Starting there and living from this place all along creates healthier, happier, more productive (issues regarding the greater good), and more peaceful living.

In addition, I would like to offer retreats for parents and their children, offer consultations to systems of care where this idea aligns with their mission and purpose, and/or facilitate seminar style dialogues with counselors and mental health providers. In fact, I am open to what the universe has planned for this work, whether it be something listed above or a combination or individual element of any or all of these (or something completely unforeseen by me at this time). I am open to whatever the tribe identifies as a need. I will respond to the call!

Rather than a Super Nanny or Nanny 911, we need Soul Nannies; people who can facilitate conversations with parents and children about ways to live from a soulful place, a sacred place that is unique to each person. Having sacred spaces for children to create, emote, and dive into their deeper soul self is valuable. For some, these strategies need to be shown, taught, and demonstrated.

As mentioned above, providing soulful extracurricular activities where children are not only participating in an activity with other peers, they are exploring soul gifts and abilities, is a hope that I would love to see come to fruition. Providing manifestation board classes for children, crystal grid classes, paint and purpose nights, and so much more could allow for children to not only express themselves creatively but create a space for soulful discussions with same age peers and like-minded individuals. Connection and belonging are paramount when trying to live a self and soul-actualized life, so allowing our children the space to do that is vital to their soul's ability to live it's intended purpose. As I like to say these days, "The possibilities are endless. In order to not be hopeless about where we may find ourselves or the state of our society, we must put action to our hope and be the change we want to see. The tribe is hopeful, not hopeless!' Let's be H.O.P.E.ful together!

As a parent I know that if things don't get on my 'to do list' they don't get done...so, here is your H.O.P.E Tribe to do list:

To DO:

Honor (self, the child, others, experience, life)
Be Curious and pay attention in a mindful way
Create a H.O.P.E tribe (for self and child)

Begin creating space for connection and
communication with my child
Put into practice a strategy or two and see how it feels,
what do I think, what is my soul informing me of?

HAVE FUN, BE CREATIVE
ALLOW SPACE FOR MY CHILD TO LIVE SOULFULLY

H.O.P.E DAILY!

Resources

Websites:
www.hayhouse.com
www.thetappingsolution.com
http://www.psychic-readings-guide.com/psychic-children/
www.yogayoga.com
http://www.metaphysical-mom.com
https://www.lightworkersworld.com
https://www.spiritual.university
http://www.arttherapyblog.com
https://en.wikipedia.org/wiki/Chromotherapy
http://www.eftnetwork.com
www.healerslibrary.com
www.mindful magazine.com
http://blissfulkids.com
https://www.bestcrystals.com/metaphysical-properties
www.buildingbeautifulsouls.com
https://psychcentral.com/
lib/10ways-to-build-and-preserve-better-boundaries/
https://www.psychologytoday.com/blog/
the-empaths-survival-guide/201706/
the-differences-between-highly-sensitive-people-and-empaths)
https://exemplore.com/auras/Indigo-Crystal-and-Rainbow-Children
www.AngelTherapy.com
https://www.consciouslifestylemag.com/
spiritual-awakening-signs-and-symptoms/
(https://en.wikipedia.org/wiki/Self-actualization

Adult Books that promote ideas and thoughts of the H.O.P.E. tribe (not exhaustive – just a launching place):

Seven Spiritual Laws of Parenting: Depak Chopra
The Empath's Survival Guide: Judith Orloff
Releasing Emotional Patterns with Essential Oils:
Rising Strong: Brene Brown
Braving the Wilderness: Brene Brown
What your clutter is trying to tell you: Kerri L. Richardson (*Also reference Denise Linn)
Unselfie: Why Empathic Kids Succeed in Our All-About-Me World: Dr. Michelle Borba
The Complete guide to Crystal Chakra Healing: Philip Permutt
The Angel Bible: Hazel Raven
Pocket Guide to Spirit Animals: Dr. Steven Farmer
The Tapping Solution: Nick Ortner
The Indigo Children: Lee Carroll & Jan Tober
Numerology (Hay House Basics): Michelle Buchanan
Mindful Parenting for ADHD: Mark Bertin
Presence: Senge, Scharmer, Jaworski, & Flowers
101 Trauma Informed Interventions: Linda Curran
The Spiritual Child: Lisa Miller Ph.D.
The Emotion Code: Nelson

Meditations and Information from The Angel Bible by Hazel Raven:
Page 159-160: Angelic Temple Meditation
Page 162: Archangel Michael Meditation
Page 164: Archangel Uriel Meditation
Page 349: reference for inner child and past abuse

Works Cited/References

Works Cited
Websites

www.oprah.com/spirit/life-lessons-we-all-need-to-learn-brene-brown (2017) Oprah.com Brene Brown's Top 4 Life Lessons

https://psychentral.com/lib/10-way-to-build-and-preserve-better-boundaries/ (2018) Psychcentral.com Margarita Tartakovsky, M.S. 10 Ways to Build and Preserve Better Boundaries

Books:
Orloff, Judith. (2017) The Empath's Survival Guide, Life Strategies for Sensitive People. Louisville, Co: Sound True, Inc.
Permutt, Philip. (2008) The Complete Guide to Crystal Chakra Healing. New York, NY: CICO Books
Brown, Brene. (2017) Braving the wilderness. New York, NY: Random House
Brown, Brene. (2015) Rising Strong. New York, NY: Random House
Curran, Lisa. (2013) 101 Trauma Informed Interventions: Activities, Exercises, and Assignments to Move the client and Therapy Forward. Premier Publishing and Media
Miller, Lisa. (2016) The Spiritual Child, The New Science on Parenting for Health and Lifelong Thriving. London, United Kingdom:Picador Publishing

Crawford, Catherine Crawford. (2008) The Highly Intuitive Child. Nashville, TN:Turner Publishing Company

Raven, Hazel. (2006) The Angel Bible, the Definitive Guide to Angel Wisdom. New York, NY: Sterling Publishing Company

Printed in the United States
By Bookmasters